GOD'S WORD
FOR CHILDREN

THE BIBLE FOR ALL GENERATIONS™

Illustrated by
José Pérez Montero

GOD'S
WORD®
TRANSLATION

GOD'S WORD for Children

Original edition published in Denmark
under the title *The Children's Bible*
by Scandinavia Publishing House,
Copenhagen, Denmark

Drejervej 11-21
DK-2400 Copenhagen NV
Denmark
E-mail: jvo@scanpublishing.dk
Telephone: +45 35 31 03 30

Illustrations: © José Pérez Montero

Text:

GOD'S WORD.
TRANSLATION

For quotation policies or questions, write to:
GOD'S WORD® Permissions
God's Word to the Nations
P.O. Box 400
Orange Park, FL 32067-0400, U.S.A.
or contact us at www.godsword.org

ISBN 978-0-9984477-0-4

Printed in China

Presented to

_____

By

_____

On

_____

MY FAMILY

_____

Name

_____

Father

_____

Father's Parents

_____

Mother

_____

Mother's Parents

_____

Brothers & Sisters

_____

Brothers & Sisters

_____

Brothers & Sisters

GOD'S WORD
FOR CHILDREN

GOD'S WORD® TRANSLATION

Illustrated by
José Pérez Montero

THE BIBLE FOR ALL GENERATIONS™

CONTENTS

The New Testament

The Old Testament

GOD MAKES EVERYTHING

Genesis 1:1-25

¹In the beginning God created heaven and earth.

²The earth was formless and empty, and darkness covered the deep water. The Spirit of God was hovering over the water.

³Then God said, "Let there be light!" So there was light. ⁴God saw the light was good. So God separated the light from the darkness. ⁵God named the light *day*, and the darkness he named *night*. There was evening, then morning—the first day.

⁶Then God said, "Let there be a horizon in the middle of the water in order to separate the water." ⁷So God made the horizon and separated the water above and below the horizon. And so it was. ⁸God named ⌊what was above⌋ the horizon *sky*. There was evening, then morning—a second day.

⁹Then God said, "Let the water under the sky come together in one area, and let the dry land appear." And so it was. ¹⁰God named the dry land *earth*. The water which came together he named *sea*. God saw that it was good. ¹¹Then God said, "Let the earth produce vegetation: plants bearing seeds, each according to its own type, and fruit trees bearing fruit with seeds, each according to its own type." And so it was. ¹²The earth produced vegetation: plants bearing seeds, each according to its own type, and trees bearing fruit with seeds, each according to its own type. God saw that they were good. ¹³There was evening, then morning—a third day.

¹⁴Then God said, "Let there be lights in the sky to separate the day from the night. They will be signs and will mark religious festivals, days, and years.

¹⁵ They will be lights in the sky to shine on the earth." And so it was. ¹⁶ God made the two bright lights: the larger light to rule the day and the smaller light to rule the night. He also made the stars. ¹⁷ God put them in the sky to give light to the earth, ¹⁸ to dominate the day and the night, and to separate the light from the darkness. God saw that it was good. ¹⁹ There was evening, then morning—a fourth day.

²⁰ Then God said, "Let the water swarm with swimming creatures, and let birds fly through the sky over the earth." ²¹ So God created the large sea creatures, every type of creature that swims around in the water and every type of flying bird. God saw that they were good. ²² God blessed them and said, "Be fertile, increase in number, fill the sea, and let there be many birds on the earth." ²³ There was evening, then morning—a fifth day.

²⁴ Then God said, "Let the earth produce every type of living creature: every type of domestic animal, crawling animal, and wild animal." And so it was. ²⁵ God made every type of wild animal, every type of domestic animal, and every type of creature that crawls on the ground. God saw that they were good.

IT LOOKS GOOD

Genesis 1:20-25

20 Then God said, "Let the water swarm with swimming creatures, and let birds fly through the sky over the earth." 21 So God created the large sea creatures, every type of creature that swims around in the water and every type of flying bird. God saw that they were good. 22 God blessed them and said, "Be fertile, increase in number, fill the sea, and let there be many birds on the earth." 23 There was evening, then morning—a fifth day.

24 Then God said, "Let the earth produce every type of living creature: every type of domestic animal, crawling animal, and wild animal." And so it was. 25 God made every type of wild animal, every type of domestic animal, and every type of creature that crawls on the ground. God saw that they were good.

Genesis 2:3-6

3 Then God blessed the seventh day and set it apart as holy, because on that day he stopped all his work of creation.

4 This is the account of heaven and earth when they were created, at the time when the LORD God made earth and heaven.

5 Wild bushes and plants were not on the earth yet because the LORD God hadn't sent rain on the earth. Also, there was no one to farm the land. 6 Instead, underground water would come up from the earth and water the entire surface of the ground.

THE FIRST MAN AND WOMAN

Genesis 1:26-27

26 Then God said, "Let us make humans in our image, in our likeness. Let them rule the fish in the sea, the birds in the sky, the domestic animals all over the earth, and all the animals that crawl on the earth."

27 So God created humans in his image.
   In the image of God he created them.
      He created them male and female.

Genesis 2:7,18-23

7 Then the LORD God formed the man from the dust of the earth and blew the breath of life into his nostrils. The man became a living being.

18 Then the LORD God said, "It is not good for the man to be alone. I will make a helper who is right for him."

19 The LORD God had formed all the wild animals and all the birds out of the ground. Then he brought them to the man to see what he would call them. Whatever the man called each creature became its name. 20 So the man named all the domestic animals, all the birds, and all the wild animals.

But the man found no helper who was right for him. 21 So the LORD God caused him to fall into a deep sleep. While the man was sleeping, the LORD God took out one of the man's ribs and closed up the flesh at that place. 22 Then the LORD God formed a woman from the rib that he had taken from the man. He brought her to the man.

23 The man said,

"This is now bone of my bones
      and flesh of my flesh.
   She will be named *woman*
      because she was taken from man."

[28] God blessed them and said, "Be fertile, increase in number, fill the earth, and be its master. Rule the fish in the sea, the birds in the sky, and all the animals that crawl on the earth."

[29] God said, "I have given you every plant with seeds on the face of the earth and every tree that has fruit with seeds. This will be your food. [30] I have given all green plants as food to every land animal, every bird in the sky, and every animal that crawls on the earth— every living, breathing animal." And so it was.

[31] And God saw everything that he had made and that it was very good. There was evening, then morning—the sixth day.

[1] Heaven and earth and everything in them were finished. [2] By the seventh day God had finished the work he had been doing. On the seventh day he stopped the work he had been doing.
[3] Then God blessed the seventh day and set it apart as holy, because on that day he stopped all his work of creation.

ALL FOR A PIECE OF FRUIT

Genesis 3:1-13

[1] The snake was more clever than all the wild animals the LORD God had made. He asked the woman, "Did God really say, 'You must never eat the fruit of any tree in the garden'?"

[2] The woman answered the snake, "We're allowed to eat the fruit from any tree in the garden [3] except the tree in the middle of the garden. God said, 'You must never eat it or touch it. If you do, you will die!'"

[4] "You certainly won't die!" the snake told the woman. [5] "God knows that when you eat it your eyes will be opened. You'll be like God, knowing good and evil."

[6] The woman saw that the tree had fruit that was good to eat, nice to look at, and desirable for making someone wise. So she took some of the fruit and ate it. She also gave some to her husband, who was with her, and he ate it.

[7] Then their eyes were opened, and they both realized that they were naked. They sewed fig leaves together and made clothes for themselves.

[8] In the cool of the evening, the man and his wife heard the LORD God walking around in the garden. So they hid from the LORD God among the trees in the garden. [9] The LORD God called to the man and asked him, "Where are you?"

[10] He answered, "I heard you in the garden. I was afraid because I was naked, so I hid."

[11] God asked, "Who told you that you were naked? Did you eat fruit from the tree I commanded you not to eat from?"

[12] The man answered, "That woman, the one you gave me, gave me some fruit from the tree, and I ate it."

[13] Then the LORD God asked the woman, "What have you done?"

"The snake deceived me, and I ate," the woman answered.

OUT OF EDEN

Genesis 3:20-23

²⁰ Adam named his wife Eve [Life] because she became the mother of every living person.

²¹ The LORD God made clothes from animal skins for the man and his wife and dressed them.

²² Then the LORD God said, "The man has become like one of us, since he knows good and evil. He must not reach out and take the fruit from the tree of life and eat. Then he would live forever." ²³ So the LORD God sent the man out of the Garden of Eden to farm the ground from which the man had been formed. ²⁴ After he sent the man out, God placed angels and a flaming sword that turned in all directions east of the Garden of Eden. He placed them there to guard the way to the tree of life.

TWO BROTHERS

Genesis 4:1-2

¹ Adam made love to his wife Eve. She became pregnant and gave birth to Cain. She said, "I have gotten the man that the LORD promised." ² Then she gave birth to another child, Abel, Cain's brother. Abel was a shepherd, and Cain was a farmer.

THE FIRST MURDER

Genesis 4:3-16

³ Later Cain brought some crops from the land as an offering to the LORD. ⁴ Abel also brought some choice parts of the firstborn animals from his flock. The LORD approved of Abel and his offering, ⁵ but he didn't approve of Cain and his offering. So Cain became very angry and was disappointed. ⁶ Then the LORD asked Cain, "Why are you angry, and why do you look disappointed? ⁷ If you do well, won't you be accepted? But if you don't do well, sin is lying outside your door ready to attack. It wants to control you, but you must master it."

⁸ Cain talked to his brother Abel. Later, when they were in the fields, Cain attacked his brother Abel and killed him.

⁹ The Lord asked Cain, "Where is your brother Abel?"

"I don't know," he answered. "Am I supposed to take care of my brother?"

¹⁰ The Lord asked, "What have you done? Your brother's blood is crying out to me from the ground. ¹¹ So now you are cursed from the ground, which has received the blood of your brother whom you killed. ¹² When you farm the ground, it will no longer yield its best for you. You will be a fugitive, a wanderer on the earth."

¹³ But Cain said to the Lord, "My punishment is more than I can stand! ¹⁴ You have forced me off this land today. I have to hide from you and become a fugitive, a wanderer on the earth. Now anyone who finds me will kill me!"

¹⁵ So the Lord said to him, "Not so! Anyone who kills Cain will suffer vengeance seven times over." The Lord gave Cain a sign so that anyone meeting him would not kill him.

¹⁶ Then Cain left the Lord's presence and lived in Nod [The Land of Wandering], east of Eden.

NOAH BUILDS A BOAT

Genesis 6:5-22

[5] The LORD saw how evil humans had become on the earth. All day long their deepest thoughts were nothing but evil. [6] The LORD was sorry that he had made humans on the earth, and he was heartbroken. [7] So he said, "I will wipe off the face of the earth these humans that I created. I will wipe out not only humans, but also domestic animals, crawling animals, and birds. I'm sorry that I made them." [8] But the LORD was pleased with Noah.

[9] This is the account of Noah and his descendants.

Noah had God's approval and was a man of integrity among the people of his time. He walked with God. [10] He had three sons: Shem, Ham, and Japheth.

[11] The world was corrupt in God's sight and full of violence. [12] God saw the world and how corrupt it was because all people on earth lived evil lives.

[13] God said to Noah, "I have decided to put an end to all people because the earth is full of their violence. Now I'm going to destroy them along with the earth. [14] Make yourself a ship of cypress wood. Make rooms in the ship and coat it inside and out with tar. [15] This is how you should build it: the ship is to be 450 feet long, 75 feet wide, and 45 feet high. [16] Make a roof for the ship, and leave an 18-inch-high opening at the top. Put a door in the side of the ship. Build the ship with lower, middle, and upper decks. [17] I'm about to send a flood on the earth to destroy all people under the sky—every living, breathing human. Everything on earth will die.

[18] "But I will make my promise to you. You, your sons, your wife, and your sons' wives will go into the ship. [19] Bring two of every living creature into the ship in order to keep them alive with you. They must be male and female. [20] Two of every type of bird, every type of domestic animal, and every type of creature that crawls on the ground will come to you to be kept alive. [21] Take every kind of food that can be eaten and store it. It will be food for you and the animals."

[22] Noah did this. He did everything that God had commanded him.

THE VOYAGE OF THE ARK

Genesis 7:1-16

[1] The LORD said to Noah, "Go into the ship with your whole family because I have seen that you alone are righteous among the people of today. [2] Take with you seven pairs of every kind of clean animal (a male and a female of each) and one pair of every kind of unclean animal (a male and a female). [3] Also, take seven pairs of every kind of bird (a male and a female of each) to preserve animal life all over the earth after the flood. [4] In seven days I will send rain to the earth for 40 days and 40 nights. I will wipe off the face of the earth every living creature that I have made."

[5] So Noah did everything that the LORD commanded him.

[6] Noah was 600 years old when the flood came to the earth. [7] Noah, his sons, his wife, and his sons' wives went into the ship to escape the floodwaters. [8] Clean and unclean animals, birds, and creatures that crawl on the ground [9] came to Noah to go into the ship in pairs (a male and female of each) as God had commanded Noah.

[10] Seven days later the flood came on the earth. [11] On the seventeenth day of the second month of the six hundredth year of Noah's life, all the deep springs burst open. The sky opened, [12] and rain came pouring down on the earth for 40 days and 40 nights.

[13] On that same day Noah and his sons Shem, Ham, and Japheth, as well as Noah's wife and his three daughters-in-law went into the ship. [14] They had with them every type of wild animal, every type of domestic animal, every type of creature that crawls on the earth, and every type of bird (every creature with wings). [15] A pair of every living, breathing animal came to Noah to go into the ship. [16] A male and a female of every animal went in as God had commanded Noah. Then the LORD closed the door behind them.

P. Montero

THE RESCUE

Genesis 7:17-7:24

[17] The flood continued for 40 days on the earth. The water increased and lifted the ship so that it rose high above the ground. [18] As the water rose and became very deep, the ship floated on top of the water. [19] The water rose very high above the earth. It covered all the high mountains everywhere under the sky. [20] It rose 23 feet above the mountaintops.

[21] Every creature that crawls on the earth died, including birds, domestic and wild animals, and everything that swarms over the earth, along with every human. [22] Everything on dry land (every living, breathing creature) died. [23] Every living creature on the face of the earth was wiped out. Humans, domestic animals, crawling creatures, and birds were wiped off the earth. Only Noah and those with him in the ship were left.

[24] The floodwaters were on the earth for 150 days.

THE END OF THE STORM

Genesis 8:1-9:17

[1] God remembered Noah and all the wild and domestic animals with him in the ship. So God made a wind blow over the earth, and the water started to go down. [2] The deep springs and the sky had been shut, and the rain had stopped pouring. [3] The water began to recede from the land. At the end of 150 days the water had decreased. [4] On the seventeenth day of the seventh month, the ship came to rest in the mountains of Ararat. [5] The water kept decreasing until the tenth month. On the first day of the tenth month, the tops of the mountains appeared.

[6] After 40 more days Noah opened the window he had made in the ship [7] and sent out a raven. It kept flying back and forth until the water on the land had dried up. [8] Next, he sent out a dove to see if the water was gone from the surface of the ground. [9] The dove couldn't find a place to land because the water was still all over the earth. So it came back to Noah in the ship. He reached out and brought the dove back into the ship. [10] He waited seven more days and again sent the dove out of the ship. [11] The dove came to him in the evening, and in its beak was a freshly plucked olive leaf. Then Noah knew that the water was gone from

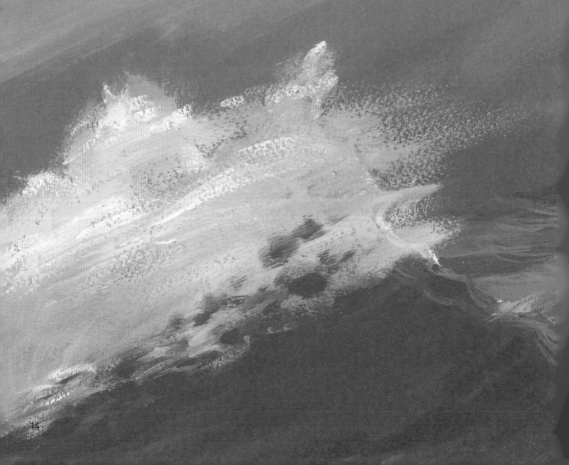

the earth. ¹²He waited seven more days and sent out the dove again, but it never came back to him.

¹³By the first day of the first month of Noah's six hundred and first year, the water on the land had dried up. Noah opened the top of the ship, looked out, and saw the surface of the ground. ¹⁴By the twenty-seventh day of the second month the land was dry.

¹⁵Then God spoke to Noah, ¹⁶"Come out of the ship with your wife, your sons, and your sons' wives. ¹⁷Bring out every animal that's with you: birds, domestic animals, and every creature that crawls on the earth. Be fertile, increase in number, and spread over the earth."

¹⁸So Noah came out with his sons, his wife, and his sons' wives. ¹⁹Every animal, crawling creature, and bird—everything that moves on the earth—came out of the ship, one kind after another.

²⁰Noah built an altar to the Lord. On it he made a burnt offering of each type of clean animal and clean bird. ²¹The Lord smelled the soothing aroma. He said to himself, "I will never again curse the ground because of humans, even though from birth their hearts are set on nothing but evil. I will never again kill every living creature as I have just done.

²²As long as the earth exists,
    planting and harvesting,
    cold and heat,
    summer and winter,
    day and night
        will never stop."

¹God blessed Noah and his sons and said to them, "Be fertile, increase in number, and fill the earth. ²All the wild animals and all the birds will fear you and be terrified of you. Every creature that crawls on the ground and all the fish in the sea have been put under your control. ³Everything that lives and moves will be your food. I gave you green plants as food; I now give you everything else.

⁴"But you are not to eat meat with blood in it. (Blood is life.) ⁵In addition, I will demand your blood for your life. I will demand it from any animal or from any person. I will demand the life of any person ⌐who kills⌐ another person.

⁶Whoever sheds human blood,
    by humans his blood will be shed,
    because in the image of God,
        God made humans.

7 Be fertile, and increase in number. Spread over the earth, and increase."

8 God also said to Noah and his sons, **9** "I am going to make my promise to you, your descendants, **10** and every living being that is with you—birds, domestic animals, and all the wild animals, all those that came out of the ship—every living thing on earth. **11** I am making my promise to you. Never again will all life be killed by floodwaters. Never again will there be a flood that destroys the earth."

12 God said, "This is the sign of the promise I am giving to you and every living being that is with you for generations to come. **13** I will put my rainbow in the clouds to be a sign of my promise to the earth. **14** Whenever I form clouds over the earth, a rainbow will appear in the clouds. **15** Then I will remember my promise to you and every living animal. Never again will water become a flood to destroy all life. **16** Whenever the rainbow appears in the clouds, I will see it and remember my everlasting promise to every living animal on earth."

17 So God said to Noah, "This is the sign of the promise I am making to all life on earth."

THE CITY BUILDERS

Genesis 10:1-11:9

1 This is the account of Noah's sons Shem, Ham, and Japheth, and their descendants. Shem, Ham and Japheth had children after the flood.

2 Japheth's descendants were
Gomer, Magog, Madai, Javan, Tubal, Meshech, and Tiras.

3 Gomer's descendants were
Ashkenaz, Riphath, and Togarmah.

4 Javan's descendants were
the people from Elishah, Tarshish, Cyprus, and Rhodes.

5 From these descendants the people of the coastlands spread into their own countries. Each nation had its own language and families.

6 Ham's descendants were
Cush, Egypt, Put, and Canaan.

7 Cush's descendants were
Seba, Havilah, Sabtah, Raamah, and Sabteca.
Raamah's descendants were
Sheba and Dedan.

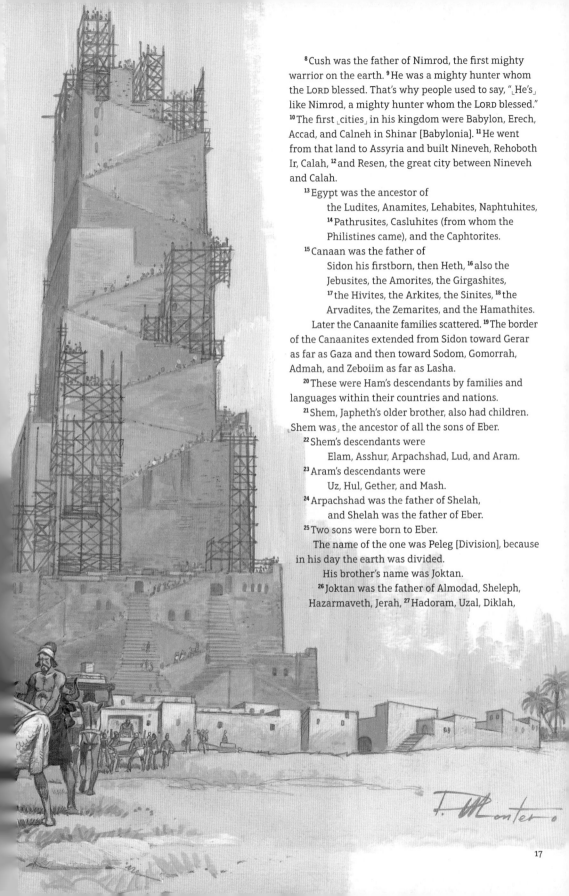

⁸ Cush was the father of Nimrod, the first mighty warrior on the earth. ⁹ He was a mighty hunter whom the Lᴏʀᴅ blessed. That's why people used to say, "⌊He's⌋ like Nimrod, a mighty hunter whom the Lᴏʀᴅ blessed." ¹⁰ The first ⌊cities⌋ in his kingdom were Babylon, Erech, Accad, and Calneh in Shinar [Babylonia]. ¹¹ He went from that land to Assyria and built Nineveh, Rehoboth Ir, Calah, ¹² and Resen, the great city between Nineveh and Calah.

¹³ Egypt was the ancestor of
　　the Ludites, Anamites, Lehabites, Naphtuhites,
　　¹⁴ Pathrusites, Casluhites (from whom the
　　Philistines came), and the Caphtorites.
¹⁵ Canaan was the father of
　　Sidon his firstborn, then Heth, ¹⁶ also the
　　Jebusites, the Amorites, the Girgashites,
　　¹⁷ the Hivites, the Arkites, the Sinites, ¹⁸ the
　　Arvadites, the Zemarites, and the Hamathites.

Later the Canaanite families scattered. ¹⁹ The border of the Canaanites extended from Sidon toward Gerar as far as Gaza and then toward Sodom, Gomorrah, Admah, and Zeboiim as far as Lasha.

²⁰ These were Ham's descendants by families and languages within their countries and nations.

²¹ Shem, Japheth's older brother, also had children. ⌊Shem was⌋ the ancestor of all the sons of Eber.

²² Shem's descendants were
　　Elam, Asshur, Arpachshad, Lud, and Aram.
²³ Aram's descendants were
　　Uz, Hul, Gether, and Mash.
²⁴ Arpachshad was the father of Shelah,
　　and Shelah was the father of Eber.
²⁵ Two sons were born to Eber.
　　The name of the one was Peleg [Division], because in his day the earth was divided.
　　His brother's name was Joktan.
²⁶ Joktan was the father of Almodad, Sheleph, Hazarmaveth, Jerah, ²⁷ Hadoram, Uzal, Diklah,

²⁸ Obal, Abimael, Sheba, ²⁹ Ophir, Havilah, and Jobab. These were Joktan's sons. ³⁰ The region where they lived extended from Mesha toward Sephar in the eastern mountains.

³¹ These were Shem's descendants by families and languages within their countries according to their nations.

³² These were the families of Noah's sons listed by their genealogies, nation by nation. From these ⌊descendants⌋ the nations spread over the earth after the flood.

¹ The whole world had one language with a common vocabulary. ² As people moved toward the east, they found a plain in Shinar [Babylonia] and settled there.

³ They said to one another, "Let's make bricks and bake them thoroughly." They used bricks as stones and tar as mortar.

⁴ Then they said, "Let's build a city for ourselves and a tower with its top in the sky. Let's make a name for ourselves so that we won't become scattered all over the face of the earth."

⁵ The Lord came down to see the city and the tower that the descendants of Adam were building.

⁶ The Lord said, "They are one people with one language. This is only the beginning of what they will do! Now nothing they plan to do will be too difficult for them. ⁷ Let us go down there and mix up their language so that they won't understand each other."

⁸ So the Lord scattered them all over the face of the earth, and they stopped building the city. ⁹ This is why it was named Babel, because there the Lord turned the language of the whole earth into babble. From that place the Lord scattered them all over the face of the earth.

THE LORD CHOOSES ABRAM

Genesis 12:1-9

¹ The Lord said to Abram,

"Leave your land,
   your relatives,
      and your father's home.
Go to the land that I will show you.
² I will make you a great nation,
I will bless you.
I will make your name great,
   and you will be a blessing.

³ I will bless those who bless you,
   and whoever curses you, I will curse.
      Through you every family on earth
         will be blessed."

⁴ So Abram left, as the Lord had told him, and Lot went with him. Abram was 75 years old when he left Haran. ⁵ Abram set out for Canaan. He took along his wife Sarai, his nephew Lot, and all the possessions they had accumulated and the servants they had acquired in Haran.

⁶ They arrived in Canaan, and Abram traveled through the land to the oak tree belonging to Moreh at Shechem. At that time the Canaanites were in the land. ⁷ Then the Lord appeared to Abram and said, "I'm going to give this land to your descendants." So he built an altar there to the Lord, who had appeared to him.

⁸ He moved on to the hills east of Bethel, and he put up his tent—with Bethel on the west and Ai on the east. He also built an altar to the Lord there and worshiped the Lord. ⁹ Abram kept moving toward the Negev.

THE LORD'S PROMISE TO ABRAM

Genesis 15:1-7

¹Later the Lord spoke his word to Abram in a vision. He said,

> "Abram, don't be afraid.
> I am your shield.
> Your reward will be very great."

²Abram asked, "Almighty Lord, what will you give me? Since I'm going to die without children, Eliezer of Damascus will inherit my household. ³You have given me no children, so this member of my household will be my heir."

⁴Suddenly, the Lord spoke his word to Abram again. He said, "This man will not be your heir. Your own son will be your heir." ⁵He took Abram outside and said, "Now look up at the sky and count the stars, if you are able to count them." He also said to him, "That's how many descendants you will have!" ⁶Then Abram believed the Lord, and that faith was regarded as the basis of Abram's approval by the Lord. ⁷Then the Lord said to him, "I am the Lord, who brought you out of Ur of the Chaldeans to give you this land so that you will take possession of it."

Genesis 17:4-5

4 "My promise is still with you. You will become the father of many nations. **5** So your name will no longer be Abram [Exalted Father], but Abraham [Father of Many] because I have made you a father of many nations.

ON THE WAY TO SODOM

Genesis 18:20-26

20 The LORD also said, "Sodom and Gomorrah have many complaints against them, and their sin is very serious. **21** I must go down and see whether these complaints are true. If not, I will know it."

22 From there the men turned and went on toward Sodom, but Abraham remained standing in front of the LORD. **23** Abraham came closer and asked, "Are you really going to sweep away the innocent with the guilty? **24** What if there are 50 innocent people in the city? Are you really going to sweep them away? Won't you spare that place for the sake of the 50 innocent people who are in it? **25** It would be unthinkable for you to do such a thing, to treat the innocent and the guilty alike and to kill the innocent with the guilty. That would be unthinkable! Won't the judge of the whole earth do what is fair?"

26 The LORD said, "If I find 50 innocent people inside the city of Sodom, I will spare the whole place for their sake."

LOT IS RESCUED

Genesis 19:1-29

1 The two angels came to Sodom in the evening as Lot was sitting in the gateway. When Lot saw them, he got up to meet them and bowed with his face touching the ground. **2** He said, "Please, gentlemen, why don't you come to my home and spend the night? ⌊You can⌋ wash your feet there. Then early tomorrow morning you can continue your journey."

"No," they answered, "we'd rather spend the night in the city square."

³ But he insisted so strongly that they came with him and went into his home. He prepared a special dinner for them, baked some unleavened bread, and they ate. ⁴ Before they had gone to bed, all the young and old male citizens of Sodom surrounded the house. ⁵ They called to Lot, "Where are the men who came to ⌐stay with⌐ you tonight? Bring them out to us so that we can have sex with them."

⁶ Then Lot went outside and shut the door behind him. ⁷ "Please, my friends, don't be so wicked," he said. ⁸ "Look, I have two daughters who have never had sex. Why don't you let me bring them out to you? Do whatever you like with them. But don't do anything to these men, since I'm responsible for them."

⁹ But the men yelled, "Get out of the way! This man came here to stay awhile. Now he wants to be our judge! We're going to treat you worse than those men." They pushed hard against Lot and lunged forward to break down the door. ¹⁰ The men ⌐inside⌐ reached out, pulled Lot into the house with them, and shut the door. ¹¹ Then they struck all the men who were in the doorway of the house, young and old alike, with blindness so that they gave up trying to find the door.

¹² Then the men asked Lot, "Do you have anyone else here—any in-laws, sons, daughters, or any other relatives in the city? Get them out of here ¹³ because we're going to destroy this place. The complaints to the LORD against its people are so loud that the LORD has sent us to destroy it."

¹⁴ So Lot went out and spoke to the men engaged to his daughters. He said, "Hurry! Get out of this place, because the LORD is going to destroy the city." But they thought he was joking.

¹⁵ As soon as it was dawn, the angels urged Lot by saying, "Quick! Take your wife and your two daughters who are here, or you'll be swept away when the city is punished." ¹⁶ When he hesitated, the men grabbed him, his wife, and his two daughters by their hands, because the LORD wanted to spare Lot. They brought them safely outside the city. ¹⁷ As soon as they were outside, one ⌐of the angels⌐ said, "Run for your lives! Don't look behind you, and don't stop on the plain. Run for the hills, or you'll be swept away!"

¹⁸ Lot answered, "Oh no! ¹⁹ Even though you've been so good to me and though you've been very kind to me by saving my life, I can't run as far as the hills. This disaster will overtake me, and I'll die. ²⁰ Look, there's a city near enough to flee to, and it's small. Why don't you let me run there? Isn't it small? Then my life will be saved."

²¹ The angel said to him, "Alright, I will grant you this request too. I will not destroy the city you're talking about. ²² Run there quickly, because I can't do anything until you get there." (The city is named Zoar [Small].)

²³ The sun had just risen over the land as Lot came to Zoar. ²⁴ Then the LORD made burning sulfur and fire rain out of heaven on Sodom and Gomorrah. ²⁵ He destroyed those cities, the whole plain, all who lived in the cities, and whatever grew on the ground. ²⁶ Lot's wife looked back and turned into a column of salt.

²⁷ Early the next morning Abraham came to the place where he had stood in front of the LORD. ²⁸ When he looked toward Sodom and Gomorrah and all the land in the plain, he saw smoke rising from the land like the thick smoke of a furnace.

²⁹ When God destroyed the cities on the plain, he remembered Abraham. Lot was allowed to escape from the destruction that came to the cities where he was living.

ISAAC IS BORN

Genesis 21:1-7

¹ The LORD came to help Sarah and did for her what he had promised. ² So she became pregnant, and at the exact time God had promised, she gave birth to a son for Abraham in his old age. ³ Abraham named his newborn son Isaac. ⁴ When Isaac was eight days old, Abraham circumcised him as God had commanded. ⁵ Abraham was 100 years old when his son Isaac was born.

⁶ Sarah said, "God has brought me laughter, and everyone who hears about this will laugh with me. ⁷ Who would have predicted to Abraham that Sarah would nurse children? Yet, I have given him a son in his old age."

ABRAHAM AND ISAAC

Genesis 22:1-13

[1] Later God tested Abraham and called to him, "Abraham!"

"Yes, here I am!" he answered.

[2] God said, "Take your son, your only son Isaac, whom you love, and go to Moriah. Sacrifice him there as a burnt offering on one of the mountains that I will show you."

[3] Early the next morning Abraham saddled his donkey. He took with him two of his servants and his son Isaac. When he had cut the wood for the burnt offering, he set out for the place that God had told him about. [4] Two days later Abraham saw the place in the distance. [5] Then Abraham said to his servants, "You stay here with the donkey while the boy and I go over there. We'll worship. After that we'll come back to you."

[6] Then Abraham took the wood for the burnt offering and gave it to his son Isaac. Abraham carried the burning coals and the knife. The two of them went on together.

[7] Isaac spoke up and said, "Father?"

"Yes, Son?" Abraham answered.

Isaac asked, "We have the burning coals and the wood, but where is the lamb for the burnt offering?"

[8] Abraham answered, "God will provide a lamb for the burnt offering, Son."

The two of them went on together. [9] When they came to the place that God had told him about, Abraham built the altar and arranged the wood on it. Then he tied up his son Isaac and laid him on top of the wood on the altar. [10] Next, Abraham picked up the knife and took it in his hand to sacrifice his son. [11] But the Messenger of the LORD called to him from heaven and said, "Abraham! Abraham!"

"Yes?" he answered.

[12] "Do not lay a hand on the boy," he said. "Do not do anything to him. Now I know that you fear God, because you did not refuse to give me your son, your only son."

[13] When Abraham looked around, he saw a ram behind him caught by its horns in a bush. So Abraham took the ram and sacrificed it as a burnt offering in place of his son.

Genesis 22:15-18

[15] Then the Messenger of the LORD called to Abraham from heaven a second time [16] and said, "I am taking an oath on my own name, declares the LORD, that because you have done this and have not refused to give me your son, your only son, [17] I will certainly bless you and make your descendants as numerous as the stars in the sky and the grains of sand on the seashore. Your descendants will take possession of their enemies' cities. [18] Through your descendant all the nations of the earth will be blessed, because you have obeyed me."

[19] Then Abraham returned to his servants, and together they left for Beersheba. Abraham remained in Beersheba.

MISSION IMPOSSIBLE

Genesis 24:1-67

¹By now Abraham was old, and the Lord had blessed him in every way. ²So Abraham said to the senior servant of his household who was in charge of all that he owned, "Take a solemn oath. ³I want you to swear by the Lord God of heaven and earth that you will not get my son a wife from the daughters of the Canaanites among whom I'm living. ⁴Instead, you will go to the land of my relatives and get a wife for my son Isaac."

⁵The servant asked him, "What if the woman doesn't want to come back to this land with me? Should I take your son all the way back to the land you came from?"

⁶"Make sure that you do not take my son back there," Abraham said to him. ⁷"The LORD God of heaven took me from my father's home and the land of my family. He spoke to me and swore this oath: 'I will give this land to your descendants.'

"God will send his angel ahead of you, and you will get my son a wife from there. ⁸If the woman doesn't want to come back with you, then you'll be free from this oath that you swear to me. But don't take my son back there." ⁹So the servant did as his master Abraham commanded and swore the oath to him concerning this.

¹⁰Then the servant took ten of his master's camels and left, taking with him all of his master's best things. He traveled to Aram Naharaim, Nahor's city.

¹¹The servant had the camels kneel down outside the city by the well. It was evening, when the women would go out to draw water. ¹²Then he prayed, "LORD, God of my master Abraham, make me successful today. Show your kindness to Abraham. ¹³Here I am standing by the spring, and the girls of the city are coming out to draw water. ¹⁴I will ask a girl, 'May I please have a drink from your jar?' If she answers, 'Have a drink, and I'll also water your camels,' let her be the one you have chosen for your servant Isaac. This way I'll know that you've shown your kindness to my master."

¹⁵Before he had finished praying, Rebekah came with her jar on her shoulder. She was the daughter of Bethuel, son of Milcah, who was the wife of Abraham's brother Nahor. ¹⁶The girl was a very attractive virgin. No man had ever had sexual intercourse with her. She went down to the spring, filled her jar, and came back.

¹⁷The servant ran to meet her and said, "Please give me a drink of water."

¹⁸"Drink, sir," she said. She quickly lowered her jar to her hand and gave him a drink. ¹⁹When she had finished giving him a drink, she said, "I'll also keep drawing water for your camels until they've had enough to drink." ²⁰So she quickly emptied her jar into the water trough, ran back to the well to draw more water, and drew enough for all his camels. ²¹The man was silently watching her to see whether or not the LORD had made his trip successful.

²²When the camels had finished drinking, the man took out a gold nose ring weighing a fifth of an ounce and two gold bracelets weighing four ounces.

²³He asked, "Whose daughter are you? Please tell me whether there is room in your father's house for us to spend the night."

²⁴She answered him, "I'm the daughter of Bethuel, son of Milcah and Nahor. ²⁵We have plenty of straw and feed ⌊for your camels⌋ and room for you to spend the night."

²⁶The man knelt, bowing to the LORD with his face touching the ground. ²⁷He said, "Praise the LORD, the God of my master Abraham. The LORD hasn't failed to be kind and faithful to my master. The LORD has led me on this trip to the home of my master's relatives."

²⁸ The girl ran and told her mother's household about these things. ²⁹ Rebekah had a brother whose name was Laban. ³⁰ He saw the nose ring and the bracelets on his sister's wrists and heard her tell what the man had said to her. Immediately, Laban ran out to the man by the spring. He came to the man, who was standing with the camels by the spring. ³¹ He said, "Come in, you whom the LORD has blessed. Why are you standing out here? I have straightened up the house and made a place for the camels."

³² So the man went into the house. The camels were unloaded and given straw and feed. Then water was brought for him and his men to wash their feet.

³³ When the food was put in front of him, he said, "I won't eat until I've said what I have to say."

"Speak up," Laban said.

³⁴ "I am Abraham's servant," he said. ³⁵ "The LORD has blessed my master, and he has become wealthy. The LORD has given him sheep and cattle, silver and gold, male and female slaves, camels and donkeys. ³⁶ My master's wife Sarah gave him a son in her old age, and my master has given that son everything he has. ³⁷ My master made me swear this oath: 'Don't get a wife for my son from the daughters of the Canaanites, in whose land I'm living. ³⁸ Instead, go to my father's home and to my relatives, and get my son a wife.'

39 "I asked my master, 'What if the woman won't come back with me?'

40 "He answered me, 'I have been living the way the LORD wants me to. The LORD will send his angel with you to make your trip successful. You will get my son a wife from my relatives and from my father's family. **41** Then you will be free from your oath to me. You will also be free of your oath to me if my relatives are not willing to do this when you go to them.'

42 "When I came to the spring today, I prayed, 'LORD God of my master Abraham, please make my trip successful. **43** I'm standing by the spring. I'll say to the young woman who comes out to draw water, "Please give me a drink of water." **44** If she says to me, "Not only may you have a drink, but I will also draw water for your camels," let her be the woman the LORD has chosen for my master's son.'

45 "Before I had finished praying, Rebekah came with her jar on her shoulder. She went down to the spring and drew water.

"So I asked her, 'May I have a drink?' **46** She quickly lowered her jar and said, 'Have a drink, and I'll water your camels too.' So I drank, and she also watered the camels.

47 "Then I asked her, 'Whose daughter are you?'

"She answered, 'The daughter of Bethuel, son of Nahor and Milcah.'

"I put the ring in her nose and the bracelets on her wrists. **48** I knelt, bowing down to the LORD. I praised the LORD, the God of my master Abraham. The LORD led me in the right direction to get the daughter of my master's relative for his son. **49** Tell me whether or not you're going to show my master true kindness so that I will know what to do."

50 Laban and Bethuel answered, "This is from the LORD. We can't say anything to you one way or another. **51** Here's Rebekah! Take her and go! She will become the wife of your master's son, as the LORD has said."

52 When Abraham's servant heard their answer, he bowed down to the LORD. **53** The servant took out gold and silver jewelry and clothes and gave them to Rebekah. He also gave expensive presents to her brother and mother. **54** Then he and the men who were with him ate and drank and spent the night. When they got up in the morning, he said, "Let me go back to my master."

55 Her brother and mother replied, "Let the girl stay with us ten days or so. After that she may go."

56 He said to them, "Don't delay me now that the LORD has made my trip successful. Let me go back to my master."

⁵⁷ So they said, "We'll call the girl and ask her."
⁵⁸ They called for Rebekah and asked her, "Will you go with this man?"

She said, "Yes, I'll go."
⁵⁹ So they let their sister Rebekah and her nurse go with Abraham's servant and his men. ⁶⁰ They gave Rebekah a blessing:

"May you, our sister, become the mother
of many thousands of children.
May your descendants take possession
of their enemies' cities."

⁶¹ Then Rebekah and her maids left. Riding on camels, they followed the man. The servant took Rebekah and left.
⁶² Isaac had just come back from Beer Lahai Roi, since he was living in the Negev. ⁶³ Toward evening Isaac went out into the field to meditate. When he looked up, he saw camels coming. ⁶⁴ When Rebekah saw Isaac, she got down from her camel. ⁶⁵ She asked the servant, "Who is that man over there coming through the field to meet us?"

"That is my master," the servant answered. Then she took her veil and covered herself. ⁶⁶ The servant reported to Isaac everything he had done. ⁶⁷ Isaac took her into his mother Sarah's tent. He married Rebekah. She became his wife, and he loved her. So Isaac was comforted after his mother's death.

TWIN BROTHERS

Genesis 25:19-26

¹⁹ This is the account of Abraham's son Isaac and his descendants. Abraham was the father of Isaac. ²⁰ Isaac was 40 years old when he married Rebekah, daughter of Bethuel the Aramean from Paddan Aram and sister of Laban the Aramean. ²¹ Isaac prayed to the Lord for his wife because she was childless. The Lord answered his prayer, and his wife Rebekah became pregnant. ²² When the children inside her were struggling with each other, she said, "If it's like this now, what will become of me?" So she went to ask the Lord.
²³ The Lord said to her,

"Two countries are in your womb.
Two nations will go their separate ways from birth.
One nation will be stronger than the other,
and the older will serve the younger."

²⁴ When the time came for her to give birth, she had twins. ²⁵ The first one born was red. His whole body was covered with hair, so they named him Esau [Hairy]. ²⁶ Afterwards, his brother was born with his hand holding on to Esau's heel, and so he was named Jacob [Heel]. Isaac was 60 years old when they were born.

AN EXPENSIVE MEAL

Genesis 25:27-34

²⁷They grew up. Esau became an expert hunter, an outdoorsman. Jacob remained a quiet man, staying around the tents. ²⁸Because Isaac liked to eat the meat of wild animals, he loved Esau. However, Rebekah loved Jacob.

²⁹Once, Jacob was preparing a meal when Esau, exhausted, came in from outdoors. ³⁰So Esau said to Jacob, "Let me have the whole pot of red stuff to eat—that red stuff—I'm exhausted." This is why he was called Edom.

³¹Jacob responded, "First, sell me your rights as firstborn."

³²"I'm about to die." Esau said. "What good is my inheritance to me?"

³³"First, swear an oath," Jacob said. So Esau swore an oath to him and sold him his rights as firstborn. ³⁴Then Jacob gave Esau a meal of bread and lentils. He ate and drank, and then he got up and left.

This is how Esau showed his contempt for his rights as firstborn.

REBEKAH IS CUNNING

Genesis 27:1-40

¹When Isaac was old and going blind, he called his older son Esau and said to him, "Son!"

Esau answered, "Here I am."

²Isaac said, "I'm old. I don't know when I'm going to die. ³Now take your hunting equipment, your quiver and bow, and go out into the open country and hunt some wild game for me. ⁴Prepare a good-tasting meal for me, just the way I like it. Bring it to me to eat so that I will bless you before I die."

⁵Rebekah was listening while Isaac was speaking to his son Esau. When Esau went into the open country to hunt for some wild game to bring back, ⁶Rebekah said to her son Jacob, "I've just heard your father speaking to your brother Esau. ⁷He said, 'Bring me some wild game, and prepare a good-tasting meal for me to eat so that I will bless you in the presence of the LORD before I die.' ⁸Now listen to me, Son, and do what I tell you. ⁹Go to the flock, and get me two good young goats. I'll prepare them as a good-tasting meal for your father, just the way he likes it. ¹⁰Then take it to your father to eat so that he will bless you before he dies."

¹¹Jacob said to his mother Rebekah, "My brother Esau is a hairy man, and my skin is smooth. ¹²My father will feel ⌐my skin⌐ and think I'm mocking him. Then I'll bring a curse on myself instead of a blessing

¹³His mother responded, "Let any curse on you fall on me, Son. Just obey me and go! Get me ⌜the young goats⌟."

¹⁴He went and got them and brought them to his mother. She prepared a good-tasting meal, just the way his father liked it. ¹⁵Then Rebekah took her older son Esau's good clothes, which she had in the house, and put them on her younger son Jacob. ¹⁶She put the skins from the young goats on his hands and on the back of his neck. ¹⁷Then she gave her son Jacob the good-tasting meal and the bread she had prepared.

¹⁸He went to his father and said, "Father?"

"Yes?" he answered. "Who are you, Son?"

¹⁹Jacob answered his father, "I'm Esau, your firstborn. I've done what you told me. Sit up and eat this meat I've hunted for you so that you may bless me."

²⁰Isaac asked his son, "How did you find it so quickly, Son?"

"The Lord your God brought it to me," he answered.

²¹Then Isaac said to Jacob, "Come over here so that I can feel your skin, Son, ⌜to find out⌟ whether or not you really are my son Esau." ²²So Jacob went over to his father. Isaac felt ⌜his skin⌟. "The voice is Jacob's," he said, "but the hands are Esau's." ²³He didn't recognize Jacob, because his hands were hairy like his brother Esau's hands. So he blessed him. ²⁴"Are you really my son Esau?" he asked him.

"I am," Jacob answered.

²⁵Isaac said, "Bring me some of the game, and I will eat it, Son, so that I will bless you." Jacob brought it to Isaac, and he ate it. Jacob also brought him wine, and he drank it.

²⁶Then his father Isaac said to him, "Come here and give me a kiss, Son." ²⁷He went over and gave him a kiss. When Isaac smelled his clothes, he blessed him and said,

"The smell of my son
    is like the smell of open country
        that the Lord has blessed.
²⁸May God give you dew from the sky,
    fertile fields on the earth,
        and plenty of fresh grain and new wine.
²⁹May nations serve you.
May people bow down to you.
    Be the master of your brothers,
        and may the sons of your mother
            bow down to you.
May those who curse you be cursed.
May those who bless you be blessed."

³⁰ Isaac finished blessing Jacob. Jacob had barely left when his brother Esau came in from hunting. ³¹ He, too, prepared a good-tasting meal and brought it to his father. Then he said to his father, "Please, Father, eat some of the meat I've hunted for you so that you will bless me."

³² "Who are you?" his father Isaac asked him.

"I'm your firstborn son Esau," he answered.

³³ Trembling violently all over, Isaac asked, "Who hunted game and brought it to me? I ate it before you came in. I blessed him, and he will stay blessed."

³⁴ When Esau heard these words from his father, he shouted out a very loud and bitter cry and said to his father, "Bless me too, Father!"

³⁵ Isaac said, "Your brother came and deceived me and has taken away your blessing."

³⁶ Esau said, "Isn't that why he's named Jacob? He's cheated me twice already: He took my rights as firstborn, and now he's taken my blessing." So he asked, "Haven't you saved a blessing for me?"

³⁷ Isaac answered Esau, "I have made him your master, and I have made all his brothers serve him. I've provided fresh grain and new wine for him. What is left for me to do for you, Son?"

³⁸ Esau asked, "Do you have only one blessing, Father? Bless me too, Father!" And Esau sobbed loudly.

³⁹ His father Isaac answered him,

"The place where you live will lack
        the fertile fields of the earth
    and the dew from the sky above.
⁴⁰ You will use your sword to live,
    and you will serve your brother.
        But eventually you will gain your freedom
        and break his yoke off your neck."

A FAMILY IS DIVIDED

Genesis 27:41-45

⁴¹ So Esau hated Jacob because of the blessing that his father had given him. Esau said to himself, "The time to mourn for my father is near. Then I'll kill my brother Jacob."

⁴² When Rebekah was told what her older son Esau had said, she sent for her younger son Jacob and said to him, "Watch out! Your brother Esau is comforting himself by planning to kill you. ⁴³ So now, Son, obey me. Quick! Run away to my brother Laban in Haran. ⁴⁴ Stay with him awhile, until your brother's anger cools down. ⁴⁵ When your brother's anger is gone and he has forgotten what you did to him, I'll send for you and get you back. Why should I lose both of you in one day?"

THE WRESTLING MATCH AND JACOB'S NEW NAME

Genesis 32:3-31

³ Jacob sent messengers ahead of him to his brother Esau in Seir, the country of Edom. ⁴ He commanded them to give this message to Esau, "Sir, this is what Jacob has to say, 'I've been living with Laban and have stayed until now. ⁵ I have cattle and donkeys, sheep and goats, and male and female slaves. I've sent ⌐these messengers⌐ to tell you ⌐this news⌐ in order to win your favor.' "

⁶ When the messengers came back to Jacob, they said, "We went to your brother Esau. He is coming to meet you with 400 men."

⁷ Jacob was terrified and distressed. So he divided the people, the sheep and goats, the cattle, and the camels into two camps. ⁸ He thought, "If Esau attacks the one camp, then the other camp will be able to escape."

⁹ Then Jacob prayed, "God of my grandfather Abraham and God of my father Isaac! LORD, you said to me, 'Go back to your land and to your relatives, and I will make you prosperous.' ¹⁰ I'm not worthy of all the love and faithfulness you have shown me. I only had a shepherd's staff when I crossed the Jordan River, but now I have two camps. ¹¹ Please save me from my brother Esau, because I'm afraid of him. I'm afraid that he'll come and attack me and the mothers and children too. ¹² But you did say, 'I will make sure that you are prosperous and that your descendants will be as many as the grains of sand on the seashore. No one will be able to count them because there are so many.' "

¹³ He stayed there that night. Then he prepared a gift for his brother Esau from what he had brought with him: ¹⁴ 200 female goats and 20 male goats, 200 female sheep and 20 male sheep, ¹⁵ 30 female camels with their young, 40 cows and 10 bulls, 20 female donkeys and 10 male donkeys.

¹⁶ He placed servants in charge of each herd. Then he said to his servants, "Go ahead of me, and keep a distance between the herds." ¹⁷ He commanded the first servant, "When my brother Esau meets you and asks you, 'To whom do you belong, and where are you going, and whose animals are these ahead of you?' ¹⁸ then say, 'Sir, they belong to your servant Jacob. This is a gift sent to you. Jacob is right behind us.'" ¹⁹ He also commanded the second servant, the third, and all the others who followed the herds. He said, "Say the same thing to Esau when you find him. ²⁰ And be sure to add, 'Jacob is right behind us, sir.'" He thought, "I'll make peace with him by giving him this gift that I'm sending ahead of me. After that I will see him, and he'll welcome me back." ²¹ So Jacob sent the gift ahead of him while he stayed in the camp that night.

²² During that night he got up and gathered his two wives, his two slaves and his eleven children and crossed at the shallow part of the Jabbok River. ²³ After he sent them across the stream, he sent everything else across. ²⁴ So Jacob was left alone. Then a man wrestled with him until dawn. ²⁵ When the man saw that he could not win against Jacob, he touched the socket of Jacob's hip so that it was dislocated as they wrestled. ²⁶ Then the man said, "Let me go; it's almost dawn."

But Jacob answered, "I won't let you go until you bless me."

²⁷ So the man asked him, "What's your name?"

"Jacob," he answered.

²⁸ The man said, "Your name will no longer be Jacob but Israel [He Struggles With God], because you have struggled with God and with men—and you have won."

²⁹ Jacob said, "Please tell me your name."

The man answered, "Why do you ask for my name?" Then he blessed Jacob there. ³⁰ So Jacob named that place Peniel [Face of God], because he said, "I have seen God face to face, but my life was saved." ³¹ The sun rose as he passed Penuel. He was limping because of his hip.

FIGHTING IN THE TENT

Genesis 37:1-4

¹ Jacob continued to live in the land of Canaan, where his father had lived.

² This is the account of Jacob and his descendants.

Joseph was a seventeen-year-old young man. He took care of the flocks with the sons of Bilhah and Zilpah, his father's wives. Joseph told his father about the bad things his brothers were doing.

³ Israel loved Joseph more than all his sons because Joseph had been born in Israel's old age. So he made Joseph a special robe with long sleeves. ⁴ Joseph's brothers saw that their father loved him more than any of them. They hated Joseph and couldn't speak to him on friendly terms.

JOSEPH'S DREAM

Genesis 37:5-11

⁵ Joseph had a dream and when he told his brothers, they hated him even more. ⁶ He said to them, "Please listen to the dream I had. ⁷ We were tying grain into bundles out in the field, and suddenly mine stood up. It remained standing while your bundles gathered around my bundle and bowed down to it."

⁸ Then his brothers asked him, "Are you going to be our king or rule us?" They hated him even more for his dreams and his words.

⁹ Then he had another dream, and he told it to his brothers. "Listen," he said, "I had another dream: I saw the sun, the moon, and 11 stars bowing down to me."

¹⁰ When he told his father and his brothers, his father criticized him by asking, "What's this dream you had? Will your mother and I and your brothers come and bow down in front of you?" ¹¹ So his brothers were jealous of him, but his father kept thinking about these things.

JOSEPH IS THROWN INTO A WELL BY HIS BROTHERS

Genesis 37:12-24

¹² His brothers had gone to take care of their father's flocks at Shechem. ¹³ Israel then said to Joseph, "Your brothers are taking care of the flocks at Shechem. I'm going to send you to them."

Joseph responded, "I'll go."

¹⁴ So Israel said, "See how your brothers and the flocks are doing, and bring some news back to me." Then he sent Joseph away from the Hebron Valley.

When Joseph came to Shechem, ¹⁵ a man found him wandering around in the open country. "What are you looking for?" the man asked.

¹⁶ Joseph replied, "I'm looking for my brothers. Please tell me where they're taking care of their flocks."

¹⁷ The man said, "They moved on from here. I heard them say, 'Let's go to Dothan.'" So Joseph went after his brothers and found them at Dothan.

¹⁸ They saw him from a distance. Before he reached them, they plotted to kill him. ¹⁹ They said to each other, "Look, here comes that master dreamer! ²⁰ Let's kill him, throw him into one of the cisterns, and say that a wild animal has eaten him. Then we'll see what happens to his dreams."

²¹ When Reuben heard this, he tried to save Joseph from their plot. "Let's not kill him," he said. ²² "Let's not have any bloodshed. Put him into that cistern that's out in the desert, but don't hurt him." Reuben wanted to rescue Joseph from them and bring him back to his father.

²³ So when Joseph reached his brothers, they stripped him of his special robe with long sleeves. ²⁴ Then they took him and put him into an empty cistern. It had no water in it.

JOSEPH IS TAKEN TO EGYPT

Genesis 37:25-35

²⁵ As they sat down to eat, they saw a caravan of Ishmaelites coming from Gilead. Their camels were carrying the materials for cosmetics, medicine, and embalming. They were on their way to take them to Egypt.

²⁶ Judah asked his brothers, "What will we gain by killing our brother and covering up his death? ²⁷ Let's sell him to the Ishmaelites. Let's not hurt him, because he is our brother, our own flesh and blood." His brothers agreed.

²⁸ As the Midianite merchants were passing by, the brothers pulled Joseph out of the cistern. They sold him to the Ishmaelites for eight ounces of silver. The Ishmaelites took him to Egypt.

²⁹ When Reuben came back to the cistern and saw that Joseph was no longer there, he tore his clothes in grief. ³⁰ He went back to his brothers and said, "The boy isn't there! What am I going to do?"

³¹ So they took Joseph's robe, killed a goat, and dipped the robe in the blood. ³² Then they brought the special robe with long sleeves to their father and said, "We found this. You better examine it to see whether it's your son's robe or not."

³³ He recognized it and said, "It is my son's robe! A wild animal has eaten him! Joseph must have been torn to pieces!" ³⁴ Then, to show his grief, Jacob tore his clothes, put sackcloth around his waist, and mourned for his son a long time. ³⁵ All his other sons and daughters came to comfort him, but he refused to be comforted. He said, "No, I will mourn for my son until I die." This is how Joseph's father cried over him.

JOSEPH MUST WORK HARD

Genesis 37:36

36 Meanwhile, in Egypt the Midianites sold Joseph to Potiphar, one of Pharaoh's officials and captain of the guard.

Genesis 39:1-6

1 Joseph had been taken to Egypt. Potiphar, one of Pharaoh's Egyptian officials and captain of the guard, bought him from the Ishmaelites who had taken him there.

2 The LORD was with Joseph, so he became a successful man. He worked in the house of his Egyptian master. 3 Joseph's master saw that the LORD was with him and that the LORD made everything he did successful. 4 Potiphar liked Joseph so much that he made him his trusted servant. He put him in charge of his household and everything he owned. 5 From that time on the LORD blessed the Egyptian's household because of Joseph. Therefore, the LORD's blessing was on everything Potiphar owned in his house and in his fields. 6 So he left all that he owned in Joseph's care. He wasn't concerned about anything except the food he ate.

Joseph was well-built and handsome.

JOSEPH IS THROWN INTO PRISON

Genesis 39:7-20

7 After a while his master's wife began to desire Joseph, so she said, "Come to bed with me."

8 But Joseph refused and said to her, "My master doesn't concern himself with anything in the house. He trusts me with everything he owns. 9 No one in this house is greater than I. He's kept nothing back from me except you, because you're his wife. How could I do such a wicked thing and sin against God?" 10 Although she kept asking Joseph day after day, he refused to go to bed with her or be with her.

11 One day he went into the house to do his work, and none of the household servants were there. 12 She grabbed him by his clothes and said, "Come to bed with me!" But he ran outside and left his clothes in her hand.

13 When she realized that he had gone but had left his clothes behind, 14 she called her household servants and said to them, "Look! My husband brought this Hebrew here to fool around with us. He came in and tried to go to bed with me, but I screamed as loud as I could. 15 As soon as he heard me scream, he ran outside and left his clothes with me."

¹⁶ She kept Joseph's clothes with her until his master came home. ¹⁷ Then she told him the same story: "The Hebrew slave you brought here came in and tried to fool around with me. ¹⁸ But when I screamed, he ran outside and left his clothes with me."

¹⁹ When Potiphar heard his wife's story, especially when she said, "This is what your slave did to me," he became very angry. ²⁰ So Joseph's master arrested him and put him in the same prison where the king's prisoners were kept.

JOSEPH INTERPRETS THE DREAMS OF TWO MEN IN PRISON

Genesis 40:1-23

[1] Later the king's cupbearer and his baker offended their master, the king of Egypt. [2] Pharaoh was angry with his chief cupbearer and his chief baker. [3] He put them in the prison of the captain of the guard, the same place where Joseph was a prisoner. [4] The captain of the guard assigned them to Joseph, and he took care of them.

After they had been confined for some time, [5] both prisoners—the cupbearer and the baker for the king of Egypt—had dreams one night. Each man had a dream with its own special meaning.

[6] When Joseph came to them in the morning, he saw that they were upset. [7] So he asked these officials of Pharaoh who were with him in his master's prison, "Why do you look so unhappy today?"

[8] "We both had dreams," they answered him, "but there's no one to tell us what they mean."

"Isn't God the only one who can tell what they mean?" Joseph asked them. "Why don't you tell me all about them."

9 So the chief cupbearer told Joseph his dream. He said "In my dream a grapevine with three branches appeared in front of me. 10 Soon after it sprouted it blossomed. Then its clusters ripened into grapes. 11 Pharaoh's cup was in my hand, so I took the grapes and squeezed them into it. I put the cup in Pharaoh's hand."

12 "This is what it means," Joseph said to him. "The three branches are three days. 13 In the next three days Pharaoh will release you and restore you to your position. You will put Pharaoh's cup in his hand as you used to do when you were his cupbearer. 14 Remember me when things go well for you, and please do me a favor. Mention me to Pharaoh, and get me out of this prison. 15 I was kidnapped from the land of the Hebrews, and even here I've done nothing to deserve being put in this prison."

16 The chief baker saw that the meaning Joseph had given to the cupbearer's dream was good. So he said to Joseph, "I had a dream too. In my dream three baskets of white baked goods were on my head. 17 The top basket contained all kinds of baked goods for Pharaoh, but the birds were eating them out of the basket on my head."

18 "This is what it means," Joseph replied. "The three baskets are three days. 19 In the next three days Pharaoh will cut off your head and hang your dead body on a pole. The birds will eat the flesh from your bones."

20 Two days later, on his birthday, Pharaoh had a special dinner prepared for all his servants. Of all his servants he gave special attention to the chief cupbearer and the chief baker. 21 He restored the chief cupbearer to his position. So the cupbearer put the cup in Pharaoh's hand. 22 But he hung the chief baker just as Joseph had said in his interpretation.

23 Nevertheless, the chief cupbearer didn't remember Joseph. He forgot all about him.

THE PHARAOH'S DREAM

Genesis 41:1-8

1 After two full years Pharaoh had a dream. He dreamed he was standing by the Nile River. 2 Suddenly, seven nice-looking, well-fed cows came up from the river and began to graze among the reeds. 3 Seven other cows came up from the river behind them. These cows were sickly and skinny. They stood behind the first seven cows on the riverbank. 4 The cows that were sickly and skinny ate the seven nice-looking, well-fed cows. Then Pharaoh woke up.

5 He fell asleep again and had a second dream. Seven good, healthy heads of grain were growing on a single stalk. 6 Seven other heads of grain, thin and scorched by the east wind, sprouted behind them. 7 The thin heads of grain swallowed the seven full, healthy heads. Then Pharaoh woke up. It was only a dream.

8 In the morning he was so upset that he sent for all the magicians and wise men of Egypt. Pharaoh told them his dreams, but no one could tell him what they meant.

JOSEPH INTERPRETS PHARAOH'S DREAM ABOUT THE FAT AND SKINNY COWS

Genesis 41:9-32

⁹ Then the chief cupbearer spoke to Pharaoh, "I remember a promise I failed to keep. ¹⁰ Some time ago when Pharaoh was angry with his servants, he confined me and the chief baker to the captain of the guard's prison. ¹¹ We both had dreams the same night. Each dream had its own meaning. ¹² A young Hebrew, a slave of the captain of the guard, was with us. We told him our dreams, and he told each of us what they meant. ¹³ What he told us happened: Pharaoh restored me to my position, but he hung the baker on a pole."

¹⁴ Then Pharaoh sent for Joseph, and immediately he was brought from the prison. After he had shaved and changed his clothes, he came in front of Pharaoh.

¹⁵ Pharaoh said to Joseph, "I had a dream, and no one can tell me what it means. I heard that when you are told a dream, you can say what it means."

¹⁶ Joseph answered Pharaoh, "I can't, but God can give Pharaoh the answer that he needs."

¹⁷ Then Pharaoh said to Joseph, "In my dream I was standing on the bank of the Nile. ¹⁸ Suddenly, seven nice-looking, well-fed cows came up from the river and began to graze among the reeds. ¹⁹ Seven other cows came up behind them. These cows were scrawny, very sick, and thin. I've never seen such sickly cows in all of Egypt! ²⁰ The thin, sickly cows ate up the seven well-fed

ones. **21** Even though they had eaten them, no one could tell they had eaten them. They looked just as sick as before. Then I woke up.

22 "In my second dream I saw seven good, full heads of grain growing on a single stalk. **23** Seven other heads of grain, withered, thin, and scorched by the east wind, sprouted behind them. **24** The thin heads of grain swallowed the seven good heads. I told this to the magicians, but no one could tell me what it meant."

25 Then Joseph said to Pharaoh, "Pharaoh had the same dream twice. God has told Pharaoh what he's going to do. **26** The seven good cows are seven years, and the seven good heads of grain are seven years. It's all the same dream. **27** The seven thin, sickly cows that came up behind them are seven years. The seven empty heads of grain scorched by the east wind are also seven years. Seven years of famine are coming.

28 "It's just as I said to Pharaoh. God has shown Pharaoh what he's going to do. **29** Seven years are coming when there will be plenty of food in Egypt. **30** After them will come seven years of famine. People will forget that there was plenty of food in Egypt, and the famine will ruin the land. **31** People won't remember that there once was plenty of food in the land, because the coming famine will be so severe. **32** The reason Pharaoh has had a recurring dream is because the matter has been definitely decided by God, and he will do it very soon.

JOSEPH HELPS PHARAOH

Genesis 41:33-42:3

[33] "Pharaoh should look for a wise and intelligent man and put him in charge of Egypt. [34] Make arrangements to appoint supervisors over the land to take a fifth of Egypt's harvest during the seven good years. [35] Have them collect all the food during these good years and store up grain under Pharaoh's control, to be kept for food in the cities. [36] This food will be a reserve supply for our country during the seven years of famine that will happen in Egypt. Then the land will not be ruined by the famine."

[37] Pharaoh and all his servants liked the idea. [38] So Pharaoh asked his servants, "Can we find anyone like this—a man who has God's Spirit in him?"

[39] Then Pharaoh said to Joseph, "Because God has let you know all this, there is no one as wise and intelligent as you. [40] You will be in charge of my palace, and all my people will do what you say. I will be more important than you, only because I'm Pharaoh."

41 Then Pharaoh said to Joseph, "I now put you in charge of Egypt." **42** Then Pharaoh took off his signet ring and put it on Joseph's finger. He had Joseph dressed in robes of fine linen and put a gold chain around his neck. **43** He had him ride in the chariot of the second-in-command. Men ran ahead of him and shouted, "Make way!" Pharaoh put Joseph in charge of Egypt.

44 He also said to Joseph, "Even though I am Pharaoh, no one anywhere in Egypt will do anything without your permission." **45** Pharaoh named Joseph Zaphenathpaneah and gave him Asenath as his wife. She was the daughter of Potiphera, priest from the city of On. Joseph traveled around Egypt.

46 Joseph was 30 years old when he entered the service of Pharaoh (the king of Egypt). He left Pharaoh and traveled all around Egypt. **47** During the seven good years the land produced large harvests. **48** Joseph collected all the food grown in Egypt during those seven years and put this food in the cities. In each city he put the food from the fields around it. **49** Joseph stored up grain in huge quantities like the sand on the seashore. He had so much that he finally gave up keeping any records because he couldn't measure it all.

50 Before the years of famine came, Joseph had two sons by Asenath, daughter of Potiphera, priest from the city of On. **51** Joseph named his firstborn son Manasseh [He Helps Me Forget], because God helped him forget all his troubles and all about his father's family. **52** He named the second son Ephraim [Blessed Twice With Children], because God gave him children in the land where he had suffered.

53 The seven years when there was plenty of food in Egypt came to an end. **54** Then the seven years of famine began as Joseph had said they would. All the other countries were experiencing famine. Yet, there was food in Egypt. **55** When everyone in Egypt began to feel the effects of the famine, the people cried to Pharaoh for food. But Pharaoh said to all the Egyptians, "Go to Joseph! Do what he tells you!"

56 When the famine had spread all over the country, Joseph opened all the storehouses and sold grain to the Egyptians. He did this because the famine was severe in Egypt. **57** The whole world came to Joseph in Egypt to buy grain, since the famine was so severe all over the world.

1 When Jacob found out that grain was for sale in Egypt, he said to his sons, "Why do you keep looking at each other? **2** I've heard there's grain for sale in Egypt. Go there and buy some for us so that we won't starve to death."

3 Ten of Joseph's brothers went to buy grain in Egypt.

JOSEPH'S BROTHERS LEARN THEIR LESSON

Genesis 42:6-38

⁶ As governor of the country, Joseph was selling grain to everyone. So when Joseph's brothers arrived, they bowed in front of him with their faces touching the ground. ⁷ As soon as Joseph saw his brothers, he recognized them. But he acted as if he didn't know them and spoke harshly to them. "Where did you come from?" he asked them.

"From Canaan, to buy food," they answered.

⁸ Even though Joseph recognized his brothers, they didn't recognize him. ⁹ Then he remembered the dreams he once had about them. "You're spies!" he said to them, "And you've come to find out where our country is unprotected."

¹⁰ "No, sir!" they answered him. "We've come to buy food. ¹¹ We're all sons of one man. We're honest men, not spies."

¹² He said to them, "No! You've come to find out where our country is unprotected."

¹³ They answered him, "We were 12 brothers, sons of one man in Canaan. The youngest brother stayed with our father, and the other one is no longer with us."

¹⁴ "It's just as I told you," Joseph said to them. "You're spies! ¹⁵ This is how you'll be tested: I solemnly swear, as surely as Pharaoh lives, that you won't leave this place unless your youngest brother comes here. ¹⁶ One of you must be sent to get your brother while the rest of you stay in prison. We'll see if you're telling the truth. If not, I solemnly swear, as surely as Pharaoh lives, you are spies!" ¹⁷ Then he put them in jail for three days.

¹⁸ On the third day Joseph said to them, "Do this, and you will live. I, too, fear God. ¹⁹ If you are honest men, you will let one of your brothers stay here in prison. The rest of you will go and take grain back to your starving families. ²⁰ But you must bring me your youngest brother. This will show that you've been telling the truth. Then you won't die." So they agreed.

²¹ They said to each other, "We're surely being punished for what we did to our brother. We saw how troubled he was when he pleaded with us for mercy, but we wouldn't listen. That's why we're in trouble now."

²² Reuben said to them, "Didn't I tell you not to sin against the boy? But you wouldn't listen. Now we must pay for this bloodshed."

²³ They didn't know that Joseph could understand them, because he was speaking through an interpreter. ²⁴ He stepped away from them to cry. When he could speak to them again, he came back. Then he picked Simeon and had him arrested right in front of their eyes.

25 Joseph gave orders to fill their bags with grain. He put each man's money back into his sack and gave them supplies for their trip. After their bags were filled, **26** they loaded their grain on their donkeys and left.

27 At the place where they stopped for the night, one of them opened his sack to feed his donkey. His money was right inside his sack. **28** He said to his brothers, "My money has been put back! It's right here in my sack!"

They wanted to die. They trembled and turned to each other and asked, "What has God done to us?"

29 When they came to their father Jacob in Canaan, they told him all that had happened to them. They said, **30** "The governor of that land spoke harshly to us and treated us like spies. **31** But we said to him, 'We're honest men, not spies. **32** We were 12 brothers, sons of the same father. One is no longer with us. The youngest brother stayed with our father in Canaan.'

33 "Then the governor of that land said to us, 'This is how I'll know that you're honest men: Leave one of your brothers with me. Take food for your starving families and go. **34** But bring me your youngest brother. Then I'll know that you're not spies but honest men. I'll give your brother back to you, and you'll be able to move about freely in this country.'"

35 As they were emptying their sacks, each man found his bag of money in his sack. When they and their father saw the bags of money, they were frightened. **36** Their father Jacob said to them, "You're going to make me lose all my children! Joseph is no longer with us, Simeon is no longer with us, and now you want to take Benjamin. Everything's against me!"

37 So Reuben said to his father, "You may put my two sons to death if I don't bring him back to you. Let me take care of him, and I'll bring him back to you."

38 Jacob replied, "My son will not go with you. His brother is dead, and he's the only one left. If any harm comes to him on the trip you're taking, the grief would drive this gray-haired old man to his grave!"

BENJAMIN MAY GO ALONG

Genesis 43:1-34

1 The famine was severe in the land. **2** When they finished eating the grain they had brought from Egypt, Israel said to his sons, "Go back and buy us a little more food."

3 Judah said to him, "The man gave us a severe warning: 'You won't be allowed to see me again unless your brother is with you.' **4** If you let our brother go with us, we'll go and buy food for you. **5** If you won't let him go, we won't go. The man said to us, 'You won't be allowed to see me again unless your brother is with you.'"

6 Israel asked, "Why have you made trouble for me by telling the man you had another brother?"

7 They answered, "The man kept asking about us and our family: 'Is your father still alive? Do you have another brother?' We simply answered his questions. How could we possibly know he would say, 'Bring your brother here'?"

49

[8] Then Judah said to his father Israel, "Send the boy along with me. Let's get going so that we won't starve to death. [9] I guarantee that he will come back. You can hold me responsible for him. If I don't bring him back to you and place him here in front of you, you can blame me the rest of my life. [10] If we hadn't waited so long, we could have made this trip twice by now."

[11] Then their father Israel said to them, "If that's the way it has to be, then take the man a gift. Put some of the best products of the land in your bags. Take a little balm, a little honey, gum, myrrh, pistachio nuts, and almonds. [12] Take twice as much money with you. You must return the money that was put back in your sacks. Maybe it was a mistake. [13] Take your brother, and go back to the man. [14] May God Almighty make him merciful to you so that he will send your other brother and Benjamin ⌊home⌋ with you. If I lose my children, I lose my children."

[15] The men took the gifts, twice as much money, and Benjamin. They went to Egypt, where they presented themselves to Joseph.

[16] When Joseph saw Benjamin with them, he said to the man in charge of his house, "Take these men to my house. Butcher an animal, and prepare a meal, because they are going to eat with me at noon."

[17] So the man did as Joseph said and took them to Joseph's house. [18] The men were frightened, because they had been brought to Joseph's house. They thought, "We've been brought here because of the money that was put back into our sacks the first time. They're going to attack us, overpower us, take our donkeys, and make us slaves."

[19] So they came to the man in charge of Joseph's house and spoke to him at the door. [20] "Please, sir," they said, "we came here to buy food once before. [21] When we stopped for the night, we opened our sacks, and each man found all of his money inside. So we brought it back with us. [22] We also brought more money to buy food. We have no idea who put our money back in our sacks."

[23] "It's alright," he said. "Don't be afraid! Your God, the God of your father, must have given you treasure in your sacks. I received your money." Then he brought Simeon out to them.

[24] The man took the brothers into Joseph's house. He gave them water to wash their feet and feed for their donkeys. [25] They got their gifts ready for Joseph's return at noon, because they had heard they were going to eat there.

[26] When Joseph came home, they gave him the gifts they had brought to the house. Then they bowed to him with their faces touching the ground. [27] He asked them how they were. Then he said, "You told me about your elderly father. How is he? Is he still alive?"

[28] They answered, "Yes, sir. Our father is alive and well." Then they knelt, bowing down.

[29] As Joseph looked around, he saw his brother Benjamin, his mother's son. "Is this your youngest brother, the one you told me about?" he asked. "God be gracious to you, my son," he said. [30] Deeply moved at the sight of his brother, he hurried away, looking for a place to cry. He went into his private room and cried there.

[31] Then he washed his face and came out. He was in control of his emotions when he said, "Serve the food."

[32] He was served separately from his brothers. The Egyptians who were there with him were also served separately, because they found it offensive to eat with Hebrews. [33] The brothers were seated facing him according to their ages—from the oldest to the youngest. They looked at each other in amazement.

[34] Joseph had portions of food brought to them from his table, but Benjamin's portion was five times more than any of the others. So they ate and drank with Joseph until they were drunk.

THE STOLEN CUP

Genesis 44:1-34

[1] Joseph commanded the man in charge of his house, "Fill the men's sacks with as much food as they can carry. Put each man's money in his sack. [2] Then put my silver cup in the youngest brother's sack along with the money for his grain." He did what Joseph told him.

[3] At dawn the men were sent on their way with their donkeys. [4] They had not gone far from the city when Joseph said to the man in charge of his house, "Go after those men at once, and when you catch up with them, say to them, 'Why have you paid me back with evil when I was good to you? [5] Isn't this the cup that my master drinks from and that he uses for telling the future? What you have done is evil!'"

⁶ When he caught up with them, he repeated these words to them. ⁷ They answered him, "Sir, how can you say such things? We would never think of doing anything like that! ⁸ We brought the money we found in our sacks back from Canaan. So why would we steal any silver or gold from your master's house? ⁹ If one of us has it, he will die, and the rest of us will become your slaves."

¹⁰ "I agree," he said. "We'll do what you've said. The man who has the cup will be my slave, and the rest of you can go free."

¹¹Each one quickly lowered his sack to the ground and opened it. ¹²Then the man made a thorough search. He began with the oldest and ended with the youngest. The cup was found in Benjamin's sack. ¹³When they saw this, they tore their clothes in grief. Then each one loaded his donkey and went back into the city.

¹⁴Judah and his brothers arrived at Joseph's house while Joseph was still there. Immediately, they bowed with their faces touching the ground. ¹⁵Joseph asked them, "What have you done? Don't you know that a man like me can find things out because he knows the future?"

¹⁶"Sir, what can we say to you?" Judah asked. "How else can we explain it? How can we prove we're innocent? God has uncovered our guilt. Now all of us are your slaves, including the one who had the cup."

¹⁷But Joseph said, "I would never think of doing that! Only the man who had the cup will be my slave. The rest of you can go back to your father in peace."

¹⁸Then Judah went up to Joseph and said, "Please, sir, let me speak openly with you. Don't be angry with me, although you are equal to Pharaoh. ¹⁹Sir, you asked us, 'Do you have a father or a brother?' ²⁰We answered, 'We have a father who is old and a younger brother born to him when he was already old. The boy's brother is dead, so he's the only one of his mother's sons left, and his father loves him.'

²¹"Then you said to us, 'Bring him here to me so that I can see him myself.' ²²We replied, 'The boy can't leave his father. If the boy leaves him, his father will die.' ²³Then you told us, 'If your youngest brother doesn't come here with you, you will never be allowed to see me again.' ²⁴When we went back to our father, we told him what you had said.

²⁵"Then our father said, 'Go back and buy us a little more food.' ²⁶We answered, 'We can't go back. We can only go back if our youngest brother is with us. The man won't see us unless our youngest brother is with us.'

²⁷"Then our father said to us, 'You know that my wife ⌞Rachel⌟ gave me two sons. ²⁸One is gone, and I said, "He must have been torn to pieces!" I haven't seen him since. ²⁹If you take this one away from me too and anything happens to him, you'll drive this gray-haired old man to his grave.'

³⁰"Our father's life is wrapped up with the boy's life. If I come ⌞home⌟ without the boy ³¹and he sees that the boy isn't ⌞with me⌟, he'll die. The grief would drive our gray-haired old father to his grave.

³²"I guaranteed my father that the boy would come back. I said, 'If I don't bring him back to you, then you can blame me the rest of my life, Father.' ³³Sir, please let me stay and be your slave in the boy's place, and let the boy go back with his brothers. ³⁴How could I go back to my father if the boy isn't with me? I couldn't bear to see my father's misery!"

THE TRUTH COMES OUT

Genesis 45:1-28

¹Joseph could no longer control his emotions in front of everyone who was standing around him, so he cried out, "Have everyone leave me!" No one else was there when Joseph told his brothers who he was. ²He cried so loudly that the Egyptians heard him, and Pharaoh's household heard about it.

³Joseph said to his brothers, "I am Joseph! Is my father still alive?" His brothers could not answer him because they were afraid of him.

⁴"Please come closer to me," Joseph said to his brothers. When they did so, he said, "I am Joseph, the brother you sold into slavery in Egypt! ⁵Now, don't be sad or angry with yourselves that you sold me. God sent me ahead of you to save lives. ⁶The famine has been in the land for two years. There will be five more years without plowing or harvesting. ⁷God sent me ahead of you to make sure that you would have descendants on the earth and to save your lives in an amazing way. ⁸It wasn't you who sent me here, but God. He has made me ⌊like⌋ a father to Pharaoh, lord over his entire household, and ruler of Egypt.

⁹"Hurry back to my father, and say to him, 'This is what your son Joseph says, "God has made me lord of Egypt. Come here to me right away! ¹⁰Live in the land of Goshen, where you will be near me. Live there with your children and your grandchildren, as well as your flocks, your herds, and everything you have. ¹¹I will provide for you in Egypt, since there will be five more years of famine. Then you, your family, and all who belong to you won't lose everything."'

¹²"You and my brother Benjamin can see for yourselves that I am the one who is speaking to you. ¹³Tell my father how greatly honored I am in Egypt and about everything you have seen. Hurry and bring my father here!"

¹⁴He threw his arms around his brother Benjamin and cried with Benjamin, who was crying on his shoulder. ¹⁵He kissed all his brothers and cried with them. After that his brothers talked with him.

¹⁶When Pharaoh's household heard the news that Joseph's brothers had come, Pharaoh and his officials were pleased. ¹⁷So Pharaoh said to Joseph, "Say to your brothers, 'Load up your animals, and go back to Canaan. ¹⁸Take your father and your families, and come to me. I will give you the best land in Egypt. Then you can enjoy the best food in the land.'

¹⁹"Give them this order: 'Take wagons with you from Egypt for your children and your wives. Bring your father, and come back. ²⁰Don't worry about your belongings because the best of everything in Egypt is yours.'"

²¹Israel's sons did as they were told. Joseph gave them wagons and supplies for their trip as Pharaoh had ordered. ²²He gave each of them a change of clothes, but he gave Benjamin three hundred pieces of silver and five changes of clothes. ²³He sent his father ten male donkeys carrying Egypt's best products and ten female donkeys carrying grain, bread, and food for his father's trip. ²⁴So Joseph sent his brothers on their way. As they were leaving, he said to them, "Don't quarrel on your way back!"

²⁵ So they left Egypt and came to their father Jacob in Canaan. ²⁶ They told him, "Joseph is still alive! Yes, he is ruler of Egypt." Jacob was stunned and didn't believe them. ²⁷ Yet, when they told their father everything Joseph had said to them and he saw the wagons Joseph had sent to bring him back, his spirits were lifted.

²⁸ "You have convinced me!" Israel said. "My son Joseph is still alive. I will go and see him before I die."

A BABY IN A BOAT

Exodus 1:1-19

[1] These are the names of the sons of Israel (that is, Jacob) who came with him to Egypt with their families: [2] Reuben, Simeon, Levi, and Judah; [3] Issachar, Zebulun, and Benjamin; [4] Dan and Naphtali; Gad and Asher. [5] Joseph was already in Egypt. The total number of Jacob's descendants was 70.

[6] Eventually, Joseph, all his brothers, and that entire generation died. [7] But the descendants of Israel had many children. They became so numerous and strong that the land was filled with them.

[8] Then a new king, who knew nothing about Joseph, began to rule in Egypt. [9] He said to his people, "There are too many Israelites, and they are stronger than we are. [10] We have to outsmart them, or they'll increase in number. Then, if war breaks out, they will join our enemies, fight against us, and leave the country."

[11] So the Egyptians put slave drivers in charge of them in order to oppress them through forced labor. They built Pithom and Rameses as supply cities for Pharaoh. [12] But the more the Israelites were oppressed, the more they increased in number and spread out. The Egyptians couldn't stand them ⌊any longer⌋. [13] So they forced the Israelites to work hard as slaves. [14] They made their lives bitter with back-breaking work in mortar and bricks and every kind of work in the fields. All the jobs the Egyptians gave them were brutally hard.

[15] Then the king of Egypt told the Hebrew midwives, whose names were Shiphrah and Puah, [16] "When you help the Hebrew women in childbirth, look at the child when you deliver it. If it's a boy, kill it, but if it's a girl, let it live."

[17] However, the midwives feared God and didn't obey the king of Egypt's orders. They let the boys live. [18] So the king of Egypt called for the midwives. He asked them, "Why have you done this? Why have you let the boys live?"

[19] The midwives answered Pharaoh, "Hebrew women are not like Egyptian women. They are so healthy that they have their babies before a midwife arrives."

MOSES IS SAVED BY PHARAOH'S DAUGHTER

Exodus 2:5-10

[1] A man from Levi's family married a Levite woman. [2] The woman became pregnant and had a son. She saw how beautiful he was and hid him for three months. [3] When she couldn't hide him any longer, she took a basket made of papyrus plants and coated it with tar and pitch. She put the baby in it and set it among the papyrus plants near the bank of the Nile River. [4] The baby's sister stood at a distance to see what would happen to him.

⁵While Pharaoh's daughter came to the Nile to take a bath, her servants walked along the bank of the river. She saw the basket among the papyrus plants and sent her slave girl to get it. ⁶Pharaoh's daughter opened the basket, looked at the baby, and saw it was a boy. He was crying, and she felt sorry for him. She said, "This is one of the Hebrew children."

⁷Then the baby's sister asked Pharaoh's daughter, "Should I go and get one of the Hebrew women to nurse the baby for you?"

⁸She answered, "Yes!" So the girl brought the baby's mother.

⁹Pharaoh's daughter said to the woman, "Take this child, nurse him for me, and I will pay you."

She took the child and nursed him. ¹⁰When the child was old enough, she brought him to Pharaoh's daughter, and he became her son. Pharaoh's daughter named him Moses [Pulled Out] and said, "I pulled him out of the water."

MOSES STRIKES A BLOW FOR FREEDOM

Exodus 2:11-14

¹¹In the course of time Moses grew up. Then he went to ⌊see⌋ his own people and watched them suffering under forced labor. He saw a Hebrew, one of his own people, being beaten by an Egyptian. ¹²He looked all around, and when he didn't see anyone, he beat the Egyptian to death and hid the body in the sand.

¹³When Moses went there the next day, he saw two Hebrew men fighting. He asked the one who started the fight, "Why are you beating another Hebrew?"

¹⁴The man asked, "Who made you our ruler and judge? Are you going to kill me as you killed the Egyptian?" Then Moses was afraid and thought that everyone knew what he had done.

MOSES AT THE BURNING BUSH

Exodus 2:15-3:10

¹⁵When Pharaoh heard what Moses had done, he tried to have him killed. But Moses fled from Pharaoh and settled in the land of Midian.

One day, while Moses was sitting by a well, ¹⁶seven daughters of the priest of Midian came. They drew water and filled the troughs to water their father's sheep. ¹⁷But some shepherds came and chased them away. So Moses got up, came to their defense, and then watered their sheep.

¹⁸When they came back to their father Reuel, he asked them, "Why have you come home so early today?"

¹⁹They answered, "An Egyptian rescued us from some shepherds. He even drew water for us and watered the sheep."

²⁰Reuel asked his daughters, "Where is he? Why did you leave the man there? Go, invite him to supper."

²¹Moses decided to stay with the man. So Reuel gave his daughter Zipporah to Moses as his wife. ²²She gave birth to a son. Moses named him Gershom [Foreigner] because he said, "I was a foreigner living in another country."

²³After a long time passed, the king of Egypt died. The Israelites still groaned because they were slaves. So they cried out, and their cries for help went up to God. ²⁴God heard their groaning, and he remembered his promise to Abraham, Isaac, and Jacob. ²⁵God saw the Israelites ⌊being oppressed⌋ and was concerned about them.

¹Moses was taking care of the sheep of his father-in-law Jethro, the priest of Midian. As he led the sheep to the far side of the desert, he came to Horeb, the mountain of God.

²The Messenger of the LORD appeared to him there as flames of fire coming out of a bush. Moses looked, and although the bush was on fire, it was not burning up. ³So he thought, "Why isn't this bush burning up? I must go over there and see this strange sight."

⁴When the LORD saw that Moses had come over to see it, God called to him from the bush, "Moses, Moses!"

Moses answered, "Here I am!"

⁵God said, "Don't come any closer! Take off your sandals because this place where you are standing is holy ground. ⁶I am the God of your ancestors, the God of Abraham, Isaac, and Jacob." Moses hid his face because he was afraid to look at God.

⁷The LORD said, "I have seen the misery of my people in Egypt, and I have heard them crying out because of the slave drivers. I know how much they're suffering. ⁸I have come to rescue them from the power of the Egyptians and to bring them from that land to a good land with plenty of room ⌊for everyone⌋. It is a land flowing with milk and honey where the Canaanites, Hittites, Amorites, Perizzites, Hivites, and Jebusites live. ⁹I have heard the cry of the people of Israel. I have seen how the Egyptians are oppressing them. ¹⁰Now, go! I am sending you to Pharaoh so that you can bring my people Israel out of Egypt."

MOSES IS CHOSEN BY GOD TO CONFRONT PHARAOH AND PERFORM MIRACLES TO FREE GOD'S PEOPLE

Exodus 3:11-4:5

¹¹ But Moses said to God, "Who am I that I should go to Pharaoh and bring the people of Israel out of Egypt?"

¹² God answered, "I will be with you. And this will be the proof that I sent you: When you bring the people out of Egypt, all of you will worship God on this mountain."

¹³ Then Moses replied to God, "Suppose I go to the people of Israel and say to them, 'The God of your ancestors has sent me to you,' and they ask me, 'What is his name?' What should I tell them?"

¹⁴ God answered Moses, "I Am Who I Am. This is what you must say to the people of Israel: 'I Am has sent me to you.'"

¹⁵ Again God said to Moses, "This is what you must say to the people of Israel: The LORD God of your ancestors, the God of Abraham, Isaac, and Jacob, has sent me to you. This is my name forever. This is my title throughout every generation.

¹⁶ "Go, assemble the leaders of Israel. Say to them, 'The LORD God of your ancestors, the God of Abraham, Isaac, and Jacob, appeared to me. He said, "I have paid close attention to you and have seen what has been done to you in Egypt. ¹⁷ I promise I will take you away from your misery in Egypt to the land of the Canaanites, Hittites, Amorites, Perizzites, Hivites, and Jebusites, a land flowing with milk and honey."'

¹⁸ "The leaders of Israel will listen to you. Then you and the leaders must go to the king of Egypt and say to him, 'The LORD God of the Hebrews has met with us. Please let us travel three days into the desert to offer sacrifices to the LORD our God.' ¹⁹ I know that the king of Egypt will not let you go, even if he is forced to. ²⁰ So I will use my power to strike Egypt. After all the miracles that I will do there, he will let you go. ²¹ I will make the Egyptians kind to the people of Israel so that, when you leave, you will not leave empty-handed.

²² "Every Hebrew woman should ask her Egyptian neighbor and any woman living in her home for silver and gold jewelry and for clothes. Put them on your sons and daughters. This way you will strip Egypt of its wealth."

"They will never believe me or listen to me!" Moses protested. "They will say, 'The LORD didn't appear to you.'"

² Then the LORD asked him, "What's that in your hand?"

He answered, "A shepherd's staff."

³ The LORD said, "Throw it on the ground." When Moses threw it on the ground, it became a snake, and he ran away from it.

⁴ Then the LORD said to Moses, "Reach out and grab the snake by its tail." He reached out and grabbed it, and it turned back into a staff as he held it. ⁵ ⌐The LORD explained,⌐ "This is to convince the people that the LORD God of their ancestors, the God of Abraham, Isaac, and Jacob, appeared to you."

PHARAOH SAYS NO

Exodus 4:19-5:2

¹⁹ Now, the LORD had said to Moses in Midian, "Go back to Egypt, because all the men who wanted to kill you are dead."

²⁰ So Moses took his wife and sons, put them on a donkey, and started out for Egypt. He also brought with him the staff God had told him to take.

²¹ The LORD said to Moses, "When you get back to Egypt, see that you show Pharaoh all the amazing things that I have given you the power to do. But I will make him stubborn so that he will not let the people go. ²² Then tell Pharaoh, 'This is what the LORD says: Israel is my firstborn son. ²³ I told you to let my son go so that he may worship me. But you refused to let him go. So now I'm going to kill your firstborn son.'"

²⁴ Along the way they stopped for the night. The LORD met Moses and tried to kill him. ²⁵ Then Zipporah took a flint knife, cut off her son's foreskin, and touched Moses' feet ⌊with it⌋. She said, "You are a bridegroom of blood to me!" ²⁶ So the LORD let him alone. It was because of the circumcision that she said at that time, "You are a bridegroom of blood!"

²⁷ Meanwhile, the LORD had told Aaron to meet Moses in the desert.

When Aaron met Moses at the mountain of God, he kissed him. ²⁸ Moses told Aaron everything the LORD had sent him to say and all the miraculous signs the LORD had commanded him to do.

²⁹ Then Moses and Aaron went ⌊to Egypt⌋ and assembled all the leaders of the people of Israel. ³⁰ Aaron told them everything the LORD had said to Moses. He also did the miraculous signs for the people, ³¹ and the people believed them. When they heard that the LORD was concerned about the people of Israel and that he had seen their misery, they knelt, bowing with their faces touching the ground.

¹ Later Moses and Aaron went to Pharaoh and said, "This is what the LORD God of Israel says: Let my people go into the desert to celebrate a festival in my honor."

² Pharaoh asked, "Who is the LORD? Why should I obey him and let Israel go? I don't know the LORD, and I won't let Israel go."

THE LORD PROMISES ACTION

Exodus 5:22-7:13

²² Moses went back to the LORD and asked, "Why have you brought this trouble on your people? Why did you send me? ²³ Ever since I went to Pharaoh to speak for you, he has treated your people cruelly, and you have done nothing at all to rescue your people."

¹ Then the LORD said to Moses, "Now you will see what I will do to Pharaoh. I will show him my power, and he will let my people go. I will show him my power, and he will throw them out of his country."

² God spoke to Moses, "I am the LORD. ³ I appeared to Abraham, Isaac, and Jacob as God Almighty, but I didn't make myself known to them by my name, the LORD. ⁴ I even made a promise to give them Canaan, the land where they lived as foreigners. ⁵ Now I have heard the groaning of the Israelites, whom the Egyptians hold in slavery, and I have remembered my promise.

⁶ "Tell the Israelites, 'I am the LORD. I will bring you out from under the oppression of the Egyptians, and I will free you from slavery. I will rescue you with my powerful arm and with mighty acts of judgment. ⁷ Then I will make you my people, and I will be your God. You will know that I am the LORD your God, who brought you out from under the forced labor of the Egyptians. ⁸ I will bring you to the land I solemnly swore to give to Abraham, Isaac, and Jacob. I will give it to you as your own possession. I am the LORD.'"

⁹ Moses reported this to the Israelites. But they would not listen to him because they were so discouraged by their back-breaking work.

¹⁰ Then the LORD spoke to Moses, ¹¹ "Go tell Pharaoh (the king of Egypt) to let the Israelites leave his country."

¹² But Moses protested to the LORD, "The Israelites wouldn't listen to me. Why would Pharaoh listen to me? I'm such a poor speaker."

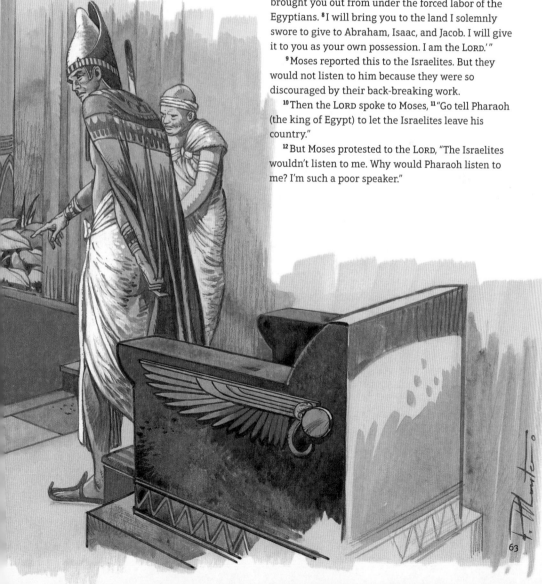

¹³The Lord spoke to Moses and Aaron about the Israelites and Pharaoh (the king of Egypt). He commanded them to bring the Israelites out of Egypt.

¹⁴These were the heads of the families:

The sons of Reuben, Israel's firstborn, were Hanoch, Pallu, Hezron, and Carmi.

These were the families descended from Reuben.

¹⁵The sons of Simeon were Jemuel, Jamin, Ohad, Jachin, Zohar, and Shaul, the son of a Canaanite woman. These were the families descended from Simeon.

¹⁶These are the names of the sons of Levi listed in birth order: Gershon, Kohath, and Merari. Levi lived 137 years.

¹⁷The sons of Gershon listed by their families were Libni and Shimei.

¹⁸The sons of Kohath were Amram, Izhar, Hebron, and Uzziel. Kohath lived 133 years.

¹⁹The sons of Merari were Mahli and Mushi.

These were the families descended from Levi listed in birth order.

²⁰Amram married his father's sister Jochebed. She gave birth to Aaron and Moses. Amram lived 137 years.

²¹The sons of Izhar were Korah, Nepheg, and Zichri.

²²The sons of Uzziel were Mishael, Elzaphan, and Sithri.

²³Aaron married Elisheba, daughter of Amminadab and sister of Nahshon. She gave birth to Nadab, Abihu, Eleazar, and Ithamar.

²⁴The sons of Korah were Assir, Elkanah, and Abiasaph.

These were the families descended from Korah.

²⁵Eleazar, son of Aaron, married one of the daughters of Putiel. She gave birth to Phinehas.

These were the heads of Levite households listed by their families.

²⁶This was the same Aaron and Moses to whom the Lord said, "Bring the Israelites out of Egypt in organized family groups." ²⁷They—this same Moses and Aaron—told Pharaoh (the king of Egypt) to let the Israelites leave Egypt.

²⁸At that time the Lord spoke to Moses in Egypt. ²⁹He said to Moses, "I am the Lord. Tell Pharaoh (the king of Egypt) everything I tell you."

³⁰But Moses said to the Lord, "Why would Pharaoh listen to me?"

¹The Lord answered Moses, "I have made you a god to Pharaoh, and your brother Aaron is your prophet. ²Tell your brother Aaron everything I command you, and he must tell Pharaoh to let the Israelites leave the country. ³But I will make Pharaoh stubborn. Even though I will do many miraculous signs and amazing things in Egypt, ⁴Pharaoh will not listen to you. Then I will use my power to punish Egypt severely, and I will bring my people, the Israelites, out of Egypt in organized family groups. ⁵The Egyptians will know that I am the Lord when I use my power against Egypt and bring the Israelites out of there."

⁶Moses and Aaron did as the Lord had commanded them. ⁷Moses was 80 years old and Aaron was 83 when they talked to Pharaoh.

⁸The Lord said to Moses and Aaron, ⁹"When Pharaoh says to you, 'Give me a sign to prove that

God has sent you,' tell Aaron, 'Take your shepherd's staff and throw it down in front of Pharaoh,' and it will become a large snake."

[10] Moses and Aaron went to Pharaoh and did as the LORD had commanded. Aaron threw his staff down in front of Pharaoh and his officials, and it became a large snake. [11] Then Pharaoh sent for his wise men and sorcerers. These Egyptian magicians did the same thing using their magic spells. [12] Each of them threw his staff down, and they all became large snakes. But Aaron's staff swallowed theirs. [13] Yet, Pharaoh continued to be stubborn and would not listen to them, as the LORD had predicted.

TEN TERRIBLE PLAGUES

Exodus 7:14-25

[14] Then the LORD said to Moses, "Pharaoh is being stubborn. He refuses to let my people go. [15] In the morning meet Pharaoh when he's on his way to the Nile. Wait for him on the bank of the river. Take along the staff that turned into a snake. [16] Say to him, 'The LORD God of the Hebrews sent me to tell you, "Let my people go to worship me in the desert." So far you have not listened. [17] Here is what the LORD says: This is the way you will recognize that I am the LORD: With this staff in my hand, I'm going to strike the Nile, and the water will turn into blood. [18] The fish in the Nile will die, and the river will stink. The Egyptians will not be able to drink any water from the Nile.'"

[19] The LORD said to Moses, "Tell Aaron, 'Take your staff and stretch out your hand over the waters of Egypt—its rivers, canals, ponds, and all its reservoirs—so that they turn into blood. There will be blood everywhere in Egypt, even in the wooden and stone containers.'"

[20] Moses and Aaron did as the LORD had commanded. In front of Pharaoh and his officials, Aaron raised his staff and struck the Nile. All the water in the river turned into blood. [21] The fish in the Nile died, and it smelled so bad that the Egyptians couldn't drink any water from the river. There was blood everywhere in Egypt.

[22] But the Egyptian magicians did the same thing using their magic spells. So Pharaoh continued to be stubborn and would not listen to Moses and Aaron, as the LORD had predicted. [23] Pharaoh turned and went back to his palace. He dismissed the entire matter from his mind.

[24] All the Egyptians dug along the Nile for water to drink because they couldn't drink any of the water from the river.

[25] Seven days passed after the LORD struck the Nile.

THE TENTH AND FINAL PLAGUE

Exodus 11:1-10

¹Then the LORD said to Moses, "I will bring one more plague on Pharaoh and Egypt. After that he will let you go. When he does, he will be certain to force all of you out of here. ²Now announce to the people ⌐of Israel⌐ that each man and woman must ask the Egyptians for silver and gold jewelry."

³The LORD made the Egyptians kind to the people. And Moses was highly respected by Pharaoh's officials and all the Egyptians.

⁴Moses said, "This is what the LORD says: About midnight I will go out among the Egyptians. ⁵Every firstborn son in Egypt will die, from the firstborn of Pharaoh who rules the land, to the firstborn children of female slaves who use their handmills, including every firstborn domestic animal. ⁶There will be loud crying throughout Egypt, such as there has never been or ever will be again. ⁷But where the Israelites are, not even a dog will be startled by any person or animal. This is how you will see that the LORD shows the distinction between Egypt and Israel. ⁸Then all these officials of yours will come, bow down to me, and say, 'You and all the people who follow you, get out!' After that I will leave." Burning with anger, Moses left Pharaoh.

⁹The LORD had said to Moses, "Pharaoh will not listen to you. This is why I will do more amazing things in Egypt." ¹⁰Moses and Aaron showed Pharaoh all these amazing things. Yet, the LORD made Pharaoh stubborn, so he wouldn't let the Israelites leave his country.

THE JEWISH PASSOVER

Exodus 12:1-41

¹The LORD said to Moses and Aaron in Egypt, ²"This month will be the very first month of the year for you. ³Tell the whole community of Israel: On the tenth ⌐day⌐ of this month each man must take a lamb or a young goat for his family—one animal per household. ⁴A household may be too small to eat a whole animal. That household and the one next door can share one animal. Choose your animal based on the number of people and what each person can eat. ⁵Your animal must be a one-year-old male that has no defects. You may choose a lamb or a young goat. ⁶Take care of it until the fourteenth ⌐day⌐ of this month.

"Then at dusk, all the assembled people from the community of Israel must slaughter their animals. ⁷They must take some of the blood and put it on the sides and tops of the doorframes of the houses where they will eat the animals. ⁸The meat must be eaten that same night. It must be roasted over a fire and eaten with bitter herbs and unleavened bread. ⁹Don't eat any of it raw or boiled but roast the whole animal over a fire. ¹⁰Don't leave any of it until morning. Anything left over in the morning must be burned up. ¹¹This is how ⌐you should be dressed when⌐ you eat it: with your belt on, your sandals on your feet, and your shepherd's staff in your hand. You must eat it in a hurry. It is the LORD's Passover.

¹²"On that same night I will go throughout Egypt and kill every firstborn male, both human and animal. I will severely punish all the gods of Egypt, ⌐because⌐ I am the LORD. ¹³But the blood on your houses will be a sign for your protection. When I see the blood, I will pass over you. Nothing will touch or destroy you when I strike Egypt.

¹⁴"This day will be one for you to remember. This is a permanent law for generations to come: You will celebrate this day as a pilgrimage festival in the LORD's honor. ¹⁵For seven days you must eat unleavened bread. On the very first day you must remove any yeast that you have in your houses. Whoever eats

66

anything with yeast in it from the first day through the seventh day must be excluded from Israel. **16** You must have a holy assembly on the first day and another one on the seventh. You must not work on these days except to prepare your own meals. That's all you may do.

17 You must celebrate the Festival of Unleavened Bread because it was on this very day that I brought you out of Egypt in organized family groups. This is a permanent law for future generations: You must celebrate this day. **18** From the evening of the fourteenth day of the first month until the evening of the twenty-first day you must eat unleavened bread. **19** There should be no yeast in your houses for seven days. Whoever eats anything with yeast in it must be excluded from the community of Israel, whether he is an Israelite or not. **20** Eat nothing made with yeast. Wherever you live, you must eat ˻only˼ unleavened bread."

21 Then Moses called for all the leaders of Israel. He said to them, "Pick out a lamb or a young goat for your families, and kill the Passover animal. **22** Take the branch of a hyssop plant, dip it in the blood which is in a bowl, and put some of the blood on the top and sides of the doorframes ˻of your houses˼. No one may leave the house until morning. **23** The LORD will go throughout Egypt to kill the Egyptians. When he sees the blood on the top and sides of the doorframe, he will pass over that doorway, and he will not let the destroyer come into your home to kill you.

24 "You must follow these instructions. They are a permanent law for you and your children. **25** When you enter the land that the LORD will give you as he promised, observe this ceremony. **26** When your children ask you what this ceremony means to you, **27** you must answer, 'It's the Passover sacrifice in the LORD's honor. The LORD passed over the houses of the Israelites in Egypt and spared our homes when he killed the Egyptians.'"

Then the people knelt, bowing with their faces touching the ground. **28** The Israelites did as the LORD had commanded Moses and Aaron.

29 At midnight the LORD killed every firstborn male in Egypt from the firstborn son of Pharaoh who ruled the land to the firstborn son of the prisoner in jail, and also every firstborn animal. **30** Pharaoh, all his officials, and all the ˻other˼ Egyptians got up during the night. There was loud crying throughout Egypt because in every house someone had died.

31 Pharaoh called for Moses and Aaron during the night. He said, "You and the Israelites must leave my people at once. Go, worship the LORD as you asked. **32** Take your flocks and herds, too, as you asked. Just go! And bless me, too!"

33 The Egyptians begged the people to leave the country quickly. They said, "Soon we'll all be dead!" **34** So the people picked up their bread dough before it had risen and carried it on their shoulders in bowls, wrapped up in their clothes.

35 The Israelites did what Moses had told them and asked the Egyptians for gold and silver jewelry and for clothes. **36** The LORD made the Egyptians generous to the people, and they gave them what they asked for. So the Israelites stripped Egypt of its wealth.

37 The Israelites left Rameses to go to Succoth. There were about six hundred thousand men on foot, plus all the women and children. **38** Many other people also went with them, along with large numbers of sheep, goats, and cattle.

39 With the dough they had brought from Egypt, they baked round, flat bread. The dough hadn't risen because they'd been thrown out of Egypt and had no time to prepare food for the trip.

40 The Israelites had been living in Egypt for 430 years. **41** After exactly 430 years all the LORD's people left Egypt in organized family groups.

THE LORD LEADS THE WAY

Exodus 13:17-14:14

17 When Pharaoh let the people go, God didn't lead them on the road through Philistine territory, although that was the shortest route. God said, "If they see that they have to fight a war, they may change their minds and go back to Egypt." **18** So God led the people around the other way, on the road through the desert toward the Red Sea. The Israelites were ready for battle when they left Egypt.

19 Moses took the bones of Joseph with him, because Joseph had made the Israelites solemnly swear to do this. Joseph had said, "God will definitely come to help you. When he does, take my bones with you."

20 They moved from Succoth and camped at Etham, on the edge of the desert. **21** By day the LORD went ahead of them in a column of smoke to lead them on their way. By night he went ahead of them in a column of fire to give them light so that they could travel by day or by night. **22** The column of smoke was always in front of the people during the day. The column of fire was always there at night.

Then the LORD said to Moses, **2** "Tell the Israelites to go back and set up their camp facing Pi Hahiroth, between Migdol and the sea. Set up your camp facing north—by the sea. **3** Pharaoh will think, 'The Israelites are ⌊just⌋ wandering around. The desert is blocking their escape.' **4** I will make Pharaoh so stubborn that he will pursue them. Then, because of what I do to Pharaoh and his entire army, I will receive honor, and the Egyptians will know that I am the LORD." So that is what the Israelites did.

5 When Pharaoh (the king of Egypt) was told that the people had fled, he and his officials changed their minds about them. They said, "What have we done? We've lost our slaves because we've let Israel go." **6** So Pharaoh prepared his chariot and took his army with him. **7** He took 600 of his best chariots as well as all the other chariots in Egypt, placing an officer in each

of them. **8** The LORD made Pharaoh (the king of Egypt) so stubborn that he pursued the Israelites, who were boldly leaving Egypt. **9** The Egyptians pursued the Israelites. Pharaoh's army, including all his horse-drawn chariots and cavalry, caught up with them as they were setting up their camp by the sea at Pi Hahiroth facing north.

10 As Pharaoh approached, the Israelites looked up and saw that the Egyptians were coming after them. Terrified, the Israelites cried out to the LORD. **11** They said to Moses, "Did you bring us out into the desert to die because there were no graves in Egypt? Look what you've done by bringing us out of Egypt! **12** Didn't we tell you in Egypt, 'Leave us alone! Let us go on serving the Egyptians'? It would have been better for us to serve the Egyptians than to die in the desert!"

13 Moses answered the people, "Don't be afraid! Stand still, and see what the LORD will do to save you today. You will never see these Egyptians again. **14** The LORD is fighting for you! So be still!"

THE LORD SEPARATES THE WATER OF THE RED SEA TO SAVE HIS PEOPLE

Exodus 14:15-31

¹⁵ Then the LORD said to Moses, "Why are you crying out to me? Tell the Israelites to start moving. ¹⁶ Raise your staff, stretch out your hand over the sea, and divide the water. Then the Israelites will go through the sea on dry ground. ¹⁷ I am making the Egyptians so stubborn that they will follow the Israelites. I will receive honor because of what I will do to Pharaoh, his entire army, his chariots, and cavalry. ¹⁸ The Egyptians will know that I am the LORD when I am honored for what I did to Pharaoh, his chariots, and his cavalry."

¹⁹ The Messenger of God, who had been in front of the Israelites, moved behind them. So the column of smoke moved from in front of the Israelites and stood behind them ²⁰ between the Egyptian camp and the Israelite camp. The ⌐column of⌐ smoke was there when darkness came, and it lit up the night. Neither side came near the other all night long.

²¹ Then Moses stretched out his hand over the sea. All that night the Lord pushed back the sea with a strong east wind and turned the sea into dry ground. The water divided, ²² and the Israelites went through the middle of the sea on dry ground. The water stood like a wall on their right and on their left.

²³ The Egyptians pursued them, and all Pharaoh's horses, chariots, and cavalry followed them into the sea. ²⁴ Just before dawn, the Lord looked down from the column of fire and smoke and threw the Egyptian camp into a panic. ²⁵ He made the wheels of their chariots come off so that they could hardly move. Then the Egyptians shouted, "Let's get out of here! The Lord is fighting for Israel! He's against us!"

²⁶ Then the LORD said to Moses, "Stretch out your hand over the sea so that the water will flow back over the Egyptians, their chariots, and their cavalry."

²⁷ Moses stretched his hand over the sea, and at daybreak the water returned to its usual place. The Egyptians tried to escape, but the LORD swept them into the sea. ²⁸ The water flowed back and covered Pharaoh's entire army, as well as the chariots and the cavalry that had followed Israel into the sea. Not one of them survived.

²⁹ Meanwhile, the Israelites had gone through the sea on dry ground while the water stood like a wall on their right and on their left. ³⁰ That day the LORD saved Israel from the Egyptians, and Israel saw the Egyptians lying dead on the seashore. ³¹ When the Israelites saw the great power the LORD had used against the Egyptians, they feared the LORD and believed in him and in his servant Moses.

THE LORD PROVIDES WATER TO SAVE HIS PEOPLE

Exodus 15:1-27

¹ Then Moses and the Israelites sang this song to the LORD:

"I will sing to the LORD.
He has won a glorious victory.
He has thrown horses and their riders
into the sea.
² The LORD is my strength and my song.
He is my Savior.
This is my God, and I will praise him,
my father's God, and I will honor him.
³ The LORD is a warrior!
The LORD is his name.
⁴ He has thrown Pharaoh's chariots and army
into the sea.
Pharaoh's best officers were drowned
in the Red Sea.
⁵   The deep water covered them.
They sank to the bottom like a rock.
⁶ Your right hand, O LORD, wins glory
because it is strong.
Your right hand, O LORD, smashes your enemies.
⁷ With your unlimited majesty, you destroyed those
who attacked you.
You sent out your burning anger.
It burned them up like straw.
⁸ With a blast from your nostrils, the water piled up.
The waves stood up like a dam.
The deep water thickened
in the middle of the sea.

⁹ "The enemy said, 'I'll pursue them!
I'll catch up with them!
I'll divide the loot!
I'll take all I want!
I'll use my sword!
I'll take all they have!'
¹⁰ Your breath blew the sea over them.
They sank like lead in the raging water.

¹¹ "Who is like you among the gods, O LORD?
Who is like you?
You are glorious because of your holiness
and awe-inspiring because of your splendor.
You perform miracles.
¹² You stretched out your right hand.
The earth swallowed them.

¹³ "Lovingly, you will lead the people you have saved.
Powerfully, you will guide them
to your holy dwelling.
¹⁴   People will hear of it and tremble.
The people of Philistia will be in anguish.
¹⁵   The tribal leaders of Edom will be terrified.
The powerful men of Moab will tremble.
The people of Canaan will be deathly afraid.
¹⁶   Terror and dread will fall on them.
Because of the power of your arm,
they will be petrified
until your people pass by, O LORD,
until the people you purchased pass by.
¹⁷ You will bring them and plant them
on your own mountain,
the place where you live, O LORD,
the holy place that you built
with your own hands, O Lord.
¹⁸ The LORD will rule as king forever and ever."

¹⁹ When Pharaoh's horses, chariots, and cavalry went into the sea, the LORD made the water of the sea flow back over them. However, the Israelites had gone through the sea on dry ground.

²⁰ Then the prophet Miriam, Aaron's sister, took a tambourine in her hand. All the women, dancing with tambourines, followed her. ²¹ Miriam sang to them:

"Sing to the Lord.
He has won a glorious victory.
He has thrown horses and their riders
into the sea."

²² Moses led Israel away from the Red Sea into the desert of Shur. For three days they traveled in the desert without finding water. ²³ When they came to Marah, they couldn't drink the water because it tasted bitter. That's why the place was called Marah [Bitter Place]. ²⁴ The people complained about Moses by asking, "What are we supposed to drink?"

²⁵ Moses cried out to the Lord, and the Lord showed him a piece of wood. He threw it into the water, and the water became sweet.

There the Lord set down laws and rules for them to live by, and there he tested them. ²⁶ He said, "If you will listen carefully to the Lord your God and do what he considers right, if you pay attention to his commands and obey all his laws, I will never make you suffer any of the diseases I made the Egyptians suffer, because I am the Lord, who heals you."

²⁷ Next, they went to Elim, where there were 12 springs and 70 palm trees. They camped there by the water.

THE LORD PROVIDES MEAT TO SAVE HIS PEOPLE

Exodus 16:1-36

¹ The whole community of Israelites moved from Elim and came to the desert of Sin, which is between Elim and Sinai. This was on the fifteenth day of the second month after they had left Egypt. ² In the desert the whole community complained about Moses and Aaron. ³ The Israelites said to them, "If only the Lord had let us die in Egypt! There we sat by our pots of meat and ate all the food we wanted! You brought us out into this desert to let us all starve to death!"

⁴ The Lord said to Moses, "I'm going to send you food from heaven like rain. Each day the people should go out and gather only what they need for that day. In this way I will test them to see whether or not they will follow my instructions. ⁵ But on the sixth day when they prepare what they bring home, it should be twice as much as they gather on other days."

⁶ So Moses and Aaron said to all the Israelites, "In the evening you will know that it was the Lord who brought you out of Egypt. ⁷ In the morning you will see the glory of the Lord, because he has heard you complaining about him. Why are you complaining about us?" ⁸ Moses also said, "The Lord will give you meat to eat in the evening and all the food you want in the morning. The Lord has heard you complaining about him. Who are we? You're not complaining about us but about the Lord."

⁹ Moses said to Aaron, "Tell the whole community of Israelites, 'Come into the Lᴏʀᴅ's presence. He has heard you complaining.'"

¹⁰ While Aaron was speaking to the whole community of Israelites, they looked toward the desert. Suddenly, they saw the glory of the Lᴏʀᴅ in the ⌊column of⌋ smoke.

¹¹ The Lᴏʀᴅ said to Moses, ¹² "I've heard the Israelites complaining. Tell them, 'At dusk you will eat meat, and in the morning you will eat all the food you want. Then you will know that I am the Lᴏʀᴅ your God.'"

¹³ That evening quails came and covered the camp, and in the morning there was a layer of dew around the camp. ¹⁴ When the dew was gone, the ground was covered with a thin layer of flakes like frost on the ground. ¹⁵ When the Israelites saw it, they asked each other, "What is this?" because they didn't know what it was.

Moses said to them, "It's the food the Lᴏʀᴅ has given you to eat. ¹⁶ This is what the Lᴏʀᴅ has commanded: Each of you should gather as much as you can eat. Take two quarts for each person in your tent."

¹⁷ So that is what the Israelites did. Some gathered more, some less. ¹⁸ They measured it into two-quart containers. Those who had gathered more didn't have too much. Those who had gathered less didn't have too little. They gathered as much as they could eat.

¹⁹ Then Moses said to them, "No one may keep any of it until morning."

²⁰ But some of them didn't listen to Moses. They kept part of it until morning, and it was full of worms and smelled bad. So Moses was angry with them.

²¹ Each morning they gathered as much food as they could eat. When the sun was hot, it melted away. ²² But on the sixth day they gathered twice as much food, four quarts per person. All the leaders of the community came to Moses and told him about it.

²³ He said to them, "This is what the LORD said: Tomorrow is a day of rest—a holy day dedicated to the LORD. Bake what you want to bake, and boil what you want to boil. Save all that's left over, and keep it until tomorrow morning."

²⁴ So they saved it until the next morning as Moses had commanded, but it didn't smell or have worms in it. ²⁵ "Eat it today," Moses said, "because today is a day of rest—a holy day dedicated to the LORD. You won't find anything on the ground today. ²⁶ You can gather food on six days, but on the seventh day, the day of rest, you won't find any."

²⁷ On the seventh day some people went out to gather food, but they didn't find any. ²⁸ The LORD said to Moses, "How long will you refuse to do what I have commanded and instructed you to do? ²⁹ Remember: The LORD has given you this day of rest as a holy day. That's why he gives you enough food on the sixth day for two days. On the seventh day stay in your place—no one is to go out. Everyone, stay where you are." ³⁰ So the people never worked on the seventh day of the week.

³¹ The Israelites called the food *manna*. It was like coriander seeds. It was white and tasted like wafers made with honey.

³² Moses said, "This is what the LORD has commanded: Take two quarts of manna to be kept for your descendants. This way they will see the food that I gave you to eat in the desert when I brought you out of Egypt."

³³Moses said to Aaron, "Take a jar, put two quarts of manna in it, and put it in the LORD's presence to be kept for your descendants." ³⁴Aaron put the jar of manna in front of the words of God's promise to be kept there, as the LORD commanded Moses.

³⁵The Israelites ate manna for 40 years until they came to a place to settle. They ate manna until they came to the border of Canaan.

³⁶(Now, the standard dry measure at that time held 20 quarts.)

THE LORD TALKS TO MOSES ON THE MOUNTAIN

Exodus 19:1-18

¹Two months after the Israelites left Egypt, they came to the desert of Sinai. ²Israel had moved from Rephidim and had come into the desert of Sinai. They had set up camp there in front of the mountain.

³Then Moses went up the mountain to God, and the LORD called to him from the mountain, "This is what you must say to the descendants of Jacob. Tell the Israelites, ⁴'You have seen for yourselves what I did to Egypt and how I carried you on eagles' wings and brought you to my mountain. ⁵If you carefully obey me and are faithful to the terms of my promise, then out of all the nations you will be my own special possession, even though the whole world is mine. ⁶You will be my kingdom of priests and my holy nation.' These are the words you must speak to the Israelites."

⁷So Moses went down and called for the leaders of the people. He repeated to them all the words that the LORD had commanded him. ⁸All the people answered together, "We will do everything the LORD has said." So Moses brought their answer back to the LORD.

⁹The LORD said to Moses, "I am coming to you in a storm cloud so that the people will hear me speaking with you and will always believe you." Moses told the LORD what the people had said.

¹⁰So the LORD said to Moses, "Go to the people, and tell them they have two days to get ready. They must set themselves apart as holy. Have them wash their clothes ¹¹and be ready by the day after tomorrow. On that day the LORD will come down on Mount Sinai as all the people watch. ¹²Mark off a boundary around the mountain for the people, and tell them not to go up the mountain or even touch it. Those who touch the mountain must be put to death. ¹³No one should touch them. They must be stoned or shot with arrows. No matter whether it's an animal or a person, it must not live. The people may go up the mountain ˻only˼ when the ram's horn sounds a long blast."

¹⁴After Moses went down the mountain to the people, he had them get ready, and they washed their clothes. ¹⁵Then Moses said to the people, "Be ready two days from now. Don't disqualify yourselves by having sexual intercourse."

¹⁶On the morning of the second day, there was thunder and lightning with a heavy cloud over the mountain, and a very loud blast from a ram's horn ˻was heard˼. All the people in the camp shook with fear. ¹⁷Then Moses led the people out of the camp to meet with God, and they stood at the foot of the mountain. ¹⁸All of Mount Sinai was covered with smoke because the LORD had come down on it in fire. Smoke rose from the mountain like the smoke from a kiln, and the whole mountain shook violently.

THE FIRST TEN COMMANDMENTS

Exodus 20:1-21

¹Then God spoke all these words:

²"I am the LORD your God, who brought you out of slavery in Egypt.

³"Never have any other god. ⁴Never make your own carved idols or statues that represent any creature in the sky, on the earth, or in the water. ⁵Never worship them or serve them, because I, the LORD your God, am a God who does not tolerate rivals. I punish children for their parents' sins to the third and fourth generation of those who hate me. ⁶But I show mercy to thousands of generations of those who love me and obey my commandments.

⁷"Never use the name of the LORD your God carelessly. The LORD will make sure that anyone who carelessly uses his name will be punished.

⁸"Remember the day of rest by observing it as a holy day. ⁹You have six days to do all your work. ¹⁰The seventh day is the day of rest—a holy day dedicated to the LORD your God. You, your sons, your daughters, your male and female slaves, your cattle, and the foreigners living in your city must never do any work ˻on that day˼. ¹¹In six days the LORD made heaven, earth, and the sea, along with everything in them. He didn't work on the seventh day. That's why the LORD blessed the day he stopped his work and set this day apart as holy.

¹²"Honor your father and your mother, so that you may live for a long time in the land the LORD your God is giving you.

F. Montero

¹³ "Never murder.

¹⁴ "Never commit adultery.

¹⁵ "Never steal.

¹⁶ "Never lie when you testify about your neighbor.

¹⁷ "Never desire to take your neighbor's household away from him.

"Never desire to take your neighbor's wife, his male or female slave, his ox, his donkey, or anything else that belongs to him."

¹⁸ All the people heard the thunder and saw the lightning. They heard the blast of the ram's horn and saw the mountain covered with smoke. So they shook with fear and stood at a distance. ¹⁹ Then they said to Moses, "You speak to us, and we'll listen. But don't let God speak to us, or we'll die!"

²⁰ Moses answered the people, "Don't be afraid! God has come only to test you, so that you will be in awe of him and won't sin."

²¹ The people kept their distance while Moses went closer to the dark cloud where God was.

THE LORD'S PEOPLE MAKE AN IDOL — A GOLDEN CALF

Exodus 32:1-20

¹When the people saw that Moses delayed coming down from the mountain, they gathered around Aaron. They said to him, "We don't know what has happened to this Moses, who led us out of Egypt. Make gods who will lead us."

²Aaron said to them, "Have your wives, sons, and daughters take off the gold earrings they are wearing, and bring them to me."

³So all the people took off their gold earrings and handed them to Aaron. ⁴After he had worked on the gold with a tool, he made it into a statue of a calf.

Then they said, "Israel, here are your gods who brought you out of Egypt."

⁵When Aaron saw this, he built an altar in front of it and announced, "Tomorrow there will be a festival in the LORD's honor."

⁶Early the next day the people sacrificed burnt offerings and brought fellowship offerings. Afterward, they sat down to a feast, which turned into an orgy.

⁷The LORD said to Moses, "Go back down there. Your people whom you brought out of Egypt have runed everything. ⁸They've already turned from the way I commanded them to live. They've made a statue of a calf for themselves. They've bowed down to it and offered sacrifices to it. They've said, 'Israel, here are your gods who brought you out of Egypt.'"

⁹The LORD added, "I've seen these people, and they are impossible to deal with. ¹⁰Now leave me alone. I'm so angry with them I am going to destroy them. Then I'll make you into a great nation."

¹¹But Moses pleaded with the LORD his God. "LORD," he said, "why are you so angry with your people whom you brought out of Egypt using your great power and mighty hand? ¹²Don't let the Egyptians say, 'He was planning all along to kill them in the mountains and wipe them off the face of the earth. That's why he brought them out ⌊of our land⌋.' Don't be so angry. Reconsider your decision to bring this disaster on your people. ¹³Remember your servants Abraham, Isaac, and Israel. You took an oath, swearing on yourself. You told them, 'I will make your descendants as numerous as the stars in the sky. I will give to your descendants all the land I spoke of. It will be their permanent possession.'"

¹⁴So the LORD reconsidered his threat to destroy his people.

¹⁵Moses turned and went down the mountain carrying the two tablets with God's words. They were written on both sides, front and back. ¹⁶The tablets were the work of God, and the writing was God's writing inscribed on the tablets.

¹⁷Then Joshua heard the noise of the people shouting. He said to Moses, "It's the sound of war in the camp!"

¹⁸ Moses replied,

"It's not the sound of winners shouting.
It's not the sound of losers crying.
It's the sound of a wild celebration
that I hear."

¹⁹ When he came near the camp, he saw the calf and the dancing. In a burst of anger Moses threw down the tablets and smashed them at the foot of the mountain. ²⁰ Then he took the calf they had made, burned it, ground it into powder, scattered it on the water, and made the Israelites drink it.

THE SECOND TIME THE LORD GIVES HIS PEOPLE THE TEN COMMANDMENTS

Exodus 32:31–34:8

³¹ So Moses went back to the LORD and said, "These people have committed such a serious sin! They made gods out of gold for themselves. ³² But will you forgive their sin? If not, please wipe me out of the book you have written."

³³ The LORD answered Moses, "I will wipe out of my book whoever sins against me. ³⁴ Now, go! Lead the people to the place I told you about. My Messenger will go ahead of you. But when I punish, I will punish them for their sin."

³⁵ So the LORD killed people because they had Aaron make the calf.

¹ Then the LORD said to Moses, "You and the people you brought out of Egypt must leave this place. Go to the land I promised to Abraham, Isaac, and Jacob with an oath, saying, 'I will give it to your descendants.' ² I will send a Messenger ahead of you, and I will force out the Canaanites, Amorites, Hittites, Perizzites, Hivites, and Jebusites. ³ Go to that land flowing with milk and honey. But I will not be with you, because you are impossible to deal with, and I would destroy you on the way."

⁴ When the people heard this bad news, they acted as if someone had died. No one wore any jewelry. ⁵ The LORD had said to Moses, "Tell the Israelites, 'You are impossible to deal with. If I were with you, I might destroy you at any time. Now take off your jewelry, and I'll decide what to do with you.'"

⁶ After they left Mount Horeb, the Israelites no longer wore their jewelry.

⁷ Now, Moses used to take a tent and set it up far outside the camp. He called it the tent of meeting. Anyone who was seeking the LORD's will used to go outside the camp to the tent of meeting. ⁸ Whenever Moses went out to the tent, all the people would rise and stand at the entrances to their tents and watch Moses until he went in. ⁹ As soon as Moses went into the tent, the column of smoke would come down and stay at the entrance to the tent while the LORD spoke with Moses. ¹⁰ When all the people saw the column of smoke standing at the entrance to the tent, they would all bow with their faces touching the ground at the entrance to their own tents. ¹¹ The LORD would speak to Moses personally, as a man speaks to his friend. Then Moses would come back to the camp, but his assistant, Joshua, son of Nun, stayed inside the tent.

¹² Moses said to the LORD, "You've been telling me to lead these people, but you haven't let me know whom you're sending with me. You've also said, 'I know you by name, and I'm pleased with you.' ¹³ If you really are pleased with me, show me your ways so that I can know you and so that you will continue to be pleased with me. Remember: This nation is your people."

¹⁴ The LORD answered, "My presence will go ˻with you,˼ and I will give you peace."

¹⁵ Then Moses said to him, "If your presence is not going ˻with us,˼ don't make us leave this place. ¹⁶ How will anyone ever know you're pleased with your people and me unless you go with us? Then we will be different from all other people on the face of the earth."

83

[17] The LORD answered Moses, "I will do what you have asked, because I am pleased with you, and I know you by name."

[18] Then Moses said, "Please let me see your glory."

[19] The LORD said, "I will let all my goodness pass in front of you, and there I will call out my name 'the LORD.' I will be kind to anyone I want to. I will be merciful to anyone I want to. [20] But you can't see my face, because no one may see me and live."

[21] Then the LORD said, "Look, there's a place near me. Stand by this rocky cliff. [22] When my glory passes by, I will put you in a crevice in the cliff and cover you with my hand until I have passed by. [23] Then I will take my hand away, and you'll see my back, but my face must not be seen."

[1] The LORD said to Moses, "Cut two ⌊more⌋ stone tablets like the first ones, and I will write on them the words that were on the first tablets which you smashed. [2] Be ready in the morning. Then come up on Mount Sinai, and stand in my presence on the top of the mountain. [3] No one may come with you or even be seen anywhere on the mountain. Even the flocks and herds may not graze in front of this mountain."

[4] So Moses cut two ⌊more⌋ stone tablets like the first ones. Early the next morning he went up on Mount Sinai, as the LORD had commanded him, carrying the two stone tablets.

[5] The LORD came down in a cloud and stood there with him and called out his name "the LORD."

[6] Then he passed in front of Moses, calling out, "The LORD, the LORD, a compassionate and merciful God, patient, always faithful and ready to forgive. [7] He continues to show his love to thousands of generations, forgiving wrongdoing, disobedience, and sin. He never lets the guilty go unpunished, punishing children and grandchildren for their parents' sins to the third and fourth generation."

[8] Immediately, Moses knelt, bowing with his face touching the ground.

THE LORD'S PEOPLE ARE WITHIN SIGHT OF THE PROMISED LAND

Numbers 13:1-33

[1] The LORD said to Moses, [2] "Send men to explore Canaan, which I'm giving to the Israelites. Send one leader from each of their ancestors' tribes."

[3] So at the LORD's command, Moses sent these men from the Desert of Paran. All of them were leaders of the Israelites.

[4] These are their names:

Shammua, son of Zaccur, from the tribe of Reuben; [5] Shaphat, son of Hori, from the tribe of Simeon; [6] Caleb, son of Jephunneh, from the tribe of Judah; [7] Igal, son of Joseph, from the tribe of Issachar; [8] Hoshea, son of Nun, from the tribe of Ephraim; [9] Palti, son of Raphu, from the tribe of Benjamin; [10] Gaddiel, son of Sodi, from the tribe of Zebulun; [11] Gaddi, son of Susi, from the tribe of Joseph (that is, the tribe of Manasseh); [12] Ammiel, son of Gemalli, from the tribe of Dan; [13] Sethur, son of Michael, from the tribe of Asher; [14] Nahbi, son of Vophsi, from the tribe of Naphtali; [15] Geuel, son of Machi, from the tribe of Gad.

[16] These are the names of the men Moses sent to explore the land. But Moses gave Hoshea, son of Nun, the name Joshua.

[17] When Moses sent them to explore Canaan, he told them, "Go through the Negev and then into the mountain region. [18] See what the land is like and whether the people living there are strong or weak, few or many. [19] Is the land they live in good or bad? Do their cities have walls around them or not? [20] Is the soil rich or poor? Does the land have trees or not? Do your best to bring back some fruit from the land." (It was the season when grapes were beginning to ripen.)

[21] So the men explored the land from the Desert of Zin to the border of Hamath. [22] They went through the Negev and came to Hebron, where Ahiman, Sheshai, and Talmai lived. They are descendants of Anak. (Hebron was built seven years before Zoan in Egypt.) [23] When they came to the Eshcol Valley, they cut off a branch with only one bunch of grapes on it. They carried it on a pole between two of them. They also brought some pomegranates and figs. [24] So they called that valley Eshcol [Bunch of Grapes] because of the bunch of grapes the Israelites cut off there.

[25] Forty days later, they came back from exploring the land. [26] They came back to Moses, Aaron, and the whole community of Israel at Kadesh in the Desert of Paran. They gave their report and showed them the fruit from the land.

[27] This is what they reported to Moses: "We went to the land where you sent us. It really is a land flowing with milk and honey. Here's some of its fruit. [28] But the people who live there are strong, and the cities have walls and are very large. We even saw the descendants of Anak there. [29] The Amalekites live in the Negev. The Hittites, Jebusites, and Amorites live in the mountain region. And the Canaanites live along the coast of the Mediterranean Sea and all along the Jordan River."

30 Caleb told the people to be quiet and listen to Moses. Caleb said, "Let's go now and take possession of the land. We should be more than able to conquer it."

31 But the men who had gone with him said, "We can't attack those people! They're too strong for us!"
32 So they began to spread lies among the Israelites about the land they had explored. They said, "The land we explored is one that devours those who live there. All the people we saw there are very tall.
33 We saw Nephilim there. (The descendants of Anak are Nephilim.) We felt as small as grasshoppers, and that's how we must have looked to them."

THE LORD'S PEOPLE DO NOT BELIEVE THAT THEY ARE STRONG ENOUGH

Exodus 14:1-10

¹ Then all the people in the Israelite community raised their voices and cried out loud all that night. ² They complained to Moses and Aaron, "If only we had died in Egypt or this desert! ³ Why is the LORD bringing us to this land—just to have us die in battle? Our wives and children will be taken as prisoners of war! Wouldn't it be better for us to go back to Egypt?" ⁴ They said to each other, "Let's choose a leader and go back to Egypt."

⁵ Immediately, Moses and Aaron bowed with their faces touching the ground in front of the whole community of Israel assembled there. ⁶ At the same time, two of those who had explored the land, Joshua (son of Nun) and Caleb (son of Jephunneh), tore their clothes in despair. ⁷ They said to the whole community of Israel, "The land we explored is very good. ⁸ If the LORD is pleased with us, he will bring us into this land and give it to us. This is a land flowing with milk and honey! ⁹ Don't rebel against the LORD, and don't be afraid of the people of the land. We will devour them like bread. They have no protection, and the LORD is with us. So don't be afraid of them."

¹⁰ But when the whole community of Israel talked about stoning Moses and Aaron to death, they all saw the glory of the LORD ⌊shining⌋ at the tent of meeting.

THE LORD'S FORTY-YEAR PUNISHMENT OF HIS PEOPLE FOR THEIR UNBELIEF

Numbers 14:26-35

²⁶ Then the LORD said to Moses and Aaron, ²⁷ "How long must I put up with this wicked community that keeps complaining about me? I've heard the complaints the Israelites are making about me. ²⁸ So tell them, 'As I live, declares the LORD, I solemnly swear I will do everything to you that you said I would do. ²⁹ Your bodies will drop dead in this desert. All of you who are at least 20 years old, who were registered and listed, and who complained about me will die. ³⁰ I raised my hand and swore an oath to give you this land to live in. But none of you will enter it except Caleb (son of Jephunneh) and Joshua (son of Nun). ³¹ You said your children would be taken as prisoners of war. Instead, I will bring them into the land you rejected, and they will enjoy it. ³² However, your bodies will drop dead in this desert. ³³ Your children will be shepherds in the desert for 40 years. They will suffer for your unfaithfulness until the last of your bodies lies dead in the desert. ³⁴ For 40 days you explored the land. So for 40 years—one year for each day—you will suffer for your sins and know what it means for me to be against you.' ³⁵ I, the LORD, have spoken. I swear I will do these things to all the people in this whole wicked community who have joined forces against me. They will meet their end in this desert. Here they will die!"

MOSES OFFERS THE CHOICE OF LIFE OR DEATH

Deuteronomy 30:15-31:6

¹⁵ Today I offer you life and prosperity or death and destruction. ¹⁶ This is what I'm commanding you today: Love the LORD your God, follow his directions, and obey his commands, laws, and rules. Then you will live, your population will increase, and the LORD your God will bless you in the land that you're about to enter and take possession of.

¹⁷ But your hearts might turn away, and you might not listen. You might be tempted to bow down to other gods and worship them. ¹⁸ If you do, I tell you today that you will certainly be destroyed. You will not live for a long time in the land that you're going to take possession of when you cross the Jordan River.

¹⁹ I call on heaven and earth as witnesses today that I have offered you life or death, blessings or curses. Choose life so that you and your descendants will live.

²⁰ Love the LORD your God, obey him, and be loyal to him. This will be your way of life, and it will mean a long life for you in the land that the LORD swore to give to your ancestors Abraham, Isaac, and Jacob.

¹ Moses continued to speak to all the Israelites: ² "I'm 120 years old now, and I'm not able to lead you anymore. Besides, the LORD has told me that I cannot cross the Jordan River. ³ The LORD your God is the one who will cross the river ahead of you. He will destroy those nations as you arrive, and you will take possession of their land. Joshua will also cross the river ahead of you, as the LORD told you. ⁴ The LORD will do to those nations what he did to King Sihon and King Og of the Amorites and to their lands when he destroyed them. ⁵ The LORD will hand them over to you, and you must do to them everything that I commanded you. ⁶ Be strong and courageous. Don't tremble! Don't be afraid of them! The LORD your God the one who is going with you. He won't abandon you or leave you."

THE LAST DAYS OF MOSES

Deuteronomy 34:1-10

Then Moses went up on Mount Nebo from the plains of Moab. He went to the top of Pisgah, across from Jericho. The LORD showed him the whole land. He could see Gilead as far as Dan, ²all of Naphtali, the territory of Ephraim and Manasseh, all the territory of Judah as far as the Mediterranean Sea, ³the Negev, and the Jordan Plain—the valley of Jericho (the City of Palms)—as far as Zoar.

⁴Then the LORD said to him, "This is the land I promised with an oath to Abraham, Isaac, and Jacob. I said I would give it to their descendants. I have let you see it with your own eyes, but you may not go there."

⁵As the LORD had predicted, the LORD's servant Moses died in Moab. ⁶He was buried in a valley in Moab, near Beth Peor. Even today no one knows where his grave is.

⁷Moses was 120 years old when he died. His eyesight never became poor, and he never lost his physical strength. ⁸The Israelites mourned for Moses in the plains of Moab for 30 days. Then the time of mourning for him was over.

⁹Joshua, son of Nun, was filled with the Spirit of wisdom, because Moses had laid his hands on him. The Israelites obeyed him and did what the LORD had commanded through Moses.

¹⁰There has never been another prophet in Israel like Moses, whom the LORD dealt with face to face. ¹¹He was the one the LORD sent to do all the miraculous signs and amazing things in Egypt to Pharaoh, to all his officials, and to his whole country. ¹²Moses used his mighty hand to do all the spectacular and awe-inspiring deeds that were seen by all the Israelites.

THE LORD'S PEOPLE SPY ON THE ENEMY BEFORE ENTERING THE PROMISED LAND

Joshua 1:1-2:1

¹ After the death of the LORD's servant Moses, the LORD said to Moses' assistant Joshua, son of Nun, ² "My servant Moses is dead. Now you and all these people must cross the Jordan River into the land that I am going to give the people of Israel. ³ I will give you every place on which you set foot, as I promised Moses. ⁴ Your borders will be the desert ⌐on the south⌐, nearby Lebanon to the Euphrates River (the country of the Hittites) ⌐on the north⌐, and the Mediterranean Sea on the west. ⁵ No one will be able to oppose you successfully as long as you live. I will be with you as I was with Moses. I will never neglect you or abandon you. ⁶ Be strong and courageous, because you will help these people take possession of the land I swore to give their ancestors.

⁷ "Only be strong and very courageous, faithfully doing everything in the teachings that my servant Moses commanded you. Don't turn away from them. Then you will succeed wherever you go. ⁸ Never stop reciting these teachings. You must think about them night and day so that you will faithfully do everything written in them. Only then will you prosper and succeed.

⁹ "I have commanded you, 'Be strong and courageous! Don't tremble or be terrified, because the LORD your God is with you wherever you go.'"

¹⁰ Then Joshua ordered the officers of the people, ¹¹ "Go through the camp. Tell the people, 'Get your supplies ready. In three days you will cross the Jordan River to take possession of the land the LORD your God is going to give you.'"

¹² Next, Joshua said to the tribes of Reuben and Gad and half of the tribe of Manasseh, ¹³ "Remember what the LORD's servant Moses commanded you. Moses said, 'The LORD your God will give you this land—a place to rest.' ¹⁴ Your wives, children, and livestock may stay in the land that Moses gave you east of the Jordan River. However, all your best soldiers must march in battle formation ahead of your relatives. You must help your relatives ¹⁵ take possession of the land the LORD your God is going to give them. Then they will have a place to rest like you do. After that, you may go back and take possession of the land east of the Jordan River which the LORD's servant Moses gave you."

¹⁶ The people responded to Joshua, "We'll do everything you tell us and go wherever you send us. ¹⁷ We will obey you as we obeyed Moses. May the LORD your God be with you as he was with Moses. ¹⁸ Whoever rebels against your authority or does not obey your orders will be put to death. Just be strong and courageous!"

¹ From Shittim Joshua, son of Nun, secretly sent out two men as spies. He told them, "Go, look at that country, especially the city of Jericho." So they went to Jericho and entered the house of a prostitute named Rahab to spend the night there.

THE SPIES ESCAPE

Joshua 2:2-14

² The king of Jericho was told, "Some Israelites have entered the city tonight. They came to gather information about our land." ³ So the king of Jericho sent messengers to Rahab, who told her, "Bring out the men who came to your house. They came here to gather information about the entire land."

⁴ But the woman had already taken the two men inside and hidden them. So she said, "Yes, the men did come here. But I didn't know where they had come from. ⁵ When it was dark and the gate was just about to close, they left. I don't know where they went. If you hurry, you'll catch up with them." ⁶ (She had taken them up to the roof and covered them with the flax which she had laid up there.)

⁷ The king's men pursued them on the road leading to a shallow place to cross the Jordan River. As soon as the king's men had left, the gate was closed.

⁸ Before the spies fell asleep, Rahab went up to them on the roof. ⁹ She said to them, "I know the Lᴏʀᴅ will give you this land. Your presence terrifies us. All the people in this country are deathly afraid of you. ¹⁰ We've heard how the Lᴏʀᴅ dried up the water of the Red Sea in front of you when you left Egypt. We've also heard what you did to Sihon and Og, the two kings of the Amorites, who ruled east of the Jordan River. We've heard how you destroyed them for the Lᴏʀᴅ. ¹¹ When we heard about it, we lost heart. There was no courage left in any of us because of you. The Lᴏʀᴅ your God is the God of heaven and earth. ¹² Please swear by the Lᴏʀᴅ that you'll be as kind to my father's family as I've been to you. Also give me some proof ¹³ that you'll protect my father, mother, brothers, sisters, and their households, and that you'll save us from death."

¹⁴ The men promised her, "We pledge our lives for your lives. If you don't tell anyone what we're doing here, we'll treat you kindly and honestly when the Lᴏʀᴅ gives us this land."

SAVED BY A RED CORD

Joshua 2:15-21

¹⁵ So she let them down by a rope from her window since her house was built into the city wall. (She lived in the city wall.) ¹⁶ She told them, "Go to the mountains so that the men who are pursuing you will not find you. Hide there for three days until they return to Jericho. Then you can go on your way."

¹⁷ The men told her, "We will be free from the oath which you made us swear, ⌐if you tell anyone what we're doing here⌐. ¹⁸ When we invade your land, tie this red cord in the window through which you let us down. Also, gather your father, mother, brothers, and all your father's family into your house. ¹⁹ Whoever leaves your house will be responsible for his own life. We will be free from that responsibility. But we will take responsibility if anyone inside your house is harmed. ²⁰ If you tell anyone what we're doing here, we will be free from the oath which you made us swear."

²¹ "I agree," she said. So she let them go and tied the red cord in the window.

THE LORD'S PEOPLE ARE ON THE EDGE OF THE PROMISED LAND

Joshua 2:22-3:5

²² The men went to the mountains and stayed there for three days until the king's men returned to Jericho. The king's men had searched for them all along the road but had not found them. ²³ Then the two spies came down out of the mountains, crossed the Jordan River, and returned to Joshua, son of Nun. They told him everything that had happened to them. ²⁴ They told Joshua, "The Lord has given us the whole country. The people who live there are deathly afraid of us."

¹Joshua got up early the next morning. He and all the Israelites left Shittim. They came to the Jordan River, where they camped before crossing.

²Three days later the officers went through the camp. ³They told the people, "As soon as you see the ark of the promise of the LORD your God and the Levitical priests who carry it, break camp and follow them. ⁴However, stay about half a mile behind them. Don't come any closer to them so that you will know which way to go because you have not gone this way before."

⁵Joshua told the people, "Perform the ceremonies to make yourselves holy because tomorrow the LORD will do miracles among you."

THE LORD'S PEOPLE CROSS THE RIVER JORDAN

Joshua 3:14-17

¹⁴So they broke camp to cross the Jordan River. The priests who carried the ark of the promise went ahead of the people. ¹⁵(The Jordan overflows all its banks during the harvest season.) When the priests who were carrying the ark came to the edge of the Jordan River and set foot in ¹⁶the water, the water stopped flowing from upstream. The water rose up like a dam as far away as the city of Adam near Zarethan. The water flowing down toward the Sea of the Plains (the Dead Sea) was completely cut off. Then the people crossed from the east side ⌊of the Jordan River⌋ directly opposite Jericho. ¹⁷The priests who carried the ark of the LORD's promise stood firmly on dry ground in the middle of the Jordan until the whole nation of Israel had crossed the Jordan River on dry ground.

THE BATTLE WON WITH TRUMPETS

Joshua 6:1-24

Jericho was bolted and barred shut because the people were afraid of the Israelites. No one could enter or leave.

²The LORD said to Joshua, "I am about to hand Jericho, its king, and its warriors over to you. ³All the soldiers will march around the city once a day for six days. ⁴Seven priests will carry rams' horns ahead of the ark. But on the seventh day you must march around the city seven times while the priests blow their horns. ⁵When you hear a long blast on the horn, all the troops must shout very loudly. The wall around the city will collapse. Then the troops must charge straight ahead into the city."

⁶Joshua, son of Nun, summoned the priests. He said to them, "Pick up the ark of the promise, and have seven priests carry seven rams' horns ahead of the LORD's ark."

⁷He told the troops, "March around the city. Let the armed men march ahead of the LORD's ark."

⁸After Joshua had given orders to the troops, the seven priests carrying the seven rams' horns ahead of the LORD marched off as they blew their horns. The ark of the LORD's promise followed them. ⁹The armed men went ahead of the priests, who blew their horns. The rear guard followed the ark while the priests continued to blow their horns.

¹⁰Joshua ordered the troops, "Don't shout, make any noise, or let one word come out of your mouth until I tell you to shout. Then shout!" ¹¹So the LORD's ark went around the city once. Then they went back to the camp and stayed there for the night.

¹²Joshua got up early in the morning. The priests carried the LORD's ark. ¹³The seven priests carrying the seven rams' horns were ahead of it. The priests blew their horns as they went. The armed men were ahead of them, and the rear guard followed the LORD's ark while the horns blew continually. ¹⁴They went around the city once on the second day and returned to the camp. They did this for six days.

¹⁵On the seventh day they got up at dawn. They marched around the city seven times the same way they had done it before. That was the only day they marched around it seven times. ¹⁶When they went around the seventh time, the priests blew their rams' horns.

Joshua said to the troops, "Shout, because the LORD has given you the city! ¹⁷The city has been claimed by the LORD. Everything in it belongs to the LORD. Only the prostitute Rahab and all who are in the house with her will live because she hid the messengers we sent. ¹⁸But stay away from what has been claimed by the LORD for destruction, or you, too, will be destroyed by the LORD. If you take anything that is claimed by the LORD, you will bring destruction and disaster on the camp of Israel. ¹⁹All the silver and gold and everything made of bronze and iron are holy and belong to the LORD. They must go into the LORD's treasury."

²⁰So the troops shouted very loudly when they heard the blast of the rams' horns, and the wall collapsed. The troops charged straight ahead and captured the city. ²¹They claimed everything in it for the LORD. With their swords they killed men and women, young and old, as well as cattle, sheep, and donkeys.

²²But Joshua said to the two spies, "Go to the prostitute's house. Bring the woman out, along with everything she has, as you swore you would do for her."

²³The spies went and brought out Rahab, her father, mother, brothers, everything she had, and even all of her relatives. They gave them a place outside the camp of Israel. ²⁴Then Israel burned the city and everything in it. But they put the silver and gold and everything made of bronze and iron into the LORD's treasury.

97

THE WISE JUDGES THE LORD SENT TO RESCUE HIS PEOPLE FROM THEIR WORSHIP OF FALSE GODS

Judges 2:8-4:16

[8] The LORD's servant Joshua, son of Nun, died at the age of 110. [9] He was buried at Timnath Heres within the territory he had inherited. This was in the mountains of Ephraim north of Mount Gaash. [10] That whole generation had joined their ancestors in death. So another generation grew up after them. They had no personal experience with the LORD or with what he had done for Israel.

[11] The people of Israel did what the LORD considered evil. They began to serve other gods—the Baals. [12] The Israelites abandoned the LORD God of their ancestors, the God who brought them out of Egypt. They followed the other gods of the people around them. They worshiped these gods, and that made the LORD angry. [13] They abandoned the LORD to serve the god Baal and the goddess Astarte. [14] So the LORD became angry with the people of Israel. He handed them over to people who robbed them. He also used their enemies around them to defeat them. They could no longer stand up against their enemies. [15] Whenever the Israelites went to war, the power of the LORD brought disaster on them. This was what the LORD said he would do in an oath. So he made them suffer a great deal.

[16] Then the LORD would send judges to rescue them from those who robbed them. [17] But the people wouldn't listen to the judges. The Israelites chased after other gods as though they were prostitutes and worshiped them. They quickly turned from the ways of their ancestors who had obeyed the LORD's commands. They refused to be like their ancestors. [18] But when the LORD appointed judges for the Israelites, he was with each judge. The LORD rescued them from their enemies as long as that judge was alive. The LORD was moved by the groaning of those who were tormented and oppressed. [19] But after each judge died, the people went back to their old ways and acted more corruptly than their parents. They followed, served, and worshiped other gods. They never gave up their evil practices and stubborn ways.

[20] The LORD became angry with Israel. He said, "Because the people of this nation have rejected the promise I gave their ancestors and have not obeyed me, [21] I will no longer force out the nations Joshua left behind when he died. [22] I will test the people of Israel with these nations to see whether or not they will carefully follow the LORD's ways as their ancestors did." [23] So the LORD let these nations stay. He had not handed them over to Joshua or forced them out quickly.

[1] These are the nations the LORD left behind to test all the Israelites who had not experienced any war in Canaan. [2] The LORD left them to teach Israel's descendants about war, at least those who had known nothing about it in the past. [3] He left the five rulers of the Philistines, all the Canaanites, the Sidonians, and the Hivites who lived on Mount Lebanon from Mount Baal Hermon to the border of Hamath. [4] These nations were left to test the Israelites, to find out if they would obey the commands the LORD had given their ancestors through Moses.

[5] So the people of Israel lived among the Canaanites, Hittites, Amorites, Perizzites, Hivites, and Jebusites. [6] The Israelites allowed their sons and daughters to marry these people. Israel also served their gods.

[7] The people of Israel did what the LORD considered evil. They forgot the LORD their God and served other gods and goddesses—the Baals and the Asherahs. [8] The LORD became angry with the people of Israel. He used King Cushan Rishathaim of Aram Naharaim to defeat them. So Israel served Cushan Rishathaim for eight years.

⁹Then the people of Israel cried out to the Lord for help. The Lord sent a savior to rescue them. It was Othniel, son of Caleb's younger brother Kenaz. ¹⁰When the Lord's Spirit came over him, he became the judge of Israel. He went out to war. The Lord handed King Cushan Rishathaim of Aram Naharaim over to him, and Othniel overpowered him. ¹¹So there was finally peace in the land for 40 years. Then Othniel, son of Kenaz, died.

¹²Once again, the people of Israel did what the Lord considered evil. So the Lord made King Eglon of Moab stronger than Israel, because Israel did what the Lord considered evil. ¹³Eglon got the Ammonites and the Amalekites to help him, and they defeated the Israelites and occupied the City of Palms. ¹⁴The Israelites served King Eglon of Moab for 18 years.

¹⁵Then the people of Israel cried out to the Lord for help. The Lord sent a savior to rescue them. It was Ehud, a left-handed man from the tribe of Benjamin. (Ehud was the son of Gera.)

The people sent him with their tax payment to King Eglon of Moab. ¹⁶Ehud made a two-edged dagger for himself. He fastened it to his right side under his clothes. ¹⁷Then he brought the tax payment to King Eglon. (Eglon was a very fat man.) ¹⁸When Ehud had finished delivering the payment, he sent back the men who had carried it. ¹⁹However, Ehud turned around at the stone idols near Gilgal ˻and returned to Eglon˼. He said, "Your Majesty, I have a secret message for you."

The king replied, "Keep quiet!" Then all his advisers left the room.

²⁰Ehud came up to him as he sat alone in his room on the roof. He said to the king, "I have a message from God for you." As the king rose from his throne, ²¹Ehud reached with his left hand, took the dagger from his right side, and plunged it into Eglon's belly. ²²Even the handle went in after the blade. Eglon's fat covered the blade because Ehud didn't pull the dagger out. The blade stuck out in back. ²³Ehud left the room. (He had closed and locked the doors of the room before he left.)

²⁴After Ehud went out, Eglon's advisers came in. They were surprised that the doors were locked. "He must be using the toilet," they said. ²⁵They waited and waited, but Eglon didn't open the doors. So they took the key and opened the door. They were shocked to see their ruler lying on the floor, dead.

²⁶While they had been waiting, Ehud escaped. He went past the stone idols and escaped to Seirah. ²⁷When he arrived there, he blew a ram's horn in the mountains of Ephraim ˻to summon the troops˼. So the troops of Israel came down from the mountains with him, and he led them. ²⁸He told them, "Follow me! The Lᴏʀᴅ will hand your enemy Moab over to you."

They followed him and captured the shallow crossings of the Jordan River that led to Moab and refused to let anyone cross. ²⁹At that time they killed about ten thousand of Moab's best fighting men. Not one of them escaped. ³⁰The power of Moab was crushed by Israel that day. So there was finally peace in the land for 80 years.

³¹After Ehud came Shamgar, son of Anath. He killed 600 Philistines with a sharp stick used for herding oxen. So he, too, rescued Israel.

¹After Ehud died, the people of Israel again did what the Lᴏʀᴅ considered evil. ²So the Lᴏʀᴅ used King Jabin of Canaan, who ruled at Hazor, to defeat them. The commander of King Jabin's army was Sisera, who lived at Harosheth Haggoyim. ³The people of Israel cried out to the Lᴏʀᴅ for help. King Jabin had 900 chariots made of iron and had cruelly oppressed Israel for 20 years.

⁴Deborah, wife of Lappidoth, was a prophet. She was the judge in Israel at that time. ⁵She used to sit under the Palm Tree of Deborah between Ramah and Bethel in the mountains of Ephraim. The people of Israel would come to her for legal decisions.

⁶Deborah summoned Barak, son of Abinoam, from Kedesh in Naphtali. She told him, "The Lᴏʀᴅ God of Israel has given you this order: 'Gather troops on Mount Tabor. Take 10,000 men from Naphtali and Zebulun with you. ⁷I will lead Sisera (the commander of Jabin's army), his chariots, and troops to you at the Kishon River. I will hand him over to you.'"

⁸Barak said to her, "If you go with me, I'll go. But if you don't go with me, I won't go."

⁹Deborah replied, "Certainly, I'll go with you. But you won't win any honors for the way you're going about this, because the Lᴏʀᴅ will use a woman to defeat Sisera."

So Deborah started out for Kedesh with Barak. ¹⁰Barak called the tribes of Zebulun and Naphtali together at Kedesh. Ten thousand men went to fight under his command. Deborah also went along with him.

¹¹Heber the Kenite had separated from the other Kenites (the descendants of Hobab, Moses' father-in-law). Heber went as far away as the oak tree at Zaanannim near Kedesh and set up his tent.

¹²The report reached Sisera that Barak, son of Abinoam, had come to fight at Mount Tabor. ¹³So Sisera summoned all his chariots (900 chariots made of iron) and all his troops from Harosheth Haggoyim to come to the Kishon River.

¹⁴Then Deborah said to Barak, "Attack! This is the day the Lᴏʀᴅ will hand Sisera over to you. The Lᴏʀᴅ will go ahead of you."

So Barak came down from Mount Tabor with 10,000 men behind him. ¹⁵The Lᴏʀᴅ threw Sisera, all his chariots, and his whole army into a panic in front of Barak's deadly assault. Sisera got down from his chariot and fled on foot. ¹⁶Barak pursued the chariots and the army to Harosheth Haggoyim. So Sisera's whole army was killed in combat. Not one man survived.

WHO WILL KILL SISERA?

Judges 4:17-22

¹⁷Meanwhile, Sisera fled on foot toward the tent of Jael, the wife of Heber the Kenite. Sisera did this because King Jabin of Hazor and Heber's family were on peaceful terms. ¹⁸When Jael came out ⌊of her tent⌋, she met Sisera. She told him, "Sir, come in here! Come into my tent. Don't be afraid." So he went into her tent, and she hid him under a tent curtain.

¹⁹Sisera said to her, "Please give me a little water to drink. I'm thirsty." But instead she gave him milk to drink and covered him up again.

²⁰He said to her, "Stand at the door of the tent. If anyone comes and asks if there has been a man around here, tell them no."

²¹When Sisera had fallen sound asleep from exhaustion, Jael, Heber's wife, took a tent peg and walked quietly toward him with a hammer in her hand. She hammered the tent peg through his temples into the ground. So Sisera died.

²²Barak was still pursuing Sisera. When Jael came out ⌊of her tent⌋, she met him. She said to him, "Come in! I have something to show you—the man you've been looking for." So Barak went into her tent. He saw Sisera lying there dead with the tent peg through his temples.

GIDEON BEGINS HIS WORK TO RESCUE ISRAEL

Judges 6:1-35

¹The people of Israel did what the Lord considered evil. So the Lord handed them over to Midian for seven years. ²Midian's power was too strong for Israel. The Israelites made hiding places in the mountains, caves, and mountain strongholds ˻to protect themselves˼ from Midian. ³Whenever Israel planted crops, Midian, Amalek, and Kedem came and damaged the crops. ⁴The enemy used to camp on the land and destroy the crops all the way to Gaza. They left nothing for Israel to live on—not one sheep, cow, or donkey. ⁵Like swarms of locusts, they came with their livestock and their tents. They and their camels could not be counted. They came into the land only to ruin it. ⁶So the Israelites became very poor because of Midian and cried out to the Lord for help.

⁷When the people of Israel cried out to the Lord for help because of what the Midianites had done to them, ⁸the Lord sent a prophet to them. He said, "This is what the Lord God of Israel says:

I brought you out of Egypt.
I took you away from slavery.
⁹I rescued you from the power of the Egyptians
    and from the power of those
        who oppressed you.
I forced people out of your way.
I gave you their land.
¹⁰I said to you, 'I am the Lord your God.
    You must never fear the gods of the Amorites
        in whose land you will live.'
            But you have not obeyed me."

¹¹The Messenger of the Lord came and sat under the oak tree in Ophrah that belonged to Joash from Abiezer's family. Joash's son Gideon was beating out wheat in a winepress to hide it from the Midianites. ¹²The Messenger of the Lord appeared to Gideon and said, "The Lord is with you, brave man."

¹³Gideon responded, "Excuse me, sir! But if the Lord is with us, why has all this happened to us? Where are all the miracles our ancestors have told us about? Didn't they say, 'The Lord brought us out of Egypt?' But now the Lord has abandoned us and has handed us over to Midian."

¹⁴The Lord turned to him and said, "You will rescue Israel from Midian with the strength you have. I am sending you."

¹⁵Gideon said to him, "Excuse me, sir! How can I rescue Israel? Look at my whole family. It's the weakest one in Manasseh. And me? I'm the least important member of my family."

¹⁶The Lord replied, "I will be with you. You will defeat Midian as if it were ˻only˼ one man."

¹⁷Gideon said to him, "If you find me acceptable, give me a sign that it is really you speaking to me. ¹⁸Don't leave until I come back. I want to bring my gift and set it in front of you."

"I will stay until you come back," he said.

¹⁹Then Gideon went into ˻his house˼ and prepared young goat and unleavened bread made with 18 quarts of flour. He put the meat in a basket and the broth in a pot. Then he went out and presented them to the Messenger of the Lord under the oak tree.

²⁰The Messenger of the Lord told him, "Take the meat and the unleavened bread, put them on this rock and pour the broth over them." Gideon did so. ²¹Then the Messenger of the Lord touched the meat and the bread with the tip of the staff that was in his hand. Fire flared up from the rock and burned the meat and the bread. Then the Messenger of the Lord disappeared. ²²That's when Gideon realized that this had been the Messenger of the Lord. So he said, "Lord God! I have seen the Messenger of the Lord face to face."

[23] The LORD said to him, "Calm down! Don't be afraid. You will not die." [24] So Gideon built an altar there to the LORD. He called it The LORD Calms. To this day it is still in Ophrah, which belongs to Abiezer's family.

[25] That same night the LORD said to Gideon, "Take a bull from your father's herd, a bull that is seven years old. Tear down your father's altar dedicated to the god Baal and cut down the pole dedicated to the goddess Asherah that is next to it. [26] Then, in the proper way, build an altar to the LORD your God on top of this fortified place. Take this second bull and sacrifice it as a burnt offering on the wood from the Asherah pole that you have cut down."

[27] Gideon took ten of his servants and did what the LORD had told him to do. However, he didn't do anything during the day. He was too afraid of his father's family and the men of the city, so he did it at night. [28] When the men of the city got up early in the morning, they saw that the Baal altar had been torn down. The Asherah pole next to it had also been cut down. They saw that the second bull had been sacrificed as a burnt offering on the altar that had been built. [29] They asked each other, "Who did this?" While they were investigating the matter, someone said, "Gideon, son of Joash, did this."

[30] Then the men of the city told Joash, "Bring your son out. He must die. He has torn down the Baal altar and cut down the Asherah pole that was beside it."

[31] But Joash said to everyone standing around him, "You're not going to defend Baal, are you? Do you think you should save him? Whoever defends him will be put to death in the morning. If he's a god, let him defend himself when someone tears down his altar." [32] So that day they nicknamed Gideon "Jerubbaal" [Let Baal Defend Himself], because they said, "When someone tears down Baal's altar, let Baal defend himself."

[33] All of Midian, Amalek, and Kedem combined their armies, crossed ⌊the Jordan River⌋, and camped in the valley of Jezreel. [34] Then the LORD's Spirit gave Gideon strength. So Gideon blew the ram's horn to summon Abiezer's family to follow him. [35] He also sent messengers throughout Manasseh to summon the people to follow him. The tribes of Asher, Zebulun, and Naphtali were also summoned to follow him, and they went to meet the enemy in battle.

THE LORD USES FEWER MEN TO WIN THE BATTLE

Judges 7:1-8

¹ Jerubbaal (that is, Gideon) and all the troops with him got up early and camped above En Harod. Midian's camp was north of him at the hill of Moreh in the valley.

² The LORD said to Gideon, "You have too many men with you for me to hand Midian over to you. Israel might brag and say, 'We saved ourselves.' ³ Announce to the troops, 'Whoever is scared or frightened should leave Mount Gilead and go back home.'" So 22,000 men went back home, and 10,000 were left.

⁴ The LORD said to Gideon, "There are still too many men. Bring them down to the water, and I will test them for you there. If I say to you, 'This one will go with you,' he must go with you. And if I say to you, 'This one won't go with you,' he must not go."

⁵ So Gideon took the men down to the water. The LORD said to him, "Separate those who lap water with their tongues like dogs from those who kneel down to drink." ⁶ Three hundred men lapped water with their hands to their mouths. All the rest of the men knelt down to drink water. ⁷ Then the LORD said to Gideon, "With the 300 men who lapped water I will save you and hand Midian over to you. All the other men should go home." ⁸ So Gideon sent the other men of Israel home, but the 300 men who stayed kept all the supplies and rams' horns.

The camp of Midian was below him in the valley.

LISTENING IN THE NIGHT

Judges 7:9-15

⁹ That night the LORD said to Gideon, "Attack! Go into the camp! I will hand it over to you. ¹⁰ But if you're afraid to go, take your servant Purah to the camp with you. ¹¹ Listen to what people are saying. After that, you will have the courage to go into the camp and attack it."

So Gideon and his servant Purah went to the edge of the camp. ¹² Midian, Amalek, and all of Kedem were spread out in the valley like a swarm of locusts. There were so many camels that they could not be counted. They were as numerous as the grains of sand on the seashore.

¹³ When Gideon got there, he heard a man telling his friend a dream. The man said, "I had a strange dream. There was a loaf of barley bread rolling around in the camp of Midian. When it got to the command post, the loaf of bread hit that tent so hard that the tent collapsed, turned upside down, and fell flat."

¹⁴ His friend replied, "That can only be the sword of Gideon, son of Joash, from Israel. God is going to hand Midian and the whole camp over to him."

¹⁵ When Gideon heard the dream and its interpretation, he worshiped the LORD. Then he went back to the camp of Israel and said, "Attack! The LORD will hand Midian's camp over to you."

TRUMPETS AND TORCHES

Judges 7:16–8:28

16 Gideon divided the 300 men into three companies. He gave them each rams' horns and jars with torches inside. 17 He said to them, "Watch me, and do what I do. When I come to the edge of the camp, do exactly as I do. 18 When I and those with me blow our rams' horns, then the rest of you around the camp do the same and shout, 'For the LORD and for Gideon!'"

19 Gideon and his 100 men came to the edge of the camp. It was the beginning of the midnight watch just at the change of the guards. They blew their rams' horns and smashed the jars they were holding in their hands. 20 The three companies also blew their rams' horns and broke their jars. They held the torches in their left hands and the rams' horns in their right hands so that they could blow them. They shouted, "A sword for the LORD and for Gideon!" 21 While each man kept his position around the camp, everyone in the Midianite camp began to run away, screaming as they fled. 22 The 300 men kept on blowing their rams' horns, and the LORD caused the whole camp of Midian to fight among themselves. They fled as far as Beth Shittah, toward Zererah, and as far as the bank of the stream at Abel Meholah near Tabbath.

23 The men of Israel were summoned from Naphtali, Asher, and all Manasseh to help pursue the troops of Midian. 24 Gideon also sent messengers to the whole mountain region of Ephraim with this message, "Go into battle against Midian. Capture the watering holes as far as Beth Barah and the Jordan River." All the men of Ephraim were also summoned to help. They captured the watering holes as far as Beth Barah and the Jordan River. 25 They also captured Oreb and Zeeb, the two Midianite commanders. They killed Oreb at the Rock of Oreb and Zeeb at the Winepress of Zeeb and kept on pursuing Midian. Then they brought the severed heads of Oreb and Zeeb to Gideon on the other side of the Jordan River.

1 The men from Ephraim strongly protested Gideon's actions. They said, "Why did you do this to us? You didn't invite us to go fight Midian with you."

2 Gideon replied, "I haven't done anything compared with what you have done. Aren't the grapes that Ephraim picked after the harvest better than all the grapes in Abiezer's entire harvest? 3 God handed Oreb and Zeeb, Midian's commanders, over to you. What have I done compared with that?" When they heard what Gideon said, they weren't angry with him anymore.

4 Gideon and his 300 men headed toward the Jordan River. They were exhausted when they crossed it, but they kept pursuing the enemy. 5 So Gideon said to the men of Succoth, "Please give me some food for the men under my command. They're exhausted, and I'm pursuing King Zebah and King Zalmunna of Midian."

6 The generals at Succoth replied, "We shouldn't give your army food. You haven't captured Zebah and Zalmunna yet."

[7] Gideon responded, "Alright, then. When the LORD hands Zebah and Zalmunna over to me, I'll whip your bodies with thorns and thistles from the desert."

[8] Then Gideon went to Penuel and asked the people there for the same help. But they gave him the same reply that the men of Succoth gave. [9] So he told them, "When I come back after my victory, I'll tear down this tower."

[10] Zebah and Zalmunna were in Karkor with an army of about 15,000 men. This was all that was left of Kedem's entire army. In the battle, 120,000 soldiers died. [11] So Gideon went up Tent Dwellers Road, east of Nobah and Jogbehah, and defeated the unsuspecting Midianite army. [12] Zebah and Zalmunna fled as Gideon pursued them. He captured King Zebah and King Zalmunna of Midian, and the whole Midianite army panicked.

[13] Gideon, son of Joash, returned from the battle through the Heres Pass [14] and captured a young man from Succoth. He questioned him, and the young man wrote down for him the names of the 77 officials and leaders of Succoth. [15] Gideon went to the men of Succoth and said, "Here are Zebah and Zalmunna! You insulted me when you said, 'We shouldn't give your exhausted men food before you've captured Zebah and Zalmunna.' " [16] So Gideon took the leaders of the city and taught them a lesson using thorns and thistles from the desert. [17] Then he tore down the tower of Penuel and killed the men of that city.

[18] He asked Zebah and Zalmunna, "What kind of men did you kill at Tabor?"

They answered, "They were like you. Each one looked like a king's son."

[19] Gideon replied, "They were my brothers, my mother's sons. I solemnly swear, as the LORD lives, if you had let them live, I would not have to kill you now." [20] Then he told Jether, his firstborn son, "Get up and kill them!" But Jether didn't draw his sword. He was afraid because he was only a young man.

[21] Zebah and Zalmunna said, "Get up and do it yourself! It's a man's job!" So Gideon got up and killed them. Then he took the half-moon ornaments that were on their camels' necks.

[22] The men of Israel said to Gideon, "You, then your son, and then your grandson, must rule us. You rescued us from Midian."

[23] Gideon replied, "I will not rule you nor will my son. The LORD will rule you." [24] Then Gideon said to them, "Do me a favor. Each of you give me the earrings from your loot." (Their enemies, the Ishmaelites, wore gold earrings.)

[25] The men of Israel answered, "Yes, we'll give them to you." So they spread out a coat. Each man took the earrings from his loot and dropped them on it. [26] The gold earrings Gideon had asked for weighed 40 pounds. This did not include the half-moon ornaments, the earrings, the purple clothes worn by the kings

of Midian, and the chains from their camels' necks. [27] Then Gideon used the gold to make an idol and placed it in his hometown, Ophrah. All Israel chased after it there as though it were a prostitute. It became a trap for Gideon and his family.

[28] The power of Midian was crushed by the people of Israel, and Midian never again became a threat. So the land had peace for 40 years during Gideon's life.

SAMSON KILLS A LION

Judges 13:1–14:9

[1] The people of Israel again did what the LORD considered evil. So the LORD handed them over to the Philistines for 40 years.

[2] There was a man from Zorah named Manoah. Manoah was from the family of Dan. His wife was not able to have children. [3] The Messenger of the LORD appeared to her and said, "You've never been able to have a child, but now you will become pregnant and have a son. [4] Now you must be careful. Don't drink any wine or liquor or eat any unclean food. [5] You're going to become pregnant and have a son. You must never cut his hair because the boy will be a Nazirite dedicated to God from birth. He will begin to rescue Israel from the power of the Philistines."

[6] The woman went to tell her husband. She said, "A man of God came to me. He had a very frightening appearance like the Messenger of God. So I didn't ask him where he came from, and he didn't tell me his name. [7] He told me, 'You're going to become pregnant and have a son. So don't drink any wine or liquor or eat any unclean food because the boy will be a Nazirite dedicated to God from the time he is born until he dies.'"

⁸ Then Manoah pleaded with the LORD, "Please, Lord, let the man of God you sent come back to us. Let him teach us what we must do for the boy who will be born."

⁹ God did what Manoah asked. The Messenger of God came back to his wife while she was sitting out in the fields. But her husband Manoah was not with her. ¹⁰ The woman ran quickly to tell her husband. She said, "The man who came to me the other day has just appeared to me ⌊again⌋."

¹¹ Manoah immediately followed his wife. When he came to the man, he asked him, "Are you the man who spoke to my wife?"

"Yes," he answered.

¹² Then Manoah asked, "When your words come true, how should the boy live and what should he do?"

¹³ The Messenger of the LORD answered Manoah, "Your wife must be careful to do everything I told her to do. ¹⁴ She must not eat anything that comes from the grapevines, drink any wine or liquor, or eat any unclean food. She must be careful to do everything I commanded."

¹⁵ Manoah said to the Messenger of the LORD, "Please stay while we prepare a young goat for you to eat."

¹⁶ But the Messenger of the LORD responded, "If I stay here, I will not eat any of your food. But if you make a burnt offering, sacrifice it to the LORD." (Manoah did not realize that it was the Messenger of the LORD.)

¹⁷ Then Manoah asked the Messenger of the LORD, "What is your name? When your words come true, we will honor you."

¹⁸ The Messenger of the LORD asked him, "Why do you ask for my name? It's a name that works miracles."

¹⁹ So Manoah took a young goat and a grain offering and sacrificed them to the LORD on a rock he used as an altar. While Manoah and his wife watched, the LORD did something miraculous. ²⁰ As the flame went up toward heaven from the altar, the Messenger of the LORD went up in the flame. When Manoah and his wife saw this, they immediately bowed down with their faces touching the ground.

²¹ The Messenger of the LORD didn't appear again to Manoah and his wife. Then Manoah knew that this had been the Messenger of the LORD. ²² So Manoah said to his wife, "We will certainly die because we have seen God."

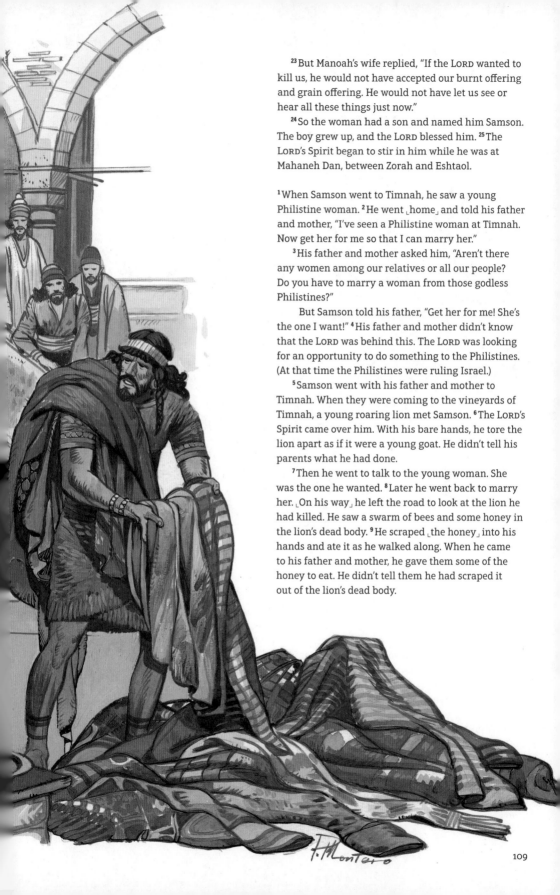

²³ But Manoah's wife replied, "If the LORD wanted to kill us, he would not have accepted our burnt offering and grain offering. He would not have let us see or hear all these things just now."

²⁴ So the woman had a son and named him Samson. The boy grew up, and the LORD blessed him. ²⁵ The LORD's Spirit began to stir in him while he was at Mahaneh Dan, between Zorah and Eshtaol.

¹ When Samson went to Timnah, he saw a young Philistine woman. ² He went ⌊home⌋ and told his father and mother, "I've seen a Philistine woman at Timnah. Now get her for me so that I can marry her."

³ His father and mother asked him, "Aren't there any women among our relatives or all our people? Do you have to marry a woman from those godless Philistines?"

But Samson told his father, "Get her for me! She's the one I want!" ⁴ His father and mother didn't know that the LORD was behind this. The LORD was looking for an opportunity to do something to the Philistines. (At that time the Philistines were ruling Israel.)

⁵ Samson went with his father and mother to Timnah. When they were coming to the vineyards of Timnah, a young roaring lion met Samson. ⁶ The LORD's Spirit came over him. With his bare hands, he tore the lion apart as if it were a young goat. He didn't tell his parents what he had done.

⁷ Then he went to talk to the young woman. She was the one he wanted. ⁸ Later he went back to marry her. ⌊On his way⌋ he left the road to look at the lion he had killed. He saw a swarm of bees and some honey in the lion's dead body. ⁹ He scraped ⌊the honey⌋ into his hands and ate it as he walked along. When he came to his father and mother, he gave them some of the honey to eat. He didn't tell them he had scraped it out of the lion's dead body.

SAMSON TELLS A RIDDLE

Judges 14:10-20

¹⁰ After his father went to see the woman, Samson threw a party. (This is what young men used to do.) ¹¹ When ₍her family₎ saw him, they chose 30 of their friends to be with him.

¹² Then Samson said to them, "Let me tell you a riddle. If you solve it during the seven days of the party, I'll give you 30 linen shirts and 30 changes of clothes. ¹³ But if you can't solve it, you will give me the same things."

They responded, "Tell us your riddle! Let's hear it!"

¹⁴ So Samson said to them,

"From the eater
    came something to eat.
From the strong one
    came something sweet."

For three days they couldn't solve the riddle. ¹⁵ On the fourth day they said to Samson's wife, "Trick your husband into solving the riddle for us. If you don't, we'll burn you and your family to death. Did the two of you invite us ₍just to make us poor₎?"

¹⁶ So Samson's wife cried on his shoulder. She said, "You hate me! You don't really love me! You gave my friends a riddle and didn't tell me the answer."

Samson replied, "I haven't even told my father and mother, so why should I tell you?"

¹⁷ But she cried on his shoulder for the rest of the ·even days of the party. Finally, on the seventh day he ·ld her the answer because she made his life miserable. ·en she told her friends the answer to the riddle.
¹⁸ So before sundown on the seventh day, the men ·the city said to him,

> "What is sweeter than honey?
> What is stronger than a lion?"

Samson replied,

> "If you hadn't used my cow to plow,
> you wouldn't know my riddle now."

¹⁹ When the Lord's Spirit came over him, he went to Ashkelon and killed 30 men there. He took their clothes and gave them to the men who solved the riddle. He was angry, and he went to his father's house. ²⁰ Samson's wife was given to his best man.

SAMSON AND DELILAH

Judges 16:4-22

⁴ After ⌊leaving Gaza⌋ he fell in love with a woman in the Sorek Valley. Her name was Delilah. ⁵ The Philistine rulers came to her and said, "Trick him, and find out what makes him so strong. Find out how we can overpower him. We want to tie him up in order to torture him. Each of us will give you 1,100 pieces of silver."

⁶ So Delilah said to Samson, "Please tell me what makes you so strong. How can you be tied up so that someone could torture you?"

⁷ Samson told her, "If someone ties me up with seven new bowstrings that are not dried out, I will be like any other man."

⁸ The Philistine rulers brought her seven new bowstrings that were not dried out. She tied Samson up with them. ⁹ Some men were hiding in the bedroom waiting for her ⌊to tie him up⌋. Then she said to him, "Samson, the Philistines are attacking!" Samson snapped the bowstrings as a thread snaps when it touches fire. So no one found out why he was so strong.

¹⁰ Delilah told Samson, "Look, you're making fun of me by telling me lies. Now, tell me how you can be tied up."

¹¹ Samson told her, "If someone ties me up tightly with new ropes that have never been used, I will be like any other man."

¹² So Delilah took some new ropes and tied him up with them. Then she said to him, "Samson, the Philistines are attacking!" Some men were in her bedroom waiting to ambush him. But Samson tore the ropes off his arms as though they were strings.

¹³ Delilah told Samson, "You're still making fun of me by telling me lies. Tell me how you can be tied up."

Samson replied, "Just weave the seven braids of my hair with the other threads in the loom."

¹⁴ So Delilah tied his braids to the loom shuttle. Then she said to him, "Samson, the Philistines are attacking!" But Samson woke up and tore his braids and the threads out of the loom shuttle.

¹⁵ Delilah said to Samson, "How can you say that you love me when your heart isn't mine? You've made fun of me three times now, but you still haven't told me what makes you so strong."

¹⁶ Every day she made his life miserable with her questions. She pestered him until he wished he were dead. ¹⁷ Finally, he told her the truth. He told her, "Because I'm a Nazirite, no one has ever cut the hair on my head. I was dedicated to God before I was born. If my hair is ever shaved off, my strength will leave me. Then I'll be like any other man."

¹⁸ When Delilah realized that he had told her everything, she sent a message to the Philistine rulers, "Come here once more." (She did this because Samson had told her everything.) So the Philistine rulers arrived with the money in their hands.

¹⁹ Delilah put Samson to sleep on her lap. She called for a man to shave off his seven braids. Then she began to torture him because his strength had left him. ²⁰ She said, "Samson, the Philistines are attacking!" Samson woke up. He thought, "I'll get out of this as usual and shake myself free." (He didn't realize that the LORD had left him.) ²¹ The Philistines grabbed him. They poked out his eyes and took him to the prison in Gaza. They tied him up with double chains and made him grind grain in the mill there.

²² But his hair started to grow back as soon as it was shaved off.

THE STRONGEST MAN WINS

Judges 16:23-31

²³ Now, the Philistine rulers gathered together to offer a great sacrifice to their god Dagon and to celebrate. They said, "Our god handed Samson, our enemy, over to us." ²⁴ When the people saw him, they praised their god. They said,

"Our god gave our enemy,
    destroyer of our land
        and killer of so many,
            into our very hand!"

²⁵ When all the Philistines were enjoying themselves, they said, "Call Samson in to entertain us."

Samson was called from the prison, and he made them laugh. They made him stand between two columns. ²⁶ Samson told the young man who was leading him by the hand, "Let me rest. Let me touch the columns on which the building stands so that I can lean against them." ²⁷ The building was filled with people. All the Philistine rulers were there. On the roof there were about three thousand men and women who watched Samson entertain them.

²⁸ Then Samson called to the LORD, "Almighty LORD, please remember me! God, give me strength just one more time! Let me get even with the Philistines for at least one of my two eyes." ²⁹ Samson felt the two middle columns on which the building stood. With his right hand on one column and his left on the other, he pushed hard against them. ³⁰ "Let me die with the Philistines," he said. With that, he pushed with all his might, and the building fell on the rulers and everyone in it. So he killed more Philistines when he died than he had when he was alive.

³¹ Then his relatives and his father's whole family went to Gaza. They took Samson and buried him between Zorah and Eshtaol in the tomb of his father Manoah.

Samson had judged Israel for 20 years.

A FAMINE IN THE LAND

Ruth 1:1-13

¹ In the days when the judges were ruling, there was a famine in the land. A man from Bethlehem in Judah went with his wife and two sons to live for a while in the country of Moab. ² The man's name was Elimelech, his wife's name was Naomi, and the names of their two sons were Mahlon and Chilion. They were descendants of Ephrathah from Bethlehem in the territory of Judah. They went to the country of Moab and lived there.

³ Now, Naomi's husband Elimelech died, and she was left alone with her two sons. ⁴ Each son married a woman from Moab. One son married a woman named Orpah, and the other son married a woman named Ruth. They lived there for about ten years. ⁵ Then both Mahlon and Chilion died as well. So Naomi was left alone, without her two sons or her husband.

⁶ Naomi and her daughters-in-law started on the way back from the country of Moab. (While they were still in Moab she heard that the LORD had come to help his people and give them food. ⁷ So she left the place where she had been living, and her two daughters-in-law went with her.) They began to walk back along the road to the territory of Judah.

⁸ Then Naomi said to her two daughters-in-law, "Go back! Each of you should go back to your mother's home. May the LORD be as kind to you as you were to me and to our loved ones who have died. ⁹ May the LORD repay each of you so that you may find security in a home with a husband."

When she kissed them goodbye, they began to cry loudly. [10] They said to her, "We are going back with you to your people."

[11] But Naomi said, "Go back, my daughters. Why should you go with me? Do I have any more sons in my womb who could be your husbands? [12] Go back, my daughters. Go, because I am too old to get married again. If I said that I still have hope…. And if I had a husband tonight…. And even if I gave birth to sons, [13] would you wait until they grew up and stay single just for them? No, my daughters. My bitterness is much worse than yours because the Lord has sent me so much trouble."

RUTH GOES TO WORK IN THE FIELDS

Ruth 2:1-21

¹ Naomi had a relative. He was from Elimelech's side of the family. He was a man of outstanding character named Boaz.

² Ruth, who was from Moab, said to Naomi, "Please let me go to the field of anyone who will be kind to me. There I will gather the grain left behind by the reapers."

Naomi told her, "Go, my daughter."

³ So Ruth went. She entered a field and gathered the grain left behind by the reapers. Now it happened that she ended up in the part of the field that belonged to Boaz, who was from Elimelech's family.

⁴ Just then, Boaz was coming from Bethlehem, and he said to his reapers, "May the Lord be with all of you!"

They answered him, "May the Lord bless you!"

⁵ Boaz asked the young man in charge of his reapers, "Who is this young woman?"

⁶ The young man answered, "She's a young Moabite woman who came back with Naomi from the country of Moab. ⁷ She said, 'Please let me gather grain. I will only gather among the bundles behind the reapers.' So she came here and has been on her feet from daybreak until now. She just sat down this minute in the shelter."

⁸ Boaz said to Ruth, "Listen, my daughter. Don't go in any other field to gather grain, and don't even leave this one. Stay here with my young women. ⁹ Watch where my men are reaping, and follow the young women in that field. I have ordered my young men not to touch you. When you're thirsty, go to the jars and drink some of the water that the young men have drawn."

¹⁰ Ruth immediately bowed down to the ground and said to him, "Why are you so helpful? Why are you paying attention to me? I'm only a foreigner."

¹¹ Boaz answered her, "People have told me about everything you have done for your mother-in-law after your husband died. They told me how you left your father and mother and the country where you were born. They also told me how you came to people

RUTH IS A WOMAN OF LOYALTY

Ruth 1:14-19

¹⁴ They began to cry loudly again. Then Orpah kissed her mother-in-law goodbye, but Ruth held on to her tightly. ¹⁵ Naomi said, "Look, your sister-in-law has gone back to her people and to her gods. Go back with your sister-in-law."

¹⁶ But Ruth answered, "Don't force me to leave you. Don't make me turn back from following you. Wherever you go, I will go, and wherever you stay, I will stay. Your people will be my people, and your God will be my God. ¹⁷ Wherever you die, I will die, and I will be buried there with you. May the Lord strike me down if anything but death separates you and me!"

¹⁸ When Naomi saw that Ruth was determined to go with her, she ended the conversation.

¹⁹ So both of them went on until they came to Bethlehem. When they entered Bethlehem, the whole town was excited about them. "This can't be Naomi, can it?" the women asked.

that you didn't know before. ¹²May the LORD reward you for what you have done! May you receive a rich reward from the LORD God of Israel, under whose protection you have come for shelter."

¹³Ruth replied, "Sir, may your kindness to me continue. You have comforted me and reassured me, and I'm not even one of your own servants."

¹⁴When it was time to eat, Boaz told her, "Come here. Have some bread, and dip it into the sour wine." So she sat beside the reapers, and he handed her some roasted grain. She ate all she wanted and had some left over.

¹⁵When she got up to gather grain, Boaz ordered his servants, "Let her gather grain even among the bundles. Don't give her any problems. ¹⁶Even pull some grain out of the bundles and leave it for her to gather. Don't give her a hard time about it."

¹⁷So Ruth gathered grain in the field until evening. Then she separated the grain from its husks. She had about half a bushel of barley. ¹⁸She picked it up and went into the town, and her mother-in-law saw what she had gathered. Ruth also took out what she had left over from lunch and gave it to Naomi.

¹⁹Her mother-in-law asked her, "Where did you gather grain today? Just where did you work? May the man who paid attention to you be blessed."

So Ruth told her mother-in-law about the person with whom she worked. She said, "The man I worked with today is named Boaz."

²⁰Naomi said to her daughter-in-law, "May the LORD bless him. The LORD hasn't stopped being kind to people—living or dead." Then Naomi told her, "That man is a relative of ours. He is a close relative, one of those responsible for taking care of us."

²¹Ruth, who was from Moab, told her, "He also said to me, 'Stay with my younger workers until they have finished the harvest.'"

RUTH IS THE GREAT-GRANDMOTHER OF A KING

Ruth 2:23-4:17

²³ So Ruth stayed with the young women who were working for Boaz. She gathered grain until both the barley harvest and the wheat harvest ended. And she continued to live with her mother-in-law.

¹ Naomi, Ruth's mother-in-law, said to her, "My daughter, shouldn't I try to look for a home that would be good for you? ² Isn't Boaz, whose young women you've been working with, our relative? He will be separating the barley from its husks on the threshing floor tonight. ³ Freshen up, put on some perfume, dress up, and go down to the threshing floor. Don't let him know that you're there until he's finished eating and drinking. ⁴ When he lies down, notice the place where he is lying. Then uncover his feet, and lie down there. He will make it clear what you must do."

⁵ Ruth answered her, "I will do whatever you say."

⁶ Ruth went to the threshing floor and did exactly as her mother-in-law had directed her. ⁷ Boaz had eaten and drunk to his heart's content, so he went and lay at the edge of a pile of grain. Then she went over to him secretly, uncovered his feet, and lay down.

⁸ At midnight the man was shivering. When he turned over, he was surprised to see a woman lying at his feet. ⁹ "Who are you?" he asked.

She answered, "I am Ruth. Spread the corner of your garment over me because you are a close relative who can take care of me."

¹⁰ Boaz replied, "May the Lᴏʀᴅ bless you, my daughter. This last kindness—that you didn't go after the younger men, whether rich or poor—is better than the first. ¹¹ Don't be afraid, my daughter. I will do whatever you say. The whole town knows that you are a woman who has strength of character. ¹² It is true that I am a close relative of yours, but there is a relative closer than I. ¹³ Stay here tonight. In the morning if he will agree to take care of you, that is good. He can take care of you. But if he does not wish to take care of you, then, I solemnly swear, as the Lᴏʀᴅ lives, I will take care of you myself. Lie down until morning."

¹⁴ So Ruth lay at his feet until morning. Then she got up early before anyone could be recognized. At that moment Boaz thought to himself, "I hope that no one will ever know that this woman came to the threshing floor."

¹⁵ Then Boaz told Ruth, "Stretch out the cape you're wearing and hold it tight." So she held it tight while he measured out six measures of barley. Then he placed it on her ⌞back⌟ and went into the town.

¹⁶ When Ruth returned, her mother-in-law Naomi asked, "How did things go, my daughter?"

Ruth told Naomi everything the man had done for her. ¹⁷ She said, "He gave me these six measures of barley and told me not to come back to you empty-handed."

¹⁸ Naomi replied, "Stay here, my daughter, until you know how it turns out. The man won't rest unless he settles this matter today."

¹Boaz went to the city gate and sat there. Just then, the relative about whom he had spoken was passing by. Boaz said, "Please come over here and sit, my friend." So the man came over and sat down.

²Then Boaz chose ten men who were leaders of that city and said, "Sit here." So they also sat down.

³Boaz said to the man, "Naomi, who has come back from the country of Moab, is selling the field that belonged to our relative Elimelech. ⁴So I said that I would inform you. Buy it in the presence of these men sitting here and in the presence of the leaders of our people. If you wish to buy back the property, you can buy back the property. But if you do not wish to buy back the property, tell me. Then I will know that I am next in line because there is no other relative except me."

The man said, "I'll buy back the property."

⁵Boaz continued, "When you buy the field from Naomi, you will also assume responsibility for the Moabite Ruth, the dead man's widow. This keeps the inheritance in the dead man's name."

⁶The man replied, "In that case I cannot assume responsibility for her. If I did, I would ruin my inheritance. Take all my rights to buy back the property for yourself, because I cannot assume that responsibility."

⁷(This is the way it used to be in Israel concerning buying back property and exchanging goods: In order to make every matter legal, a man would take off his sandal and give it to the other man. This was the way a contract was publicly approved in Israel.) ⁸So when the man said to Boaz, "Buy it for yourself," he took off his sandal.

⁹Then Boaz said to the leaders and to all the people, "Today you are witnesses that I have bought from Naomi all that belonged to Elimelech and all that belonged to Chilion and Mahlon. ¹⁰In addition, I have bought as my wife the Moabite Ruth, Mahlon's widow, to keep the inheritance in the dead man's name. In this way the dead man's name will not be cut off from his relatives or from the public records. Today you are witnesses."

¹¹All the people who were at the gate, including the leaders, said, "We are witnesses. May the LORD make this wife, who is coming into your home, like Rachel and Leah, both of whom built our family of Israel. So show your strength of character in Ephrathah and make a name for yourself in Bethlehem. ¹²Also, from the descendant whom the LORD will give you from this young woman, may your family become like the family of Perez, the son whom Tamar gave birth to for Judah."

¹³Then Boaz took Ruth home, and she became his wife. He slept with her, and the LORD gave her the ability to become pregnant. So she gave birth to a son.

¹⁴The women said to Naomi, "Praise the LORD, who has remembered today to give you someone who will take care of you. The child's name will be famous in Israel. ¹⁵He will bring you a new life and support you in your old age. Your daughter-in-law who loves you is better to you than seven sons, because she has given birth."

¹⁶Naomi took the child, held him on her lap, and became his guardian.

¹⁷The women in the neighborhood said, "Naomi has a son." So they gave him the name Obed.

He became the father of Jesse, who was the father of David.

121

HANNAH WAITS FOR A BABY

1 Samuel 1:1-5

¹There was a man named Elkanah from Ramathaim Zophim in the mountains of Ephraim. He was the son of Jeroham, grandson of Elihu, great-grandson of Tohu, whose father was Zuph from the tribe of Ephraim. ²Elkanah had two wives, one named Hannah, the other Peninnah. Peninnah had children, but Hannah had none. ³Every year this man would go from his own city to worship and sacrifice to the LORD of Armies at Shiloh. Eli's two sons, Hophni and Phinehas, served there as priests of the LORD.

⁴Whenever Elkanah offered a sacrifice, he would give portions of it to his wife Peninnah and all her sons and daughters. ⁵He would also give one portion to Hannah because he loved her, even though the LORD had kept her from having children.

PENINNAH HURTS HANNAH

1 Samuel 1:6-8

⁶Because the LORD had made her unable to have children, her rival ⌊Peninnah⌋ tormented her endlessly in order to make her miserable. ⁷This happened year after year. Whenever Hannah went to the LORD's house, Peninnah would make her miserable, and Hannah would cry and not eat. ⁸Her husband Elkanah would ask her, "Hannah, why are you crying? Why haven't you eaten? Why are you so downhearted? Don't I mean more to you than ten sons?"

123

HANNAH OFFERS A PRAYER FROM HER HEART

1 Samuel 1:9-19

⁹ One day, after Hannah had something to eat and drink in Shiloh, she got up. (The priest Eli was sitting on a chair by the door of the Lord's temple.) ¹⁰ Though she was resentful, she prayed to the Lᴏʀᴅ while she cried. ¹¹ She made this vow, "Lᴏʀᴅ of Armies, if you will look at my misery, remember me, and give me a boy, then I will give him to you for as long as he lives. A razor will never be used on his head." ¹² While Hannah was praying a long time in front of the Lᴏʀᴅ, Eli was watching her mouth. ¹³ She was praying silently. Her voice couldn't be heard; only her lips were moving. Eli thought she was drunk.

¹⁴ "How long are you going to stay drunk?" Eli asked her. "Get rid of your wine."

15 Hannah responded, "No sir. I'm not drunk. I'm depressed. I'm pouring out my heart to the LORD. **16** Don't take me to be a good-for-nothing woman. I was praying like this because I've been troubled and tormented."

17 Eli replied, "Go in peace, and may the God of Israel grant your request."

18 "May you continue to be kind to me," she said. Then the woman went her way and ate. She was no longer sad.

19 Early in the morning Elkanah and his family got up and worshiped in front of the LORD. Then they returned home to Ramah. Elkanah made love to his wife Hannah, and the LORD remembered her.

HANNAH GIVES BIRTH TO A SON – SAMUEL

1 Samuel 1:20-23

20 Hannah became pregnant and gave birth to a son. She named him Samuel [God Hears], because she said, "I asked the LORD for him."

21 To keep his vow, Elkanah and his entire household again went to offer the annual sacrifice to the LORD. **22** But Hannah didn't go. She told her husband, "I'll wait until the boy is weaned. Then I'll bring him and present him to the LORD, and he'll stay there permanently."

23 "Do what you think is best," her husband Elkanah told her. "Wait until you've weaned him. May the LORD keep his word." The woman stayed and nursed her son until she had weaned him.

HANNAH LEAVES SAMUEL WITH ELI

1 Samuel 1:24-28

²⁴ As soon as she had weaned Samuel, she took him with her. She also brought a three-year-old bull, half a bushel of flour, and a full wineskin. She brought him to the Lord's house at Shiloh while the boy was ⌊still⌋ a child.

²⁵ Then the parents butchered the bull and brought the child to Eli. ²⁶ "Sir," Hannah said, "as sure as you live, I'm the woman who stood here next to you and prayed to the Lord. ²⁷ I prayed for this child, and the Lord granted my request. ²⁸ In return, I am giving him to the Lord. He will be dedicated to the Lord for his whole life."

And they worshiped the Lord there.

SAMUEL BECOMES A PRIEST

1 Samuel 2:18-21

¹⁸ Meanwhile, Samuel continued to serve in front of the Lord. As a boy he was ⌊already⌋ wearing a linen ephod. ¹⁹ His mother would make him a robe and bring it to him every year when she went with her husband to offer the annual sacrifice.

²⁰ Eli would bless Elkanah (and his wife) and say, "May the Lord give you children from this woman in place of the one which she has given to the Lord." Then they would go home.

²¹ The Lord came to Hannah. She became pregnant ⌊five times⌋ and had three sons and two daughters. Meanwhile, the boy Samuel grew up in front of the Lord.

SAMUEL HEARS THE LORD'S VOICE

1 Samuel 3:2-18

²One night Eli was lying down in his room. His eyesight had begun to fail so that he couldn't see well. ³The lamp in God's temple hadn't gone out yet, and Samuel was asleep in the temple of the LORD where the ark of God was kept.

⁴Then the LORD called Samuel. "Here I am," Samuel responded. ⁵He ran to Eli and said, "Here I am. You called me."

"I didn't call ⌐you⌐," Eli replied. "Go back to bed." So Samuel went back and lay down.

⁶The LORD called Samuel again. Samuel got up, went to Eli, and said, "Here I am. You called me."

"I didn't call ⌐you⌐, son," he responded. "Go back to bed." ⁷Samuel had no experience with the LORD, because the Lord's word had not yet been revealed to him.

⁸The LORD called Samuel a third time. Samuel got up, went to Eli, and said, "Here I am. You called me."

Then Eli realized that the LORD was calling the boy. ⁹"Go, lie down," Eli told Samuel. "When he calls you, say, 'Speak, LORD. I'm listening.'" So Samuel went and lay down in his room.

[10] The Lord came and stood there. He called as he had called the other times: "Samuel! Samuel!" And Samuel replied, "Speak. I'm listening."

[11] Then the Lord said to Samuel, "I am going to do something in Israel that will make the ears of everyone who hears it ring. [12] On that day I am going to do to Eli and his family everything I said from beginning to end. [13] I told him that I would hand down a permanent judgment against his household because he knew about his sons' sin—that they were cursing God—but he didn't try to stop them. [14] That is why I have taken an oath concerning Eli's family line: No offering or sacrifice will ever ⌊be able to⌋ make peace for the sins that Eli's family committed."

[15] Samuel remained in bed until morning. Then he opened the doors of the Lord's house. But Samuel was afraid to tell Eli about the vision.

[16] Then Eli called Samuel. "Samuel, my son!" he said.

"Here I am," he responded.

[17] "What did the Lord tell you?" he asked. "Please don't hide anything from me. May God strike you dead if you hide anything he told you from me."

[18] So Samuel told Eli everything.

Eli replied, "He is the Lord. May he do what he thinks is right."

THE PEOPLE REFUSE TO LISTEN TO SAMUEL — THEY WANT AN EARTHLY KING

1 Samuel 8:1-20

[1] When Samuel was old, he made his sons judges over Israel. [2] The name of his firstborn son was Joel; the name of his second son was Abijah. They were judges in Beersheba. [3] The sons didn't follow their father's example but turned to dishonest ways of making money. They took bribes and denied people justice.

[4] Then all the leaders of Israel gathered together and came to Samuel at Ramah. [5] They told him, "You're old, and your sons aren't following your example. Now appoint a king to judge us so that we will be like all the other nations."

[6] But Samuel considered it wrong for them to request a king to judge them. So Samuel prayed to the Lord. [7] The Lord told Samuel, "Listen to everything the people are saying to you. They haven't rejected you; they've rejected me. [8] They're doing just what they've done since I took them out of Egypt—leaving me and serving other gods. [9] Listen to them now, but be sure to warn them and tell them about the rights of a king."

[10] Then Samuel told the people who had asked him for a king everything the Lord had said. [11] Samuel said, "These are the rights of a king:

He will draft your sons, make them serve on his chariots and horses, and make them run ahead of his chariots.

[12] He will appoint them to be his officers over 1,000 or over 50 soldiers, to plow his ground and harvest his crops, and to make weapons and equipment for his chariots.

[13] He will take your daughters and have them make perfumes, cook, and bake.

[14] He will take the best of your fields, vineyards, and olive orchards and give them to his officials.

[15] He will take a tenth of your grain and wine and give it to his aids and officials.

[16] He will take your male and female slaves, your best cattle, and your donkeys for his own use.

[17] He will take a tenth of your flocks.

In addition, you will be his servants.

18 "When that day comes, you will cry out because the king whom you have chosen for yourselves. e LORD will not answer you when that day comes."
19 But the people refused to listen to Samuel. They id, "No, we want a king! **20** Then we, too, will be like the other nations. Our king will judge us, lead us t ⌞to war⌟, and fight our battles."

THE BIG SECRET

1 Samuel 9:24-10:1

24 So the cook picked up the leg and thigh and laid it in front of Saul. Samuel said, "This was kept in order to be laid in front of you. Eat it. When I invited people to the feast, I set it aside for you." Saul ate with Samuel that day.

25 Then they left the worship site for the city. They spread blankets on the roof for Saul, and he slept there.

26 At dawn Samuel called to Saul on the roof, "Get up! ⌞It's time for⌟ me to send you away." Saul got up, and both he and Samuel went outside. 27 As they were going toward the city limits, Samuel told Saul, "Have the servant go ahead of you." (He went ahead.) "But you stay here, and I will tell you God's word."

1 Samuel took a flask of olive oil, poured it on Saul's head, kissed him, and said, "The LORD has anointed you to be ruler of his people Israel. You will rule his people and save them from all their enemies. This will be the sign that the LORD has anointed you to be ruler of his people.

SAUL BECOMES KING

1 Samuel 10:17-25

17 Samuel called the people to ⌞come into the presence of⌟ the LORD at Mizpah. 18 He said to the Israelites, "This is what the LORD God of Israel says: I brought Israel out of Egypt and rescued you from the power of the Egyptians and all the kings who were oppressing you. 19 But now you have rejected your God, who saves you from all your troubles and distresses. You said, 'No! Place a king over us.' Now then, stand in front of the LORD by your tribes and family groups."

20 When Samuel had all the tribes of Israel come forward, the tribe of Benjamin was chosen.

21 When he had the tribe of Benjamin come forward by families, the family of Matri was chosen. Then Saul, the son of Kish, was chosen. They looked for him but couldn't find him. 22 They asked the LORD again, "Has he arrived here yet?"

The LORD answered, "He's hiding among the baggage."

23 They ran and got him from there. As he stood among the people, he was a head taller than everyone else. 24 Samuel asked the people, "Do you see whom the LORD has chosen? There is no one like him among all the people."

Then all the people shouted, "Long live the king!"

25 Samuel explained the laws concerning kingship to the people. He wrote the laws on a scroll, which he placed in front of the LORD. Then Samuel sent the people back to their homes.

THE LORD CHOOSES A NEW KING

1 Samuel 15:10-16:13

¹⁰ Then the LORD spoke to Samuel: ¹¹ "I regret that I made Saul king. He turned away from me and did not carry out my instructions." Samuel was angry, and he prayed to the LORD all night. ¹² Early in the morning he got up to meet Saul. Samuel was told, "Saul went to Carmel to set up a monument in his honor. Then he left there and went to Gilgal."

¹³ Samuel came to Saul, who said, "The LORD bless you. I carried out the LORD's instructions."

¹⁴ However, Samuel asked,

> "But what is this sound of sheep in my ears
> and this sound of cows that I hear?"

¹⁵ Saul answered, "The army brought them from the Amalekites. They spared the best sheep and cows to sacrifice to the LORD your God. But the rest they claimed for God and destroyed."

¹⁶ "Be quiet," Samuel told Saul, "and let me tell you what the LORD told me last night."

"Speak," Saul replied.

¹⁷ Samuel said, "Even though you don't consider yourself great, you were the head of Israel's tribes. The LORD anointed you king of Israel. ¹⁸ And the LORD sent you on a mission. He said, 'Claim those sinners, the Amalekites, for me by destroying them. Wage war against them until they're wiped out.' ¹⁹ Why didn't you obey the LORD? Why have you taken their belongings and done what the LORD considers evil?"

²⁰ "But I did obey the LORD," Saul told Samuel. "I went where the LORD sent me, brought ⌐back⌐ King Agag of Amalek, and claimed the Amalekites for God. ²¹ The army took some of their belongings— the best sheep and cows were claimed for God— in order to sacrifice to the LORD your God in Gilgal."

²² Then Samuel said,

> "Is the LORD as delighted with burnt offerings
>   and sacrifices
>   as he would be with your obedience?
> To follow instructions is better than to sacrifice.
> To obey is better than sacrificing the fat of rams.
> ²³   The sin of black magic is rebellion.
>   Wickedness and idolatry are arrogance.
>   Because you rejected the Lord's word,
>   he rejects you as king."

²⁴ Then Saul told Samuel, "I have sinned by not following the LORD's command or your instructions. I was afraid of the people and listened to them. ²⁵ Now please forgive my sin and come back with me so that I may worship the LORD."

²⁶ Samuel told Saul, "I will not go back with you because you rejected what the LORD told you. So the LORD rejects you as king of Israel." ²⁷ When Samuel turned to leave, Saul grabbed the hem of his robe, and it tore. ²⁸ Samuel told him, "The LORD has torn the kingdom of Israel from you today. He has given it to your neighbor who is better than you. ²⁹ In addition, the Glory of Israel does not lie or change his mind, because he is not a mortal who changes his mind."

³⁰ Saul replied, "I have sinned! Now please honor me in front of the leaders of my people and in front of Israel. Come back with me, and let me worship the LORD your God." ³¹ Then Samuel turned and followed Saul, and Saul worshiped the LORD.

³² "Bring me King Agag of Amalek," Samuel said.

Agag came to him trembling. "Surely, the bitterness of death is past," Agag said.

³³ But Samuel said, "As your sword made women childless, so your mother will be made childless among women." And Samuel cut Agag in pieces in the presence of the LORD at Gilgal.

³⁴ Then Samuel went to Ramah, and Saul went to his home at Gibeah. ³⁵ Samuel didn't see Saul again before he died, though Samuel mourned over Saul. And the LORD regretted that he had made Saul king of Israel.

¹ The LORD asked Samuel, "How long are you going to mourn for Saul now that I have rejected him as king of Israel? Fill a flask with olive oil and go. I'm sending you to Jesse in Bethlehem because I've selected one of his sons to be king."

² "How can I go?" Samuel asked. "When Saul hears about it, he'll kill me."

The LORD said, "Take a heifer with you and say, 'I've come to sacrifice to the LORD.' ³ Invite Jesse to the sacrifice. I will reveal to you what you should do, and you will anoint for me the one I point out to you."

⁴ Samuel did what the LORD told him. When he came to Bethlehem, the leaders of the city, trembling with fear, greeted him and said, "May peace be with you."

133

5 "Greetings," he replied, "I have come to sacrifice to the LORD. Perform the ceremonies to make yourselves holy, and come with me to the sacrifice." He performed the ceremonies for Jesse and his sons and invited them to the sacrifice. **6** When they came, he saw Eliab and thought, "Certainly, here in the LORD's presence is his anointed king."

7 But the LORD told Samuel, "Don't look at his appearance or how tall he is, because I have rejected him. God does not see as humans see. Humans look at outward appearances, but the LORD looks into the heart."

8 Then Jesse called Abinadab and brought him to Samuel. But Samuel said, "The LORD has not chosen this one either."

9 Then Jesse had Shammah come to Samuel. "The LORD has not chosen this one either," Samuel said.
10 So Jesse brought seven ⌊more⌋ of his sons to Samuel, but Samuel told Jesse, "The LORD has not chosen ⌊any of⌋ these. **11** Are these all the sons you have?"

"There's still the youngest one," Jesse answered. "He's tending the sheep."

Samuel told Jesse, "Send someone to get him. We won't continue until he gets here."

12 So Jesse sent for him. He had a healthy complexion, attractive eyes, and a handsome appearance. The LORD said, "Go ahead, anoint him. He is the one." **13** Samuel took the flask of olive oil and anointed David in the presence of his brothers. The LORD's Spirit came over David and stayed with him from that day on. Then Samuel left for Ramah.

DAVID CARES FOR SAUL

1 Samuel 16:14-23

14 Now, the LORD's Spirit had left Saul, and an evil spirit from the LORD tormented him. **15** Saul's officials told him, "An evil spirit from God is tormenting you. **16** Your Majesty, why don't you command us to look for a man who can play the lyre well? When the evil spirit from God comes to you, he'll strum a tune, and you'll feel better."

17 Saul told his officials, "Please find me a man who can play well and bring him to me."

18 One of the officials said, "I know one of Jesse's sons from Bethlehem who can play well. He's a courageous man and a warrior. He has a way with words, he is handsome, and the LORD is with him."

19 Saul sent messengers to Jesse to say, "Send me your son David, who is with the sheep."

²⁰ Jesse took six bushels of bread, a full wineskin, and a young goat and sent them with his son David to Saul. ²¹ David came to Saul and served him. Saul loved him very much and made David his armorbearer. ²² Saul sent ⌊this message⌋ to Jesse, "Please let David stay with me because I have grown fond of him."

²³ Whenever God's spirit came to Saul, David took the lyre and strummed a tune. Saul got relief ⌊from his terror⌋ and felt better, and the evil spirit left him.

GOLIATH — THE PHILISTINE GIANT

Samuel 17:3-16

The Philistines were stationed on a hill on one side, and the Israelites were stationed on a hill on the other side. There was a ravine between the two of them.

⁴ The Philistine army's champion came out of their camp. His name was Goliath from Gath. He was ten feet tall. ⁵ He had a bronze helmet on his head, and he wore a bronze coat of armor scales weighing 125 pounds. ⁶ On his legs he had bronze shin guards and on his back a bronze javelin. ⁷ The shaft of his spear was like the beam used by weavers. The head of his spear was made of 15 pounds of iron. The man who carried his shield walked ahead of him.

⁸ Goliath stood and called to the Israelites, "Why do you form a battle line? Am I not a Philistine, and aren't you Saul's servants? Choose a man, and let him come down to ⌊fight⌋ me. ⁹ If he can fight me and kill me, then we will be your slaves. But if I overpower him and kill him, then you will be our slaves and serve us." ¹⁰ The Philistine added, "I challenge the Israelite battle line today. Send out a man so that we can fight each other." ¹¹ When Saul and all the Israelites heard what this Philistine said, they were gripped with fear.

¹² David was a son of a man named Jesse from the region of Ephrath and the city of Bethlehem in Judah. Jesse had eight sons, and in Saul's day he was an old man. ¹³ Jesse's three oldest sons joined Saul's army for the battle. The firstborn was Eliab, the second was Abinadab, the third was Shammah, ¹⁴ and David was the youngest. The three oldest joined Saul's army. David went back and forth from Saul's camp to Bethlehem, where he tended his father's flock.

¹⁶ Each morning and evening for 40 days, the Philistine came forward and made his challenge.

GOLIATH'S INSULTS

Samuel 17:17-27

[17] Jesse told his son David, "Take this half-bushel of roasted grain and these ten loaves of bread to your brothers. Take them to your brothers in the camp right away. [18] And take these ten cheeses to the captain of the regiment. See how your brothers are doing, and bring back some news about them. [19] They, along with Saul and all the soldiers of Israel, are in the Elah Valley fighting the Philistines."

[20] David got up early in the morning and had someone else watch ˏthe sheepˏ. He took ˏthe foodˏ and went, as Jesse ordered him. He went to the camp as the army was going out to the battle line shouting their war cry. [21] Israel and the Philistines formed their battle lines facing each other. [22] David left the supplies behind in the hands of the quartermaster, ran to the battle line, and greeted his brothers. [23] While he was talking to them, the Philistine champion, Goliath from Gath, came from the battle lines of the Philistines. He repeated his words, and David heard them. [24] When all the men of Israel saw Goliath, they fled from him because they were terrified. [25] The men of Israel said, "Did you see that man coming ˏfrom the Philistine linesˏ? He keeps coming to challenge Israel. The king will make the man who kills this Philistine very rich. He will give his daughter to that man to marry and elevate the social status of his family."

[26] David asked the men who were standing near him, "What will be done for the man who kills this Philistine and gets rid of Israel's disgrace? Who is this uncircumcised Philistine that he should challenge the army of the living God?"

[27] The soldiers repeated ˏto Davidˏ how the man who kills Goliath would be treated.

DAVID THE GIANT-KILLER

1 Samuel 17:31-51

[31] What David said was overheard and reported to Saul, who then sent for him. [32] David told Saul, "No one should be discouraged because of this. I will go and fight this Philistine."

[33] Saul responded to David, "You can't fight this Philistine. You're just a boy, but he's been a warrior since he was your age."

[34] David replied to Saul, "I am a shepherd for my father's sheep. Whenever a lion or a bear came and carried off a sheep from the flock, [35] I went after it, struck it, and rescued the sheep from its mouth. If it attacked me, I took hold of its mane, struck it, and killed it. [36] I have killed lions and bears, and this uncircumcised Philistine will be like one of them because he has challenged the army of the living God." [37] David added, "The Lord, who saved me from the lion and the bear, will save me from this Philistine."

"Go," Saul told David, "and may the Lord be with you."

[38] Saul put his battle tunic on David; he put a bronze helmet on David's head and dressed him in armor. [39] David fastened Saul's sword over his clothes and tried to walk, but he had never practiced doing this. "I can't walk in these things," David told Saul. "I've never had any practice doing this." So David took all those things off.

[40] He took his stick with him, picked out five smooth stones from the riverbed, and put them in his shepherd's bag. With a sling in his hand, he approached the Philistine. [41] The Philistine, preceded by the man carrying his shield, was coming closer and closer to David. [42] When the Philistine got a good look at David, he despised him. After all, David was a young man with a healthy complexion and good looks.

[43] The Philistine asked David, "Am I a dog that you come to ˏattackˏ me with sticks?" So the Philistine called on his gods to curse David. [44] "Come on," the Philistine told David, "and I'll give your body to the birds."

[45] David told the Philistine, "You come to me with sword and spear and javelin, but I come to you in the name of the Lord of Armies, the God of the army of Israel, whom you have insulted. [46] Today the Lord will hand you over to me. I will strike you down and cut off your head. And this day I will give the dead bodies of the Philistine army to the birds and the wild animals. The whole world will know that Israel has a God. [47] Then everyone gathered here will know that the Lord can save without sword or spear, because the Lord determines every battle's outcome. He will hand all of you over to us."

48 When the Philistine moved closer in order to attack, David quickly ran toward the opposing battle line to attack the Philistine. **49** Then David reached into his bag, took out a stone, hurled it from his sling, and struck the Philistine in the forehead. The stone sank into Goliath's forehead, and he fell to the ground on his face. **50** So using ⌊only⌋ a sling and a stone, David proved to be stronger than the Philistine. David struck down and killed the Philistine, even though David didn't have a sword in his hand.

51 David ran and stood over the Philistine. He took Goliath's sword, pulled it out of its sheath, and made certain the Philistine was dead by cutting off his head.

When the Philistines saw their hero had been killed, they fled.

KING SAUL IS JEALOUS

Samuel 18:5-30

5 David was successful wherever Saul sent him. Saul put him in charge of the fighting men. This pleased all the people, including Saul's officials.

6 As they arrived, David was returning from a campaign against the Philistines. Women from all of Israel's cities came to meet King Saul. They sang and danced, accompanied by tambourines, joyful music, and triangles. **7** The women who were celebrating sang,

> "Saul has defeated thousands
>   but David tens of thousands!"

8 Saul became very angry because he considered this saying to be insulting. "To David they credit tens of thousands," he said, "but to me they credit ⌊only⌋ a few thousand. The only thing left for David is my kingdom." **9** From that day on Saul kept an eye on David.

10 The next day an evil spirit from God seized Saul. He began to prophesy in his house while David strummed a tune on the lyre as he did every day. Now, Saul had a spear in his hand. **11** He raised the spear and thought, "I'll nail David to the wall." But David got away from him twice.

12 Saul was afraid of David, because the LORD was with David but had left Saul. **13** So he kept David away. He made David captain of a regiment. David led the troops out ⌊to battle⌋ and back again. **14** He was successful in everything he undertook because the LORD was with him. **15** Saul noticed how very successful he was and became ⌊even more⌋ afraid of him. **16** Everyone in Israel and Judah loved David, because he led them in and out ⌊of battle⌋.

17 Finally, Saul said to David, "Here is my oldest daughter Merab. I will give her to you as your wife if you prove yourself to be a warrior for me and fight the LORD's battles." (Saul thought, "I must not lay a hand on him. Let the Philistines do that.")

18 "Who am I?" David asked Saul. "And how important are my relatives or my father's family in Israel that I should be the king's son-in-law?"

19 But when the time came to give Saul's daughter Merab to David, she was married to Adriel from Meholah. **20** However, Saul's daughter Michal fell in love with David. When Saul was told about it, the news pleased him. **21** Saul thought, "I'll give her to David. She will trap him, and the Philistines will get him." So he said to David a second time, "You will now be my son-in-law."

22 Saul ordered his officers, "Talk to David in private. Tell him, 'The king likes you, and all his officers are fond of you. Become the king's son-in-law.'"

23 When Saul's officers made it a point to say this, David asked, "Do you think it's easy to become the king's son-in-law? I am a poor and unimportant person."

24 When the officers told Saul what David had said, **25** Saul replied, "Tell David, 'The king doesn't want any payment for the bride except 100 Philistine foreskins so that he can get revenge on his enemies.'" In this way Saul planned to have David fall into the hands of the Philistines. **26** When his officers told David this, David concluded that it was acceptable to become the king's son-in-law. Before the time was up, **27** David and his men went out and struck down 200 Philistines. David brought the foreskins, and they counted them out for the king so that David could become the king's son-in-law. Then Saul gave him his daughter Michal as his wife. **28** Saul realized that the LORD was with David and that his daughter Michal loved David. **29** Then Saul was even more afraid of David, and so Saul became David's constant enemy.

30 The Philistine generals still went out ⌞to fight Israel⌟. But whenever they went out ⌞to fight⌟, David was more successful than the rest of Saul's officers. So David gained a good reputation.

FRIENDS FOR LIFE

: Samuel 18:1-5 and 19:1-7

[1] David finished talking to Saul. After that, Jonathan became David's closest friend. He loved David as much as ⌐he loved⌐ himself. **2** (From that day on Saul kept David ⌐as his servant⌐ and didn't let him go back to his family.) **3** So Jonathan made a pledge of mutual loyalty with David because he loved him as much as ⌐he loved⌐ himself. **4** Jonathan took off the coat he had on and gave it to David along with his battle tunic, his sword, his bow, and his belt.

Saul told his son Jonathan and all his officers to kill David. But Saul's son Jonathan was very fond of David, so he reported to David, "My father Saul is trying to kill you. Please be careful tomorrow morning. Go into hiding, and stay out of sight. **3** I'll go out and stand beside my father in the field where you'll be. I'll speak with my father about you. If I find out anything, I'll tell you."

4 So Jonathan spoke well of David to his father Saul. "You should not commit a sin against your servant David," he said. "He hasn't sinned against you. Instead, he has done some very fine things for you: **5** He risked his life and killed the Philistine Goliath, and the LORD gave all Israel a great victory. When you saw it, you rejoiced. Why then should you sin by shedding David's innocent blood for no reason?"

6 Saul listened to Jonathan, and he promised, "I solemnly swear, as the LORD lives, he will not be killed." Jonathan told David all of this. Then Jonathan took David to Saul. So David was returned to his former status in Saul's court.

JONATHAN SAVES DAVID'S LIFE

: Samuel 19:9-20:41

Then an evil spirit from the LORD came over Saul while he was sitting in his house with his spear in his hand. David was strumming a tune. **10** Saul tried to nail David to the wall with his spear. But David dodged it, and Saul's spear struck the wall. David fled, escaping ⌐from Saul⌐ that night.

11 Saul sent messengers to watch David's house and kill him in the morning. But Michal, David's wife, advised him, "If you don't save yourself tonight, you'll be dead tomorrow!" **12** So Michal lowered David through a window, and he ran away to escape. **13** Then Michal took the idols, laid them in the bed, put a goat-hair blanket at its head, and covered the idols with a garment.

14 When Saul sent messengers to get David, Michal said, "He's sick." **15** Then Saul sent the messengers back to see David themselves. Saul told them, "Bring him here to me in his bed so that I can kill him." **16** The messengers came, and there in the bed were the idols with the goat-hair blanket at its head.

17 Saul asked Michal, "Why did you betray me by sending my enemy away so that he could escape?"

Michal answered, "He told me, 'Let me go! Why should I kill you?'"

18 David escaped and went to Samuel at Ramah. He told Samuel everything Saul had done to him. Then he and Samuel went to the pastures and lived there.

¹⁹When it was reported to Saul that David was in the pastures at Ramah, ²⁰Saul sent messengers to get David. But when they saw a group of prophets prophesying with Samuel serving as their leader, God's Spirit came over Saul's messengers so that they also prophesied. ²¹When they told Saul ˌabout thisˌ, he sent other messengers, but they also prophesied. Saul even sent a third group of messengers, but they also prophesied. ²²Then he went to Ramah himself. He went as far as the big cistern in Secu and asked ˌthe peopleˌ, "Where are Samuel and David?"

He was told, "Over there in the pastures at Ramah." ²³As he went toward the pastures at Ramah, God's Spirit came over him too. He continued his journey, prophesying until he came to the pastures at Ramah. ²⁴He even took off his clothes as he prophesied in front of Samuel and lay there naked all day and all night. This is where the saying, "Is Saul one of the prophets?" came from.

¹David fled from the pastures at Ramah, came to Jonathan, and asked, "What have I done? What crime am I guilty of? What sin have I committed against your father that he's trying to kill me?"

²Jonathan answered, "That's unthinkable! You're not going to die! My father does nothing without telling me, whether it's important or not. Why should my father hide this from me? It's just not that way."

³But David took an oath, saying, "Your father certainly knows that you support me, so he said ˌto himselfˌ, 'Jonathan must not know about this. It will bring him distress.' But I solemnly swear, as the LORD and you live, I'm only one step away from death."

⁴Jonathan said to David, "I'll do whatever you say."

⁵David replied, "Tomorrow is the New Moon Festival, when I should sit and eat at the king's ˌtableˌ. But let me go and hide in the countryside for two more nights. ⁶If your father really misses me, tell him, 'David repeatedly begged me to let him run to Bethlehem, his hometown, because his relatives are offering the annual sacrifice there.' ⁷If he says, 'Good!' then I will be safe. But if he gets really angry, then you'll know for sure that he has decided to harm me. ⁸Now, be kind to me. After all, you forced me into an agreement with the LORD. If I have committed any crime, kill me yourself. Why bother taking me to your father?"

⁹Jonathan answered, "That's unthinkable! If I knew for sure that my father had decided to harm you, I would have told you about it."

¹⁰ Then David asked, "Who will tell me whether or not your father gives you a harsh answer?"

¹¹ Jonathan said, "Let's go out into the country." So they went out into the country.

¹² "As the LORD God of Israel ⸤is my witness⸥," Jonathan continued, "I'll find out in the next two or three days how my father feels about you. If he does feel kindly toward you, then I will send someone to tell you. ¹³ If my father plans to harm you and I fail to tell you and send you away safely, may the LORD harm me even more. May the LORD be with you as he used to be with my father. ¹⁴ But as long as I live, promise me that you will ⸤show me kindness because of the LORD. And even when I die, ¹⁵ never stop being kind to my family. The Lord will wipe each of David's enemies off the face of the earth. ¹⁶ At that time, if Jonathan's name is cut off from David's family, then may the LORD punish David's house."

17 Once again Jonathan swore an oath to David because of his love for David. He loved David as much as he loved himself. **18** "Tomorrow is the New Moon Festival," Jonathan told him, "and you will be missed when your seat is empty. **19** The day after tomorrow you will be missed even more. So go to the place where you hid on that other occasion, and stay by the rock. **20** I will shoot three arrows from beside it toward a target. **21** Then I will send out a boy and say, 'Go, find the arrows.' Now, if I tell the boy, 'Look, the arrows are next to you; get them,' then come ⌊back with me⌋. You will be safe, and there will be no trouble. I swear it, as the LORD lives. **22** But if I tell the boy, 'The arrows are next to you,' then go, because the LORD has sent you away. **23** We have made a promise to each other, and the LORD is ⌊a witness⌋ between you and me forever."

24 So David hid in the countryside. When the New Moon Festival came, King Saul sat down to eat the festival meal. **25** He sat in his usual seat by the wall, while Jonathan stood. Abner sat beside Saul, but David's place was empty. **26** Saul didn't say anything that day, thinking, "Something has happened to him so that he's unclean. He must be unclean." **27** But on the second day of the month, David's place was still empty.

Saul asked his son Jonathan, "Why hasn't Jesse's son come to the meal either yesterday or today?"

28 Jonathan answered Saul, "David repeatedly begged me ⌊to let him go⌋ to Bethlehem. **29** David said to me 'Please let me go. Our relatives will offer a sacrifice in the city, and my brother ordered me to be there. If you will permit it, please let me go to see my brothers.' This is why he hasn't come to your banquet."

30 Then Saul got angry with Jonathan. "Son of a crooked and rebellious woman!" he called Jonathan. "I know you've sided with Jesse's son. You have no shame. ⌊You act⌋ as if you are your mother's son but not mine. **31** As long as Jesse's son lives on earth, neither you nor your right to be king is secure. Now, send some men to bring him to me. He's a dead man!"

32 Jonathan asked his father, "Why should he be killed? What has he done?"

33 Saul raised his spear to strike him. Then Jonathan knew his father was determined to kill David. **34** Jonathan got up from the table very angry and ate nothing that second day of the month. He was worried sick about David because Jonathan had been humiliated by his own father.

35 In the morning Jonathan went out to the country to the place he and David had agreed on. Jonathan had a young boy with him. **36** "Run," he told the boy, "please find the arrows I shoot."

The boy ran, and Jonathan shot the arrow over him. **37** When the boy reached the place where Jonathan's arrow ⌊had landed⌋, Jonathan called after him, "The arrows are next to you!" **38** Jonathan added, "Quick! Hurry up! Don't stand there!" Jonathan's young servant gathered the arrows and came to his master. **39** The boy had no idea what was going on, but Jonathan and David understood. **40** Then Jonathan gave his weapons to the boy. He told the boy, "Take them back into town."

41 When the boy had left, David came out from the south side ⌊of the rock⌋ and quickly bowed down three times with his face touching the ground. Then they kissed each other and cried together, but David cried the loudest.

down with his face touching the ground. [9] David asked Saul, "Why do you listen to rumors that I am trying to harm you? [10] Today you saw how the LORD handed you over to me in the cave. Although I was told to kill you, I spared you, saying, 'I will not raise my hand against Your Majesty because you are the LORD's anointed.' [11] My master, look at this! The border of your robe is in my hand! Since I cut off the border of your robe and didn't kill you, you should know and be able to see I mean no harm or rebellion. I haven't sinned against you, but you are trying to ambush me in order to take my life. [12] May the LORD decide between you and me. May the LORD take revenge on you for what you did to me. However, I will not lay a hand on you. [13] It's like people used to say long ago, 'Wickedness comes from wicked people.' But I will not lay a hand on you. [14] Against whom has the king of Israel come out? Whom are you pursuing? A dead dog? One flea? [15] So the LORD must be the judge. He will decide between you and me. He will watch and take my side in ⌊this⌋ matter and set me free from you."

[16] When David finished saying this, Saul asked, "Is that you speaking, my servant David?" and Saul cried loudly. [17] He told David, "You are more righteous than I. You treated me well while I treated you badly. [18] Today you have proved how good you've been to me. When the LORD handed me over to you, you didn't kill me. [19] When a person finds an enemy, does he send him away unharmed? The LORD will repay you completely for what you did for me today.

EVERYTHING IS LOST

1 Samuel 30:1-18

[1] Two days later, when David and his men came to Ziklag, the Amalekites had raided the Negev, including Ziklag. They had attacked Ziklag and burned it. [2] Although they captured the young and old women who were there, they killed no one. Instead, they had taken ⌊the women and other prisoners⌋ and gone away. [3] By the time David and his men came to the town, it had been burned down, and their wives, sons, and daughters had been taken captive. [4] Then David and his men cried loudly until they didn't have the strength to cry anymore. [5] The Amalekites also captured David's two wives, Ahinoam from Jezreel and Abigail (who had been Nabal's wife) from Carmel. [6] David was in great distress because the people in their bitterness said he should be stoned. (They were thinking of their sons and daughters. But David found strength in the LORD his God.)

⌊A⌋LONE IN A CAVE

⌊1 S⌋amuel 24:2-19

⌊T⌋hen Saul took 3,000 of the best-trained men from all ⌊Isr⌋ael and went to search for David and his men on the ⌊ro⌋cks of the Wild Goats. [3] He came to some sheep pens ⌊alo⌋ng the road where there was a cave. Saul went into ⌊in⌋to to relieve himself while David and his men were ⌊sit⌋ting further back in the cave.

[4] David's men told him, "Today is the day the LORD ⌊re⌋ferred to when he said, 'I'm going to hand your ⌊en⌋emy over to you. You will do to him whatever you ⌊thi⌋nk is right.'"

David quietly got up and cut off the border of ⌊Sa⌋ul's robe. [5] But afterward, David's conscience bothered ⌊hi⌋m because he had cut off the border of Saul's robe. ⌊H⌋e said to his men, "It would be unthinkable for me to ⌊ra⌋ise my hand against His Majesty, the LORD's anointed ⌊kin⌋g, since he is the LORD's anointed." [7] So David stopped ⌊hi⌋s men by saying this to them and didn't let them ⌊at⌋tack Saul.

Saul left the cave and went out onto the road. ⌊L⌋ater, David got up, left the cave, and called to Saul, ⌊"Yo⌋ur Majesty!" When Saul looked back, David knelt

147

[7] David told the priest Abiathar, Ahimelech's son, "Please bring me the priestly ephod." So Abiathar brought David the ephod.

[8] Then David asked the LORD, "Should I pursue these troops? Will I catch up with them?"

"Pursue them," the LORD told him. "You will certainly catch up with them and rescue the captives."

[9] So David and his 600 men went to the Besor Valley, where some were left behind. [10] David and 400 men went in pursuit, while 200 men who were too exhausted to cross the Besor Valley stayed behind.

[11] David's men found an Egyptian in the open country and took him to David. They gave him food to eat and water to drink. [12] They gave him a slice of fig cake and two bunches of raisins. After he had eaten, he revived. (He hadn't eaten any food or drunk any water for three whole days.) [13] David asked him, "To whom do you belong? Where do you come from?"

"I'm an Egyptian, the slave of an Amalekite," the young man answered. "My master left me behind because I got sick three days ago. [14] We raided the portion of the Negev where the Cherethites live, the territory of Judah, the portion of the Negev where Caleb settled, and we burned down Ziklag."

[15] "Will you lead me to these troops?" David asked him.

He answered, "Take an oath in front of God that you won't kill me or hand me over to my master, and I'll lead you to these troops."

[16] The Egyptian led him ⌞to them⌟. They were spread out all over the land, eating, and drinking. They were celebrating because they had taken so much loot from Philistine territory and from the land of Judah. [17] From dawn until evening the next day, David attacked them. No one escaped except 400 young men who rode away on camels. [18] David rescued everything the Amalekites had taken, including his two wives.

DAVID LOSES SAUL AND JONATHAN

1 Samuel 31:1-6

[1] When the Philistines were fighting against Israel, the men of Israel fled from the Philistines and were killed in battle on Mount Gilboa. [2] The Philistines caught up to Saul and his sons. They killed Jonathan, Abinadab, and Malchishua, Saul's sons. [3] The heaviest fighting was against Saul. When the archers got him in their range, he was badly wounded by them.

[4] Saul told his armorbearer, "Draw your sword! Stab me, or these godless men will come, stab me, and make fun of me." But his armorbearer refused because he was terrified. So Saul took the sword and fell on it. [5] When the armorbearer saw that Saul was dead, he also fell on his sword and died with him. [6] So Saul, his three sons, his armorbearer, and all his men died together that day.

DAVID IS CROWNED KING

2 Samuel 5:1-10

[1] All the tribes of Israel came to David at Hebron. "We are your own flesh and blood," they said. [2] "Even in the past when Saul ruled us, you were the one who led Israel in battle. The LORD has said to you, 'You will be shepherd of my people Israel, the leader of Israel.'"

[3] All the leaders of Israel had come to Hebron. King David made an agreement with them at Hebron in front of the LORD. So they anointed David king of Israel. [4] David was 30 years old when he became king, and he ruled for 40 years. [5] In Hebron he ruled Judah for seven years and six months. In Jerusalem he ruled for 33 years over all Israel and Judah.

[6] The king and his men went to Jerusalem to attack the Jebusites, who lived in that region. The Jebusites told David, "You will never get in here. Even the blind and the lame could turn you away" (meaning that David could never get in there). [7] But David captured the fortress Zion (that is, the City of David). [8] That day David said, "Whoever wants to defeat the Jebusites must reach the lame and the blind who hate me by using the water shaft." So there is a saying, "The blind and the lame will not get into the palace." [9] David lived in the fortress and called it the City of David. He built the city ⌞of Jerusalem⌟ around it from the Millo to the palace. [10] David continued to grow more powerful because the LORD God of Armies was with him.

8 When the Philistines heard that David had been anointed king of Israel, all of them came to attack David. But David heard about it and went out to meet them. **9** The Philistines had come and raided the valley of Rephaim.

10 David asked God, "Should I attack the Philistines? Will you hand them over to me?"

The Lᴏʀᴅ answered him, "Attack! I will hand them over to you."

11 So David ⌊and his men⌋ attacked and defeated the Philistines at Baal Perazim. David said, "Using my power like an overwhelming flood, God has overwhelmed my enemies." That is why they call that place Baal Perazim [The Lord Overwhelms]. **12** The Philistines left their gods there, so David ordered that the gods be burned.

13 The Philistines again raided the valley. **14** Once more David asked God.

God answered him, "Don't go after them. Circle around, and come at them in front of the balsam trees. **15** As you hear the sound of marching in the tops of the balsam trees, then go out and fight because God has gone ahead of you to defeat the Philistine army."

16 David did as God ordered him, and his men defeated the Philistine army from Gibeon to Gezer. **17** David's fame spread through all lands, and the Lᴏʀᴅ made all the nations fear him.

THE ARK OF GOD ARRIVES IN JERUSALEM

Chronicles 15:1–16:6

After David constructed buildings for himself in the City of David, he prepared a place for God's ark and set up a tent for it. ²Then David insisted that only the Levites carry God's ark because the LORD had chosen them to carry his ark and to serve him forever.

³David called together all Israel at Jerusalem to bring the LORD's ark to the place he had prepared for it. ⁴David also called together Aaron's descendants and the Levites. ⁵Leading Kohath's descendants was Uriel, who came with 120 of his relatives. ⁶Leading Merari's descendants was Asaiah, who came with 220 of his relatives. ⁷Leading Gershom's descendants was Joel, who came with 130 of his relatives. ⁸Leading Elizaphan's descendants was Shemaiah, who came with 200 of his relatives. ⁹Leading Hebron's descendants was Eliel, who came with 80 of his relatives. ¹⁰Leading Uzziel's descendants was Amminadab, who came with 112 of his relatives.

¹¹David called for the priests Zadok and Abiathar and for the Levites Uriel, Asaiah, Joel, Shemaiah, Eliel, and Amminadab. ¹²He said to them, "You are the heads of the Levite families. You and your relatives must perform the ceremonies to make yourselves holy. Then bring the ark of the LORD God of Israel to the place I prepared for it. ¹³Because you weren't there the first time, the LORD our God struck us. We hadn't dedicated our lives to serving him in the way ⌊he⌋ designated."

¹⁴So the priests and the Levites made themselves holy in order to move the ark of the LORD God of Israel. ¹⁵The Levites carried God's ark on their shoulders. They used poles as Moses had commanded according to the LORD's instructions.

¹⁶David told the Levite leaders to appoint some of their relatives to serve as musicians. They were expected to play music on harps, lyres, and cymbals to produce joyful music for singing. ¹⁷So the Levites appointed Heman, son of Joel, and from his relatives they appointed Asaph, Berechiah's son. From their own relatives, Merari's descendants, they appointed Ethan, son of Kushaiah. ¹⁸In addition, they appointed their relatives from the second division: Zechariah, Jaaziel, Shemiramoth, Jehiel, Unni, Eliab, Benaiah, Maaseiah, Mattithiah, Eliphelehu, and Mikneiah. Obed Edom and Jeiel were appointed gatekeepers. ¹⁹The musicians Heman, Asaph, and Ethan were appointed to play bronze cymbals. ²⁰Zechariah, Jaziel, Shemiramoth, Jehiel, Unni, Eliab, Maaseiah, and Benaiah were appointed to play harps according to *alamoth*. ²¹Mattithiah, Eliphelehu, Mikneiah, Obed Edom, Jeiel, and Azaziah were appointed to play lyres and to conduct the *sheminith*. ²²Chenaniah, a Levite leader, instructed others how to sing prophetic songs because he was skilled at it. ²³Berechiah and Elkanah were gatekeepers for the ark. ²⁴The priests Shebaniah, Joshaphat, Nethanel, Amasai, Zechariah, Benaiah, and Eliezer blew trumpets in front of God's ark. Obed Edom and Jehiah were doorkeepers for the ark.

²⁵So David, the leaders of Israel, and the army's commanders joyfully went to get the ark of the LORD's promise from Obed Edom's house. ²⁶Because God helped the Levites who carried the ark of the LORD's promise, they sacrificed seven bulls and seven rams. ²⁷David was dressed in a fine linen robe, as were all the Levites who carried the ark, the ⌊Levites who were⌋ singers, and Chenaniah, the leader of the musicians' prophetic songs. David also wore a linen ephod.

²⁸All Israel brought the ark of the LORD's promise with shouts of joy and the sounding of rams' horns, trumpets, cymbals, harps, and lyres. ²⁹When the ark of the LORD's promise came to the City of David, Saul's daughter Michal looked out of a window and saw King David dancing and celebrating, so she despised him.

¹The men carrying the ark set it inside the tent David had put up for it. They presented burnt offerings and fellowship offerings in God's presence. ²When David had finished sacrificing burnt offerings and fellowship offerings, he blessed the people in the name of the LORD. ³He also distributed to every person in Israel—both men and women—a loaf of bread, a date cake, and a raisin cake.

⁴David appointed some Levites to serve in front of the LORD's ark by offering prayers, thanks, and praise to the LORD God of Israel. ⁵Asaph was the head; Zechariah was second, then Jeiel, Shemiramoth, Jehiel, Mattithiah, Eliab, Benaiah, Obed Edom, and Jeiel with harps and lyres. Asaph played the cymbals. ⁶The priests Benaiah and Jahaziel played trumpets all the time in front of the ark of God's promise.

DAVID BECOMES A MURDERER

2 Samuel 11:2-17

2 Now, when evening came, David got up from his bed and walked around on the roof of the royal palace. From the roof he saw a woman bathing, and she was very pretty. **3** David sent someone to ask about the woman. The man said, "She's Bathsheba, daughter of Eliam and wife of Uriah the Hittite." **4** So David sent messengers and took her. She came to him, and he went to bed with her. (She had just cleansed herself after her monthly period.) Then she went home. **5** The woman had become pregnant. So she sent someone to tell David that she was pregnant.

6 Then David sent a messenger to Joab, saying, "Send me Uriah the Hittite." So Joab sent Uriah to David. **7** When Uriah arrived, David asked him how Joab and the troops were and how the war was going.

8 "Go home," David said to Uriah, "and wash your feet." Uriah left the royal palace, and the king sent a present to him. **9** But Uriah slept at the entrance of the royal palace among his superior's mercenaries. He didn't go home.

10 When they told David, "Uriah didn't go home," David asked Uriah, "Didn't you just come from a journey? Why didn't you go home?"

11 Uriah answered David, "The ark and ⌊the army of⌋ Israel and Judah are in temporary shelters, and my commander Joab and Your Majesty's mercenaries are living in the field. Should I then go to my house to eat and drink and go to bed with my wife? I solemnly swear, as sure as you're living, I won't do this!"

12 David said to Uriah, "Then stay here today, and tomorrow I'll send you back." So Uriah stayed in Jerusalem that day and the next. **13** David summoned him, ate and drank with him, and got him drunk.

But that evening Uriah went to lie down on his bed among his superior's mercenaries. He didn't go home.

¹⁴ In the morning David wrote a letter to Joab and sent it with Uriah. ¹⁵ In the letter he wrote, "Put Uriah on the front line where the fighting is heaviest. Then abandon him so that he'll be struck down and die."

¹⁶ Since Joab had kept the city under observation, he put Uriah at the place where he knew the experienced warriors were. ¹⁷ The men of the city came out and fought Joab. Some of the people, namely, some of David's mercenaries, fell and died—including Uriah the Hittite.

THE BROKEN KING

2 Samuel 12:1-15

So the LORD sent Nathan to David. Nathan came to him and said, "There were two men in a certain city. One was rich, and the other was poor. ² The rich man had a very large number of sheep and cows, ³ but the poor man had only one little female lamb that he had bought. He raised her, and she grew up in his home with his children. She would eat his food and drink from his cup. She rested in his arms and was like a daughter.

⁴ "Now, a visitor came to the rich man. The rich man thought it would be a pity to take one of his own sheep or cattle to prepare a meal for the traveler. So he took the poor man's lamb and prepared her for the traveler."

⁵ David burned with anger against the man. "I solemnly swear, as the LORD lives," he said to Nathan, "the man who did this certainly deserves to die! ⁶ And he must pay back four times the price of the lamb because he did this and had no pity."

⁷ "You are the man!" Nathan told David. "This is what the LORD God of Israel says: I anointed you king over Israel and rescued you from Saul. I gave you your master Saul's house and his wives. I gave you the house of Israel and Judah. And if this weren't enough, I would have given you even more. ⁸ Why did you despise my word by doing what I considered evil? You had Uriah the Hittite killed in battle. You took his wife as your wife. You used the Ammonites to kill him. ¹⁰ So warfare will never leave your house because you despised me and took the wife of Uriah the Hittite to be your wife.

¹¹ "This is what the LORD says: I will stir up trouble against you within your own household, and before your own eyes I will take your wives and give them to someone close to you. He will go to bed with your wives in broad daylight. ¹² You did this secretly, but I will make this happen in broad daylight in front of all Israel."

¹³ Then David said to Nathan, "I have sinned against the LORD."

Nathan replied, "The LORD has taken away your sin; you will not die. ¹⁴ But since you have shown total contempt for the LORD by this affair, the son that is born to you must die." ¹⁵ Then Nathan went home.

The LORD struck the child that Uriah's wife had given birth to for David so that the child became sick.

SOLOMON — THE YOUNG KING

1 Kings 2:10-3:15

¹⁰ David lay down in death with his ancestors and was buried in the City of David. ¹¹ He ruled as king of Israel for 40 years. He ruled for 7 years in Hebron and for 33 years in Jerusalem.

¹² Solomon sat on his father David's throne, and his power was firmly established.

¹³ Then Adonijah, son of Haggith, went to Bathsheba, Solomon's mother. "Is this a friendly visit?" she asked.

"Yes," he answered. ¹⁴ Then he added, "I have a matter ˻to discuss˼ with you."

"What is it?" she asked.

¹⁵ He said, "You know the kingship was mine. All Israel expected me to be their king. But the kingship has been turned over to my brother because the LORD gave it to him. ¹⁶ Now I want to ask you for one thing. Don't refuse me."

"What is it?" she asked.

¹⁷ He said, "Please ask King Solomon to give me Abishag from Shunem as my wife. He will not refuse you."

¹⁸ "Very well," Bathsheba answered. "I will talk to the king for you."

¹⁹ Bathsheba went to King Solomon to talk to him on Adonijah's behalf. The king got up to meet her and bowed down in front of her. Then he sat on his throne. He had a throne brought for his mother, and she sat at his right side.

²⁰ "I'm asking you for one little thing," she said. "Don't refuse me."

"Ask, Mother," the king told her. "I won't refuse yo

²¹ She replied, "Let Abishag from Shunem be given to your brother Adonijah as his wife."

²² King Solomon then said, "Why do you ask that Abishag from Shunem be given to Adonijah? That would be the same as giving him the kingship. After all, he is my older brother. The priest Abiathar and Joab (Zeruiah's son) are supporting him."

²³ King Solomon took an oath by the LORD and said, "May God strike me dead if Adonijah doesn't pay with his life for this request! ²⁴ The LORD set me on my father David's throne and gave me a dynasty as he promised. So I solemnly swear, as the LORD wh has established me lives, that Adonijah will be put to death today." ²⁵ King Solomon gave this task to Benai son of Jehoiada. Benaiah attacked and killed Adonija

²⁶ The king told the priest Abiathar, "Go to your land in Anathoth. You deserve to die, but I won't kill you at this time because you carried the ark of the Almighty LORD ahead of my father David and becaus you shared all my father's sufferings." ²⁷ So Solomon removed Abiathar as the LORD's priest and fulfilled the LORD's word spoken at Shiloh about Eli's family.

²⁸ The news reached Joab. (He had supported Adonijah, although he hadn't supported Absalom.) So Joab fled to the LORD's tent and clung to the horns of the altar. ²⁹ After King Solomon heard that Joab ha fled to the altar in the tent of the LORD, Solomon sen Benaiah, son of Jehoiada, to kill Joab.

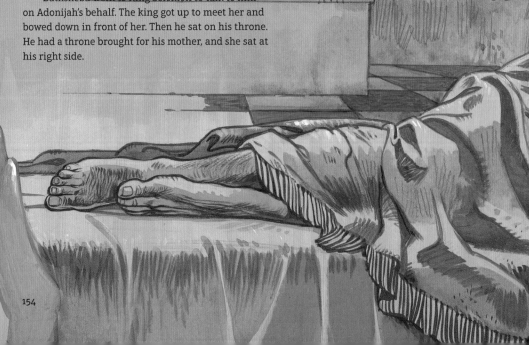

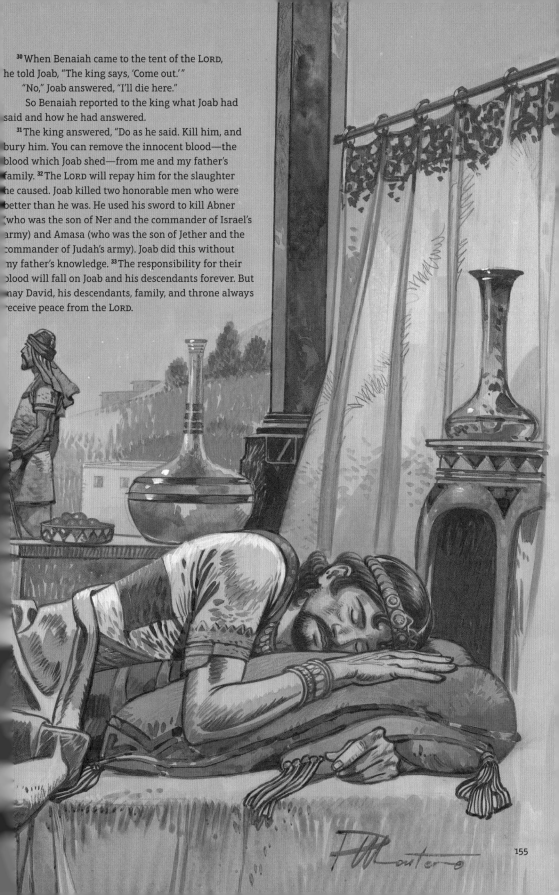

³⁰ When Benaiah came to the tent of the LORD, he told Joab, "The king says, 'Come out.'"

"No," Joab answered, "I'll die here."

So Benaiah reported to the king what Joab had said and how he had answered.

³¹ The king answered, "Do as he said. Kill him, and bury him. You can remove the innocent blood—the blood which Joab shed—from me and my father's family. ³² The LORD will repay him for the slaughter he caused. Joab killed two honorable men who were better than he was. He used his sword to kill Abner (who was the son of Ner and the commander of Israel's army) and Amasa (who was the son of Jether and the commander of Judah's army). Joab did this without my father's knowledge. ³³ The responsibility for their blood will fall on Joab and his descendants forever. But may David, his descendants, family, and throne always receive peace from the LORD."

34 Then Benaiah, son of Jehoiada, went and attacked Joab, killed him, and buried him at his home in the desert. **35** The king then appointed Benaiah, son of Jehoiada, to replace Joab as commander of the army. King Solomon also replaced Abiathar with the priest Zadok.

36 The king summoned Shimei and said to him, "Build a house for yourself in Jerusalem, and stay there. Don't leave ⌊the city⌋ to go anywhere else. **37** But the day you leave and cross the brook in the Kidron Valley, you can be certain that you will die. You will be responsible for your own death."

38 "Very well," Shimei answered. "I'll do just what Your Majesty said."

So Shimei stayed in Jerusalem for a long time. **39** But after three years, two of Shimei's slaves fled to Gath's King Achish, son of Maacah. Shimei was told that his slaves were in Gath, **40** so he saddled his donkey and went to Achish in Gath to search for his slaves. Shimei went to Gath and got his slaves.

41 After Solomon heard that Shimei had gone from Jerusalem to Gath and back, **42** he summoned Shimei. Solomon asked him, "Didn't I make you take an oath by the LORD? Didn't I warn you that if you left ⌊the city⌋ to go anywhere, you could be certain that you would die? Didn't you say to me, 'Very well. I'll do just what you said'? **43** Why didn't you keep your oath to the LORD and obey the command I gave you? **44** Shimei, you know in your heart all the evil that you did to my father David. The LORD is going to pay you back for the evil you have done. **45** But King Solomon is blessed, and David's dynasty will always be firmly established by the LORD."

46 Then the king gave orders to Benaiah, son of Jehoiada. He went to attack and kill Shimei.

Solomon's power as king was now firmly established.

1 Solomon became the son-in-law of Pharaoh (the king of Egypt). After marrying Pharaoh's daughter, Solomon brought her to the City of David until he finished building his own house, the LORD's house, and the wall around Jerusalem.

2 The people were still sacrificing at other worship sites because a temple for the name of the LORD had not yet been built. **3** Solomon loved the LORD and lived by his father

David's rules. However, he still sacrificed and burned incense at these other worship sites.

4 King Solomon went to Gibeon to sacrifice because it was the most important place of worship. Solomon sacrificed 1,000 burnt offerings on that altar.

5 In Gibeon the LORD appeared to Solomon in a dream at night. He said, "What can I give you?"

6 Solomon responded, "You've shown great love to my father David, who was your servant. He lived in your presence with truth, righteousness, and commitment. And you continued to show him your great love by giving him a son to sit on his throne tod

7 "LORD my God, although I'm young and inexperienced, you've made me king in place of my father David. **8** I'm among your people whom you hav chosen. They are too numerous to count or record. **9** Give me a heart that listens so that I can judge your people and tell the difference between good and evil After all, who can judge this great people of yours?"

157

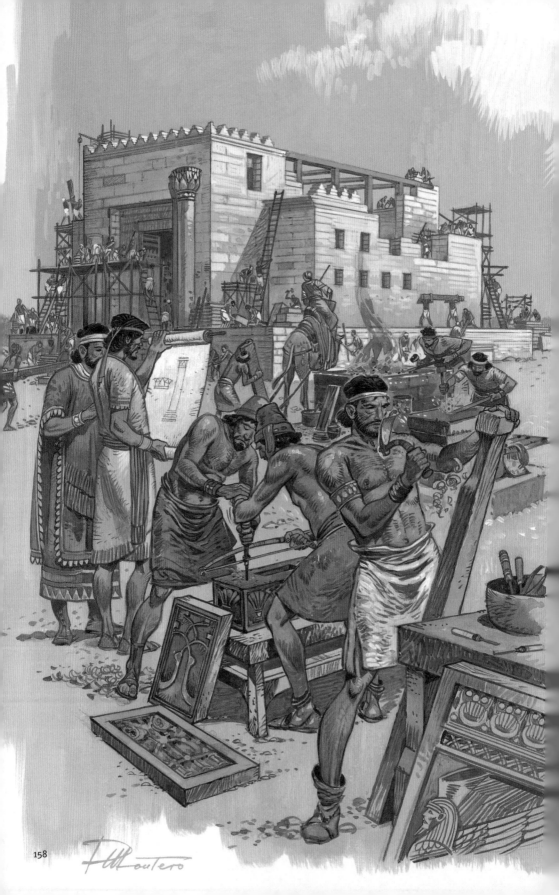

[10] The Lord was pleased that Solomon asked for s. [11] God replied, "You've asked for this and not for ong life, or riches for yourself, or the death of your emies. Instead, you've asked for understanding so at you can do what is right. [12] So I'm going to do what u've asked. I'm giving you a wise and understanding art so that there will never be anyone like you. [13] I'm o giving you what you haven't asked for—riches d honor—so that no other king will be like you as ng as you live. [14] And if you follow me and obey my vs and commands as your father David did, then ill also give you a long life."

[15] Solomon woke up and realized it had been a eam. He went to Jerusalem and stood in front of e ark of the Lord's promise. He sacrificed burnt erings and fellowship offerings and held a banquet all his officials.

E BABY WITH TWO MOTHERS

ings 3:16-28

A short time later two prostitutes came to the king d stood in front of him. [17] One woman said to him, , this woman and I live in the same house. I gave rth ⌊to a son⌋ while she was with me in the house. wo days later this woman also gave birth ⌊to a son⌋. e were alone. No one else was with us. Just the two us were in the house. [19] That night this woman's son ed because she rolled over on top of him. [20] So she got during the night and took my son, who was beside e, while I was asleep. She held him in her arms. Then e laid her dead son in my arms. [21] When I got up in the orning to nurse my son, he was dead! I took a good ok at him and realized that he wasn't my son at all!"

[22] The other woman said, "No! My son is alive—your n is dead."

The first woman kept on saying, "No! Your son dead—my son is alive." So they argued in front of e king.

[23] The king said, "This one keeps saying, 'My son is ve—your son is dead,' and that one keeps saying, ! Your son is dead—my son is alive.'"

[24] So the king told his servants to bring him a sword. hen they brought it, [25] he said, "Cut the living child in o. Give half to the one and half to the other."

[26] Then the woman whose son was still alive was eply moved by her love for the child. She said to the ng, "Please, sir, give her the living child. Please don't l him!"

But the other woman said, "He won't be mine or urs. Cut him ⌊in two⌋."

[27] The king replied, "Give the living child to the first woman. Don't kill him. She is his mother."

[28] All Israel heard about the decision the king made. They respected the king very highly, because they saw he possessed wisdom from God to do what was right.

SOLOMON BUILDS A TEMPLE FOR THE LORD

1 Kings 5:1-6:38

[1] King Hiram of Tyre sent his officials to Solomon when he heard that Solomon had been anointed king to succeed his father. Hiram had always been David's friend.

[2] Solomon sent word to Hiram, by saying, [3] "You know that my father David was surrounded by war. He couldn't build a temple for the name of the Lord our God until the Lord let him defeat his enemies. [4] But the Lord my God has surrounded me with peace. I have no rival and no trouble. [5] Now I'm thinking of building a temple for the name of the Lord my God as the Lord spoke to my father David: 'Your son, whom I will put on your throne to succeed you, will build a temple for my name.' [6] So order men to cut down cedars from Lebanon for me. My workers will work with your workers. I will pay you whatever wages you ask for your workers. You know we don't have any skilled lumberjacks like those from Sidon."

[7] Hiram was very glad to hear what Solomon had said. Hiram responded, "May the Lord be praised today. He has given David a wise son to rule this great nation."

[8] Hiram sent men to Solomon to say, "I've received the message you sent me. I will do everything you want in regard to the cedar and cypress logs. [9] My workers will bring logs from Lebanon to the sea, and I will have them make them into rafts to go by sea to any place you specify. There I will have them taken apart, and you can use them. You can pay me by providing food for my palace." [10] So Hiram gave Solomon all the cedar and cypress wood he wanted. [11] Solomon gave Hiram 120,000 bushels of wheat and 120,000 gallons of pure olive oil. Solomon paid Hiram this much every year.

[12] The Lord gave Solomon wisdom as he had promised. There was peace between Hiram and Solomon, and they made a treaty with one another.

[13] King Solomon forced 30,000 men from all over Israel to work for him. [14] He sent a shift of 10,000 men to Lebanon for a month. They would spend one month in Lebanon and two months at home. Adoniram was in charge of forced labor.

¹⁵ Solomon had 70,000 men who carried heavy loads, 70,000 who quarried stone in the mountains, ¹⁶ and 3,300 foremen who were in charge of the workers. ¹⁷ The king commanded them to quarry large, expensive blocks of stone in order to provide a foundation of cut stone for the temple. ¹⁸ Solomon's workmen, Hiram's workmen, and men from Gebal quarried the stone and prepared the logs and stone to build the temple.

¹ Solomon began to build the LORD's temple 480 years after Israel left Egypt. He began building in the month of Ziv (the second month) of the fourth year of his reign over Israel. ² The temple that King Solomon built for the LORD was 90 feet long, 30 feet wide, and 45 feet high. ³ The entrance hall in front of the main room of the temple was the same length as the shorter side of the temple. It extended 15 feet in front of the temple. ⁴ He also made latticed windows for the temple.

⁵ He built an annex containing side rooms all around the temple. This annex was next to the walls of the main building and the inner sanctuary. ⁶ The ⌊interior of⌋ the lowest story of the annex was 7½ feet wide, the second story was 9 feet wide, and the third story was 10½ feet wide. Solomon made ledges all around the temple so that this annex would not be fastened to the walls of the temple.

⁷ The temple was built with stone blocks that were finished at the quarry. No hammer, chisel, or any other iron tool made a sound at the temple construction site.

⁸ The entrance to the first story was on the south side of the temple. A staircase went up to the middle story and then to the third story.

⁹ When he had finished building the walls, he roofed the temple with rows of cedar beams and planks. ¹⁰ He built ⌊each story of the⌋ annex 7½ feet high alongside the entire temple. Its cedar beams were attached to the temple.

¹¹ The LORD spoke to Solomon, saying, ¹² "This concerns the temple you are building: If you live by my laws, follow my rules, and keep my commands, I will fulfill the promise I made about you to your father David. ¹³ I will live among the Israelites and never abandon my people."

¹⁴ When Solomon had finished building the temple's ⌊frame,⌋ ¹⁵ he began to line the inside walls of the temple with cedar boards. He paneled the inside of the temple with wood from floor to ceiling. He covered the floor of the temple with cypress planks.

¹⁶ He sectioned off a 30-foot-long room at the rear of the temple with cedar boards from the floor to the rafters. He built it to serve as an inner room, the most

holy place. ¹⁷ The 60-foot-long room at the front of the temple served as the main hall. ¹⁸ Gourds and flowers were carved into the cedar paneling inside the temple. Everything was ⌊covered with⌋ cedar. No stone could be seen.

¹⁹ He prepared the inner room of the temple in order to put the ark of the LORD's promise there. ²⁰ The inner room was 30 feet long, 30 feet wide, and 30 feet high. Solomon covered it and the cedar altar with pure gold. ²¹ He covered the inside of the temple with pure gold. He put golden chains across the front of the inner room which was covered with gold. ²² He covered the entire inside of the temple with gold. He also covered the entire altar in the inner room with gold.

[23] In the inner room he made two 15-foot-tall angels out of olive wood. [24] Each wing of the angels was 7½ feet long. The distance from the tip of one wing to the tip of the other was 15 feet. [25] Both angels had a 15-foot ⌞wingspan⌟. Both had the same measurements and the same shape. [26] Each was 15 feet high. [27] Solomon put the angels in the inner room of the temple. The wings of the angels extended so that the wing of one of the angels touched the one wall, and the wing of the other touched the other wall. Their remaining wings touched each other in the center of the room. [28] He covered the angels with gold.

[29] He carved angels, palm trees, and flowers into the walls all around the inner and outer rooms of the temple. [30] He covered the floor of the inner and outer rooms of the temple with gold.

[31] He made doors for the entrance to the inner room out of olive wood. The doorposts had five sides. [32] The two doors were ⌞made out of⌟ olive wood. He carved angels, palm trees, and flowers into them and covered them with gold. The gold was hammered onto the angels and the palm trees.

[33] In the same way he made square doorposts out of olive wood for the temple's entrance. [34] He made two doors from cypress. Each of the doors had two folding panels. [35] On them he carved angels, palm trees, and flowers. He evenly covered them with gold.

[36] He built the inner courtyard with three courses of finished stones and a course of finished cedar beams.

[37] In the month of Ziv of the fourth year of Solomon's reign, the foundation of the LORD's temple was laid. [38] In the month of Bul (the eighth month) of the eleventh year ⌞of his reign⌟, the temple was finished according to all its plans and specifications. He spent seven years building it.

THE VISIT OF THE QUEEN OF SHEBA

1 Kings 4:29-33

[29] God gave Solomon wisdom—keen insight and a mind as limitless as the sand on the seashore. [30] Solomon's wisdom was greater than that of all the eastern people and all the wisdom of the Egyptians. [31] He was wiser than anyone, than Ethan the Ezrahite, or Heman, Calcol, or Darda, Mahol's sons. His fame spread to all the nations around him.

[32] Solomon spoke 3,000 proverbs and wrote 1,005 songs. [33] He described and classified trees—from the cedar in Lebanon to the hyssop growing out of the wall. He described and classified animals, birds, reptiles, and fish.

1 Kings 10:1-7

[1] The queen of Sheba heard about Solomon's reputation. (He owed his reputation to the name of the LORD.) So she came to test him with riddles. [2] She arrived in Jerusalem with a large group of servants, with camels carrying spices, a very large quantity of gold, and precious stones. When she came to Solomon, she talked to him about everything she had on her mind. [3] Solomon answered all her questions. No question was too difficult for the king to answer.

[4] When the queen of Sheba saw all of Solomon's wisdom, the palace he built, [5] the food on his table, his officers' seating arrangement, the organization of his officials and the uniforms they wore, his cupbearers, and the burnt offerings that he sacrificed at the LORD's temple, she was breathless. [6] She told the king, "What I heard in my country about your words and your wisdom is true! [7] But I didn't believe the reports until I came and saw it with my own eyes. I wasn't even told half of it. Your wisdom and wealth surpass the stories I've heard."

THE CONTEST

1 Kings 16:29-18:24

[29] Ahab, son of Omri, began to rule Israel in Asa's thirty-eighth year as king of Judah. He ruled for 22 years in Samaria. [30] Ahab, son of Omri, did what the LORD considered evil. He was worse than all ⌞the kings⌟ who were before him. [31] It wasn't enough that he committed the same sins as Jeroboam (Nebat's son). He also married Jezebel, daughter of King Ethbaal of Sidon. Ahab then served and worshiped Baal. [32] He built the temple of Baal in Samaria and set up an altar there. [33] Ahab made poles dedicated to the goddess Asherah. He did more to make the LORD God of Israel furious than all the kings of Israel who came before him.

[34] In Ahab's time Hiel from Bethel rebuilt Jericho.

> Laying the foundation
>   cost him his firstborn son, Abiram.
> Setting up the city doors
>   cost him his youngest son, Segub.

The LORD had spoken this through Joshua, son of Nun.

163

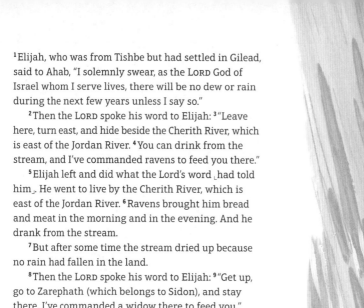

¹Elijah, who was from Tishbe but had settled in Gilead, said to Ahab, "I solemnly swear, as the LORD God of Israel whom I serve lives, there will be no dew or rain during the next few years unless I say so."

²Then the LORD spoke his word to Elijah: ³"Leave here, turn east, and hide beside the Cherith River, which is east of the Jordan River. ⁴You can drink from the stream, and I've commanded ravens to feed you there."

⁵Elijah left and did what the Lord's word ˻had told him˼. He went to live by the Cherith River, which is east of the Jordan River. ⁶Ravens brought him bread and meat in the morning and in the evening. And he drank from the stream.

⁷But after some time the stream dried up because no rain had fallen in the land.

⁸Then the LORD spoke his word to Elijah: ⁹"Get up, go to Zarephath (which belongs to Sidon), and stay there. I've commanded a widow there to feed you."

¹⁰He got up and went to Zarephath. As he came to the town's entrance, a widow was gathering wood. He called to her, "Please bring me a drink of water." ¹¹As she was going to get it, he called to her again, "Please bring me a piece of bread too."

¹²She said, "I solemnly swear, as the LORD your God lives, I didn't bake any bread. I have one handful of flour in a jar and a little oil in a jug. I'm gathering wood. I'm going to prepare something for myself and my son so that we can eat it and then die."

¹³ Then Elijah told her, "Don't be afraid. Go home, and do as you've said. But first make a small loaf and bring it to me. Then prepare something for yourself and your son. ¹⁴ This is what the LORD God of Israel says: Until the LORD sends rain on the land, the jar of flour will never be empty and the jug will always contain oil."

¹⁵ She did what Elijah had told her. So she, Elijah, and her family had food for a long time. ¹⁶ The jar of flour never became empty, and the jug always contained olive oil, as the LORD had promised through Elijah.

¹⁷ Afterwards, the son of the woman who owned the house got sick. He got so sick that finally no life was left in him. ¹⁸ The woman asked Elijah, "What do you and I have in common, man of God? Did you come here to remind me of my sin and kill my son?"

¹⁹ He said to her, "Give me your son." Elijah took him from her arms, carried him to the upstairs room where he was staying, and laid him on his own bed. ²⁰ Then he called to the LORD, "LORD my God, have you brought misery on the widow I'm staying with by killing her son?" ²¹ Then Elijah stretched himself over the boy three times and called to the LORD, "LORD my God, please make this child's life return to him." ²² The LORD heard Elijah's request, and the child's life returned to him. He was alive again.

²³ Elijah took the child, brought him down from the upstairs room of the house, and gave him to his mother. He said, "Look! Your son is alive."

²⁴ The woman said to Elijah, "Now I'm convinced that you are a man of God and that the Lord's word from your mouth is true."

¹ A while later in the third year of the drought, the LORD spoke his word to Elijah: "Present yourself to Ahab. I will allow rain to fall on the ground." ² So Elijah went to present himself to Ahab.

The famine was particularly severe in Samaria. ³ Ahab sent for Obadiah, who was in charge of the palace. Obadiah was a devout worshiper of the LORD. ⁴ (When Jezebel was killing the LORD's prophets, Obadiah had hidden 100 prophets in caves. He put 50 prophets in each cave and kept them alive by providing bread and water for them.) ⁵ Ahab told Obadiah, "Let's go throughout the countryside to every spring and stream. If we can find grass, then we can keep the horses and mules alive and not lose any animals." ⁶ So they split up in order to cover the entire countryside. Ahab went one way by himself, and Obadiah went the other way by himself.

⁷ Obadiah was on the road when he met Elijah. Obadiah recognized him and immediately bowed down to the ground. "Is it you, my master Elijah?" he asked.

⁸ "Yes," Elijah answered him. "Tell your master that Elijah is here."

⁹ Obadiah asked, "What have I done wrong to make you hand me over to Ahab to be killed? ¹⁰ I solemnly swear, as the LORD your God lives, my master has searched for you in every region and kingdom. When people would say, 'He isn't here,' my master made that kingdom or region take an oath that they hadn't found you.

¹¹ "Now you say, 'Tell your master that Elijah is here.' ¹² This is what will happen: When I leave you, the LORD's Spirit will take you away to some unknown place. I'll tell Ahab, but he won't be able to find you. Then he will kill me.

"I have been faithful to the LORD since I was a child. ¹³ Haven't you heard what I did when Jezebel killed the LORD's prophets? Haven't you heard how I hid 100 of the LORD's prophets in caves? I hid 50 prophets in each cave and provided bread and water for them. ¹⁴ Now you say that I should tell my master that Elijah is here. He will kill me."

¹⁵ Elijah said, "I solemnly swear, as the Lᴏʀᴅ of Armies whom I serve lives, I will present myself to Ahab."

¹⁶ So Obadiah went to tell Ahab.

Ahab went to meet Elijah. ¹⁷ When he saw Elijah, Ahab said, "Is that you, you troublemaker of Israel?"

¹⁸ Elijah answered, "I haven't troubled Israel. You and your father's family have done it by disobeying the Lᴏʀᴅ's commands and following the various Baal gods. ¹⁹ Order all Israel to gather around me on Mount Carmel. And bring the 450 prophets of Baal and 400 prophets of Asherah who eat at Jezebel's table."

²⁰ Ahab sent word to all the Israelites and brought the prophets together on Mount Carmel. ²¹ Elijah stood up in front of all the people and asked them, "How long will you try to have it both ways? If the Lᴏʀᴅ is God, follow him; if Baal is God, follow him." The peop didn't say a word.

²² So Elijah told the people, "I'm the only survivin prophet of the Lᴏʀᴅ, but there are 450 prophets of Baal. ²³ Give us two bulls. Let the prophets of Baal choose one for themselves, cut it into pieces, lay it o the wood, but not set it on fire. I'll do the same with the other bull.

²⁴ "You call on the name of your gods, but I will ca on the name of the Lᴏʀᴅ. The god who answers by fi is the real God."

All the people answered, "That's fine."

IJAH AND THE FALSE PHOPHETS

ngs 18:25-46

lijah told the prophets of Baal, "Choose one bull for
urselves. Prepare yours first, because there are more
you. Call on the name of your god, but don't set the
od on fire."

[26] They took the bull he gave them, prepared it, and called on the name of Baal from morning until noon. They said, "Baal, answer us!" But there wasn't a sound or an answer. So they danced around the altar they had made. [27] At noon Elijah started to make fun of them. "Shout louder, since he is a god. Maybe he's thinking, relieving himself, or traveling! Maybe he's sleeping, and you have to wake him!"

[28] So they shouted louder. They also cut themselves with swords and spears until their blood flowed. (This is what their ritual called for.) [29] In the afternoon they continued to rant and rave until the time for the evening sacrifice. But there was no sound, no answer, no attention given to them.

[30] Then Elijah said to all the people, "Come over here." So all the people came to him. He rebuilt the LORD's altar that had been torn down. [31] Elijah took 12 stones, one for each of the tribes named after Jacob's sons. (The LORD had spoken his word to Jacob: "Your name will be Israel.") [32] Elijah built an altar in the LORD's name with those stones. He also made a trench that could hold 12 quarts of grain around the altar. [33] He arranged the wood, cut up the bull, and put it on the wood.

³⁴ He said, "Fill four jars with water. Pour the water on the offering and on the wood." Then he said, "Do it again," and they did it again. Then he said, "Do it a third time," and they did it a third time. ³⁵ The water flowed around the altar, and even the trench was filled with water.

³⁶ When it was time to offer the sacrifice, the prophet Elijah stepped forward. He said, "Lord God of Abraham, Isaac, and Israel, make known today that you are God in Israel and that I'm your servant and have done all these things by your instructions. ³⁷ Answer me, Lord! Answer me! Then these people will know that you, Lord, are God and that you are winning back their hearts."

³⁸ So a fire from the Lord fell down and consumed the burnt offering, wood, stones, and dirt. The fire even dried up the water that was in the trench. ³⁹ All the people saw it and immediately bowed down to the ground. "The Lord is God!" they said. "The Lord is God!"

⁴⁰ Elijah told them, "Seize the prophets of Baal. Don't let any of them escape." The people seized them, and Elijah took them to the Kishon River and slaughtered them there.

⁴¹ Then Elijah told Ahab, "Get up, eat, and drink. It sounds like a heavy rain ˌis comingˌ." ⁴² Ahab got up to eat and drink.

Elijah went to the top of Carmel and bowed down on the ground to pray. ⁴³ He said to his servant, "Please go back to ˌMount Carmelˌ and look toward the sea."

He went up, looked, ˌcame back,ˌ and said, "There's nothing."

Seven times Elijah told him, "Go back."

⁴⁴ After the seventh time the servant said, "A little cloud like a man's hand is coming from the sea."

Elijah said, "Go and tell Ahab, 'Prepare ˌyour chariotˌ and leave before the rain delays you.'"

⁴⁵ Gradually, the sky grew darker with clouds and wind, and there was a heavy rain. Ahab got into his chariot to go back to Jezreel. ⁴⁶ The Lord's power was on Elijah. He hiked up his robe and ran ahead of Ahab until they came to Jezreel.

THE CHARIOT OF FIRE

2 Kings 2:1-11

¹ When the Lord was going to take Elijah to heaven in a windstorm, Elijah and Elisha left Gilgal. ² Elijah said to Elisha, "Please stay here because the Lord is sending me to Bethel."

Elisha answered, "I solemnly swear, as the Lord lives and as you live, I will not abandon you." So they went to Bethel.

³Some of the disciples of the prophets at Bethel came to Elisha. They asked him, "Do you know that the LORD is going to take your master from you today?"

He answered, "Yes, I know. Be quiet."

⁴Elijah said, "Elisha, please stay here because the LORD is sending me to Jericho."

Elisha answered, "I solemnly swear, as the LORD lives and as you live, I will not abandon you." So they went to Jericho.

⁵Then some of the disciples of the prophets who were in Jericho approached Elisha. They asked, "Do you know that the LORD is going to take your master from you today?"

He answered, "Yes, I know. Be quiet."

⁶Elijah said to Elisha, "Please stay here because the LORD is sending me to the Jordan River."

Elisha answered, "I solemnly swear, as the LORD lives and as you live, I will not abandon you."

⁷Fifty disciples of the prophets stood at a distance as Elijah and Elisha stood by the Jordan River. ⁸Elijah took his coat, rolled it up, and struck the water with it. The water divided to their left and their right, and the two men crossed ⌊the river⌋ on dry ground.

⁹While they were crossing, Elijah asked Elisha, "What should I do for you before I'm taken from you?"

Elisha answered, "Let me inherit a double share of your spirit."

¹⁰Elijah said, "You have asked for something difficult. If you see me taken from you, it will be yours. Otherwise, it will not."

¹¹As they continued walking and talking, a fiery chariot with fiery horses separated the two of them, and Elijah went to heaven in a windstorm.

A STRANGE WAY TO CROSS A RIVER

2 Kings 2:12-18

¹²When Elisha saw this, he cried out, "Master! Master! Israel's chariot and horses!" When he couldn't see Elijah anymore, he grabbed his own garment and tore it in two ⌐to show his grief⌐. ¹³Then he picked up Elijah's coat (which had fallen off Elijah), went back, and stood on the bank of the Jordan River. ¹⁴He took the coat and struck the water with it. He asked, "Where is the LORD God of Elijah?" As he struck the water, it divided to his left and his right, and Elisha crossed ⌐the river⌐.

¹⁵The disciples of the prophets who were at Jericho saw him from a distance. They said, "Elijah's spirit rests on Elisha!" Then they went to meet him and bowed in front of him with their faces touching the ground. ¹⁶They said to him, "There are 50 strong men here with us. Please let them go and search for your master. Maybe the LORD's Spirit lifted him up and dropped him on one of the hills or in one of the valleys."

Elisha answered, "Don't send them ⌐to look⌐."
¹⁷But the disciples kept urging him ⌐to send the men⌐ until he was embarrassed. So he said, "Send them." They sent 50 men who searched for three days without finding him. ¹⁸They returned to Elisha in Jericho, where he was waiting. He said, "Didn't I tell you not to go?"

THE BOTTOMLESS JAR OF OIL

2 Kings 4:1-7

¹One of the wives of a disciple of the prophets called to Elisha, "Sir, my husband is dead! You know how he feared the LORD. Now a creditor has come to take my two children as slaves."

²Elisha asked her, "What should I do for you? Tell me, what do you have in your house?"

She answered, "I have nothing in the house except a jar of olive oil."

³Elisha said, "Borrow many empty containers from all your neighbors. ⁴Then close the door behind you and your children, and pour oil into all those containers. When one is full, set it aside."

⁵So she left him and closed the door behind her and her children. The children kept bringing containers to her, and she kept pouring. ⁶When the containers were full, she told her son, "Bring me another container."

He told her, "There are no more containers." So the olive oil stopped flowing. ⁷She went and told the man of God.

He said, "Sell the oil, and pay your debt. The rest is for you and your children."

JONAH RUNS AWAY FROM THE LORD

Jonah 1:1-16

¹ The LORD spoke his word to Jonah, son of Amittai. He said, ² "Leave at once for the important city, Nineveh. Announce to the people that I can no longer overlook the wicked things they have done."

³ Jonah immediately tried to run away from the LORD by going to Tarshish. He went to Joppa and found a ship going to Tarshish. He paid for the trip and went on board. He wanted to go to Tarshish to get away from the LORD.

⁴ The LORD sent a violent wind over the sea. The storm was so powerful that the ship was in danger of breaking up. ⁵ The sailors were afraid, and they cried to their gods for help. They began to throw the cargo overboard to lighten the ship's load.

182

Now, Jonah had gone below deck and was lying there sound asleep. ⁶ The captain of the ship went to him and asked, "How can you sleep? Get up, and pray to your God. Maybe he will notice us, and we won't die."

⁷ Then the sailors said to each other, "Let's throw dice to find out who is responsible for bringing this disaster on us." So they threw dice, and the dice indicated that Jonah was responsible.

⁸ They asked him, "Tell us, why has this disaster happened to us? What do you do for a living? Where do you come from? What country are you from? What nationality are you?"

⁹ Jonah answered them, "I'm a Hebrew. I worship the LORD, the God of heaven. He is the God who made the sea and the land."

¹⁰ Then the men were terrified. They knew that he was running away from the LORD, because he had told them. They asked Jonah, "Why have you done this?"

¹¹ The storm was getting worse. So they asked Jonah, "What should we do with you to calm the sea?"

¹² He told them, "Throw me overboard. Then the sea will become calm. I know that I'm responsible for this violent storm."

¹³ Instead, the men tried to row harder to get the ship back to shore, but they couldn't do it. The storm was getting worse.

¹⁴ So they cried to the LORD for help: "Please, LORD, don't let us die for taking this man's life. Don't hold us responsible for the death of an innocent man, because you, LORD, do whatever you want." ¹⁵ Then they took Jonah and threw him overboard, and the sea became calm. ¹⁶ The men were terrified of the LORD. They offered sacrifices and made vows to the LORD.

THE BIG FISH

Jonah 1:17-2:10

¹⁷ The LORD sent a big fish to swallow Jonah. Jonah was inside the fish for three days and three nights.

¹ From inside the fish Jonah prayed to the LORD his God.
² Jonah prayed:

"I called to the LORD in my distress,
    and he answered me.
From the depths of my ⌞watery⌟ grave I cried for help,
    and you heard my cry.
³ You threw me into the deep, into the depths of the sea,
    and water surrounded me.
        All the whitecaps on your waves have swept over me.

⁴ "Then I thought,
    'I have been banished from your sight.
        Will I ever see your holy temple again?'

⁵ "Water surrounded me, threatening my life.
    The deep ⌞sea⌟ covered me completely.
        Seaweed was wrapped around my head.
⁶ I sank to the foot of the mountains.
  I sank to the bottom,
    where bars held me forever.
        But you brought me back from the pit, O LORD, my God.

⁷ "As my life was slipping away, I remembered the LORD.
    My prayer came to you in your holy temple.
⁸ Those who hold on to worthless idols abandon their loyalty ⌞to you⌟.
⁹   But I will sacrifice to you with songs of thanksgiving.
  I will keep my vow.
    Victory belongs to the LORD!"

¹⁰ Then the LORD spoke to the fish, and it spit Jonah out onto the shore.

JONAH CHANGES HIS MIND

Jonah 3:1-10

¹ Then the Lord spoke his word to Jonah a second time. He said, ² "Leave at once for the important city, Nineveh. Announce to the people the message I have given you."

³ Jonah immediately went to Nineveh as the Lord told him. Nineveh was a very large city. It took three days to walk through it. ⁴ Jonah entered the city and walked for about a day. Then he said, "In forty days Nineveh will be destroyed."

⁵ The people of Nineveh believed God. They decided to fast, and everyone, from the most important to the least important, dressed in sackcloth.

⁶ When the news reached the king of Nineveh, he got up from his throne, took off his robe, put on sackcloth, and sat in ashes. ⁷ Then he made this announcement and sent it throughout the city:

"This is an order from the king and his nobles: No one is to eat or drink anything. This includes all people, animals, cattle, and sheep. ⁸ Every person and animal must put on sackcloth. Cry loudly to God for help. Turn from your wicked ways and your acts of violence. ⁹ Who knows? God may reconsider his plans and turn from his burning anger so that we won't die."

¹⁰ God saw what they did. He saw that they turned from their wicked ways. So God reconsidered his threat to destroy them, and he didn't do it.

THE LORD IS GOOD

Jonah 4:1-11

¹ Jonah was very upset about this, and he became angry. ² So he prayed to the Lord, "Lord, isn't this what I said would happen when I was still in my own country? That's why I tried to run to Tarshish in the first place. I knew that you are a merciful and compassionate God, patient, and always ready to forgive and to reconsider your threats of destruction. ³ So now, Lord, take my life. I'd rather be dead than alive."

⁴ The Lord asked, "What right do you have to be angry?"

⁵ Jonah left the city and sat down east of it. He made himself a shelter there. He sat in its shade and waited to see what would happen to the city. ⁶ The Lord God made a plant grow up beside Jonah to give him shade and make him more comfortable. Jonah was very happy with the plant.

⁷ At dawn the next day, God sent a worm to attack the plant so that it withered. ⁸ When the sun rose, God made a hot east wind blow. The sun beat down on Jonah's head so that he was about to faint. He wanted to die. So he said, "I'd rather be dead than alive."

⁹ Then God asked Jonah, "What right do you have to be angry over this plant?"

Jonah answered, "I have every right to be angry– so angry that I want to die."

¹⁰ The Lord replied, "This plant grew up overnight and died overnight. You didn't plant it or make it grow. Yet, you feel sorry for this plant. ¹¹ Shouldn't I feel sorry for this important city, Nineveh? It has more than 120,000 people in it as well as many animals. These people couldn't tell their right hand from their left."

JEREMIAH STAYS BEHIND

2 Chronicles 36:11-21

[11] Zedekiah was 21 years old when he began to rule, and he ruled for 11 years in Jerusalem. [12] He did what the LORD his God considered evil and didn't humble himself in front of the prophet Jeremiah, who spoke for the LORD. [13] Zedekiah also rebelled against King Nebuchadnezzar. Nebuchadnezzar had made Zedekiah swear an oath of allegiance to him in God's name. But Zedekiah became so stubborn and so impossible to deal with that he refused to turn back to the LORD God of Israel.

[14] All the officials, the priests, and the people became increasingly unfaithful and followed all the disgusting practices of the nations. Although the LORD had made the temple in Jerusalem holy, they made the temple unclean. [15] The LORD God of their ancestors repeatedly sent messages through his messengers because he wanted to spare his people and his dwelling place. [16] But they mocked God's messengers, despised his words, and made fun of his prophets until the LORD became angry with his people. He could no longer heal them.

17 So he had the Babylonian king attack them and execute their best young men in their holy temple. He didn't spare the best men or the unmarried women, the old people or the sick people. God handed all of them over to him. **18** He brought to Babylon each of the utensils from God's temple, the treasures from the LORD's temple, and the treasures of the king and his officials. **19** They burned God's temple, tore down Jerusalem's walls, burned down all its palaces, and destroyed everything of value. **20** The king of Babylon took those who weren't executed to Babylon to be slaves for him and his sons. They remained captives until the Persian Empire began to rule. **21** This happened so that the LORD's words spoken through Jeremiah would be fulfilled. The land had its years of rest and was made acceptable ˻again˼. While it lay in ruins, ˻the land had its˼ 70 years of rest.

A SPECIAL SCHOOL

Daniel 1:3-7

³ The king told Ashpenaz, the chief-of-staff, to bring some of the Israelites, the royal family, and the nobility. ⁴ They were to be young men who were healthy, good-looking, knowledgeable in all subjects, well-informed, intelligent, and able to serve in the king's palace. They were to be taught the language and literature of the Babylonians.

⁵ The king arranged for them to get a daily allowance of the king's rich food and wine. They were to be trained for three years. After that, they were to serve the king. ⁶ Among these young men were some Judeans: Daniel, Hananiah, Mishael, and Azariah. ⁷ The chief-of-staff gave them ⌊Babylonian⌋ names: To Daniel he gave the name Belteshazzar. To Hananiah he gave the name Shadrach. To Mishael he gave the name Meshach. And to Azariah he gave the name Abednego.

A TEST OF FAITH

Daniel 1:8-14

⁸ Daniel made up his mind not to harm himself by eating the king's rich food and drinking the king's wine. So he asked the chief-of-staff for permission not to harm himself in this way.

⁹ God made the chief-of-staff kind and compassionate toward Daniel. ¹⁰ The chief-of-staff told Daniel, "I'm afraid of my master, the king. The king determined what you should eat and drink. If he sees that you look worse than the other young men your age, he would have my head cut off."

¹¹ The chief-of-staff put a supervisor in charge of Daniel, Hananiah, Mishael, and Azariah. Daniel said to the supervisor, ¹² "Please test us for ten days. Give us only vegetables to eat and water to drink. ¹³ Then compare us to the young men who are eating the king's rich food. Decide how to treat us on the basis of how we look."

¹⁴ The supervisor listened to them about this matter and tested them for ten days.

PASSING THE TEST

Daniel 1:15-21

15 After ten days they looked healthier and stronger than the young men who had been eating the king's rich food. **16** So the supervisor took away the king's rich food and wine and gave them vegetables.

17 God gave these four men knowledge, wisdom, and the ability to understand all kinds of literature. Daniel could also understand all kinds of visions and dreams.

18 At the end of the three-year training period, the chief-of-staff brought all the young men to Nebuchadnezzar. **19** The king talked to them and found no one like Daniel, Hananiah, Mishael, and Azariah among all of them. So these four men served the king. **20** Whenever the king asked them about things that required wisdom and insight, he found that they knew ten times more than all the magicians and psychics in his whole kingdom.

21 Daniel served the royal palace until the first year of King Cyrus ⌊of Persia⌋.

THE WIZARDS

Daniel 2:1-13

1 During the second year of Nebuchadnezzar's reign, he had some dreams. He was troubled, but he stayed asleep. **2** The king sent for the magicians, psychics, sorcerers, and astrologers so that they could tell him what he had dreamed. So they came to the king.

3 The king said to them, "I had a dream, and I'm troubled by it. I want to know what the dream was."

4 The astrologers spoke to the king in Aramaic, "Your Majesty, may you live forever! Tell us the dream, and we'll interpret it for you."

5 The king answered the astrologers, "I meant what I said! If you don't tell me the dream and its meaning, you will be torn limb from limb, and your houses will be turned into piles of rubble. **6** But if you tell me the dream and its meaning, I will give you gifts, awards, and high honors. Now tell me the dream and its meaning."

7 Once more they said, "Your Majesty, tell us the dream, and we'll tell you its meaning."

8 The king replied, "I'm sure you're trying to buy some time because you know that I meant what I said. **9** If you don't tell me the dream, you'll all receive the same punishment. You have agreed among yourselves to make up a phony explanation to give me, hoping that things will change. So tell me the dream. Then I'll know that you can explain its meaning to me."

10 The astrologers answered the king, "No one on earth can tell the king what he asks. No other king, no matter how great and powerful, has ever asked such a thing of any magician, psychic, or astrologer. **11** What you ask is difficult, Your Majesty. No one can tell what you dreamed except the gods, and they don't live with humans."

12 This made the king so angry and furious that he gave an order to destroy all the wise advisers in Babylon. **13** So a decree was issued that the wise advisers were to be killed, and some men were sent to find Daniel and his friends and kill them.

WHAT DOES THE KING'S DREAM MEAN?

Daniel 2:19-42

¹⁹ The secret was revealed to Daniel in a vision during the night. So Daniel praised the God of heaven. ²⁰ He said,

> "Praise God's name from everlasting to everlasting
> because he is wise and powerful.
> ²¹ He changes times and periods of history.
> He removes kings and establishes them.
> He gives wisdom to those who are wise
> and knowledge to those who have insight.
> ²² He reveals deeply hidden things.
> He knows what is in the dark,
> and light lives with him.
> ²³ God of my ancestors, I thank and praise you.
> You gave me wisdom and power.
> You told me the answer to our question.
> You told us what the king wants to know."

²⁴ Then Daniel went to Arioch, whom the king had appointed to destroy Babylon's wise advisers. Daniel told him, "Don't destroy Babylon's wise advisers. Take me to the king, and I'll explain the dream's meaning to him."

²⁵ Arioch immediately took Daniel to the king. He told the king, "I've found one of the captives from Judah who can explain the dream's meaning to you, Your Majesty."

²⁶ The king asked Daniel (who had been renamed Belteshazzar), "Can you tell me the dream I had and its meaning?"

²⁷ Daniel answered the king, "No wise adviser, psychic, magician, or fortuneteller can tell the king this secret. ²⁸ But there is a God in heaven who reveals secrets. He will tell King Nebuchadnezzar what is going to happen in the days to come. This is your dream, the vision you had while you were asleep: ²⁹ Your Majesty, while you were lying in bed, thoughts about what would happen in the future came to you. The one who reveals secrets told you what is going to happen. ³⁰ This secret wasn't revealed to me because I'm wiser than anyone else. It was revealed so that you could be told the meaning and so that you would know your innermost thoughts.

³¹ "Your Majesty, you had a vision. You saw a large statue. This statue was very bright. It stood in front of you, and it looked terrifying. ³² The head of this statue was made of fine gold. Its chest and arms were made of silver. Its stomach and hips were made of bronze. ³³ Its legs were made of iron. Its feet were made partly of iron and partly of clay. ³⁴ While you were watching, a stone was cut out, but not by humans. It struck the statue's iron-and-clay feet and smashed them. ³⁵ Then all at once, the iron, clay, bronze, silver, and gold were smashed. They became like husks on a threshing floor in summer. The wind carried them away, and not a trace of them could be found. But the stone that struck the statue became a large mountain which filled the whole world. ³⁶ This is the dream. Now we'll tell you its meaning.

³⁷ "Your Majesty, you are the greatest king. The God of heaven has given you a kingdom. He has given you power, strength, and honor. ³⁸ He has given you control over people, wild animals, and birds, wherever they live. He has made you ruler of them all. You are the head of gold. ³⁹ Another kingdom, inferior to yours, will rise to power after you. Then there will be a third kingdom, a kingdom of bronze, that will rule the whole world. ⁴⁰ There will also be a fourth kingdom. It will be as strong as iron. (Iron smashes and shatters everything.) As iron crushes things, this fourth kingdom will smash and crush all the other kingdoms. ⁴¹ You also saw the feet and toes. They were partly potters' clay and partly iron. This means that there will be a divided kingdom which has some of the firmness of iron. As you saw, iron was mixed with clay. ⁴² The toes were partly iron and partly clay. Part of the kingdom will be strong, and part will be brittle.

A NEVER-ENDING KINGDOM

Daniel 2:44-48

⁴⁴ "At the time of those kings, the God of heaven will establish a kingdom that will never be destroyed. No other people will be permitted to rule it. It will smash all the other kingdoms and put an end to them. But it will be established forever. ⁴⁵ This is the stone that you saw cut out from a mountain, but not by humans. It smashed the iron, bronze, clay, silver, and gold. The great God has told you what will happen in the future, Your Majesty. The dream is true, and you can trust that this is its meaning."

⁴⁶ King Nebuchadnezzar immediately bowed down on the ground in front of Daniel. He ordered that gifts and offerings be given to Daniel. ⁴⁷ The king said to Daniel, "Your God is truly the greatest of gods, the Lord over kings. He can reveal secrets because you were able to reveal this secret."

⁴⁸ Then the king promoted Daniel and gave him many wonderful gifts. Nebuchadnezzar made Daniel governor of the whole province of Babylon and head of all Babylon's wise advisers.

THREE BRAVE MEN

Daniel 3:1-18

[1] King Nebuchadnezzar made a gold statue 90 feet high and 9 feet wide. He set it up in a recessed area in the wall in the province of Babylon. [2] King Nebuchadnezzar sent messengers to assemble the satraps, governors, mayors, military advisers, treasurers, judges, officers, and all the other provincial officials to dedicate the statue he had set up. [3] Then the satraps, governors, mayors, military advisers, treasurers, judges, officers, and all the other provincial officials assembled to dedicate the statue King Nebuchadnezzar had set up. They stood in front of the statue.

[4] The herald called out loudly, "People of every province, nation, and language! [5] When you hear the sound of rams' horns, flutes, lyres, harps, and three-stringed harps playing at the same time with all other kinds of instruments, bow down and worship the gold statue that King Nebuchadnezzar has set up. [6] Whoever doesn't bow down and worship will immediately be thrown into a blazing furnace." [7] As soon as they heard the sound of rams' horns, flutes, lyres, harps, and three-stringed harps with all other kinds of instruments, all the people from every province, nation, and language bowed down and worshiped the gold statue King Nebuchadnezzar had set up.

[8] After that happened, some astrologers came forward and brought charges against the Jews. [9] They addressed King Nebuchadnezzar, "Your Majesty, may you live forever! [10] Your Majesty, you gave an order that everyone who hears the sound of rams' horns, flutes, lyres, harps, and three-stringed harps playing at the same time with all other kinds of instruments should bow down and worship the gold statue. [11] ⌊Your order said that⌋ whoever doesn't bow down and worship will be thrown into a blazing furnace. [12] There are certain Jews whom you appointed to govern the province of Babylon: Shadrach, Meshach, and Abednego. These men didn't obey your order, Your Majesty. They don't honor your gods or worship the statue that you set up."

¹³ Then, in a fit of rage and anger, Nebuchadnezzar summoned Shadrach, Meshach, and Abednego. Immediately, they were brought to the king. ¹⁴ Nebuchadnezzar asked them, "Shadrach, Meshach, and Abednego, is it true that you don't honor my gods or worship the gold statue that I set up? ¹⁵ When you hear the sound of the rams' horns, flutes, lyres, harps, and three-stringed harps playing at the same time with all other kinds of instruments, will you bow down and worship the gold statue I made? If you don't worship it, you will immediately be thrown into a blazing furnace. What god can save you from my power then?"

¹⁶ Shadrach, Meshach, and Abednego answered King Nebuchadnezzar, "We don't need to answer your last question. ¹⁷ If our God, whom we honor, can save us from a blazing furnace and from your power, he will, Your Majesty. ¹⁸ But if he doesn't, you should know, Your Majesty, we'll never honor your gods or worship the gold statue that you set up."

THE BLAZING FURNACE

Daniel 3:19-29

¹⁹ Nebuchadnezzar was so filled with anger toward Shadrach, Meshach, and Abednego that his face turned red. He ordered that the furnace should be heated seven times hotter than normal. ²⁰ He told some soldiers from his army to tie up Shadrach, Meshach, and Abednego so that they could be thrown into the blazing furnace. ²¹ Then the three men were thrown into the blazing furnace. They were wearing their clothes, hats, and other clothing. ²² The king's order was so urgent and the furnace was so extremely hot that the men who carried Shadrach, Meshach, and Abednego were killed by the flames from the fire. ²³ So these three men—Shadrach, Meshach, and Abednego—fell into the blazing furnace. They were still tied up.

²⁴ Then Nebuchadnezzar was startled. He sprang to his feet. He asked his advisers, "Didn't we throw three men into the fire?"

"That's true, Your Majesty," they answered.

²⁵ The king replied, "But look, I see four men. They're untied, walking in the middle of the fire, and unharmed. The fourth one looks like a son of the gods."

²⁶ Then Nebuchadnezzar went to the door of the blazing furnace and said, "Shadrach, Meshach, and Abednego—servants of the Most High God—come out here."

Shadrach, Meshach, and Abednego came out of the fire. ²⁷ The king's satraps, governors, mayors, and advisers gathered around the three men. They saw that the fire had not harmed their bodies. The hair on their heads wasn't singed, their clothes weren't burned, and they didn't smell of smoke.

²⁸ Nebuchadnezzar said, "Praise the God of Shadrach, Meshach, and Abednego. He sent his angel and saved his servants, who trusted him. They disobeyed the king and risked their lives so that they would not have to honor or worship any god except their own God. ²⁹ So I order that people from every province, nation, or language who say anything slanderous about the God of Shadrach, Meshach, and Abednego will be torn limb from limb. Their houses will be turned into piles of rubble. No other god can rescue like this."

THE KING'S FEAST

Daniel 5:1-12

¹ King Belshazzar threw a large banquet for 1,000 nobles and drank wine with them. ² As they were tasting the wine, Belshazzar ordered that the gold and silver utensils which his grandfather Nebuchadnezzar had taken from the temple in Jerusalem be brought to him. He wanted to drink from them with his nobles, his wives, and his concubines.

³ So the servants brought the gold utensils that had been taken from God's temple in Jerusalem. The king, his nobles, wives, and concubines drank from them. ⁴ They drank the wine and praised their gods made of gold, silver, bronze, iron, wood, or stone.

⁵ Suddenly, the fingers of a person's hand appeared and wrote on the plaster wall opposite the lamp stand of the royal palace. The king watched as the hand wrote. ⁶ Then the king turned pale, and his thoughts frightened him. His hip joints became loose, and his knees knocked against each other.

⁷ The king screamed for the psychics, astrologers, and fortunetellers to be brought to him. He told these wise advisers of Babylon, "Whoever reads this writing and tells me its meaning will be dressed in purple, wear a gold chain on his neck, and become the third-highest ruler in the kingdom." ⁸ All the king's wise advisers came, but they couldn't read the writing or tell the king its meaning. ⁹ King Belshazzar was terrified, and his face turned pale. His nobles didn't know what to do.

¹⁰ The discussion between the king and his nobles brought the queen herself into the banquet hall. The queen said, "Your Majesty, may you live forever! Don't let your thoughts frighten you, and don't turn pale. ¹¹ There's a man in your kingdom who has the spirit of the holy gods. In the days of your grandfather, he was found to have insight, good judgment, and wisdom like the wisdom of the gods. Your grandfather, King Nebuchadnezzar, made him head of the magicians, psychics, astrologers, and fortunetellers. ¹² This Daniel (who had been renamed Belteshazzar) was found to have knowledge, judgment, and an extraordinary spirit. He has the ability to interpret dreams, solve riddles, and untangle problems. Now, call Daniel, and he will tell ⌞you⌟ what it means."

DANIEL INTERPRETS THE WRITING ON THE WALL

Daniel 5:13-31

¹³ So Daniel was taken to the king. The king asked him, "Are you Daniel, one of the captives that my grandfather brought from Judah? ¹⁴ I've heard that you have the spirit of the gods and that you have insight, good judgment, and extraordinary wisdom. ¹⁵ The wise advisers and the psychics were brought to me to read this writing and tell me its meaning. But they couldn't tell me its meaning. ¹⁶ I have heard that you can interpret such things and untangle problems. If you can read the writing and tell ⌐me⌐ its meaning, you will be dressed in purple, wear a gold chain on your neck, and become the third-highest ruler in the kingdom."

¹⁷ Daniel told the king, "Keep your gifts. Give your gifts and awards to someone else. I'll still read the writing for you and tell you its meaning.

¹⁸ "Your Majesty, the Most High God gave your grandfather Nebuchadnezzar a kingdom, might, honor, and glory. ¹⁹ People from every province, nation, and language trembled and were terrified by him, because God gave him power. Nebuchadnezzar killed whomever he wanted to kill, and he kept alive whomever he wanted to keep alive. He promoted whomever he wanted to promote, and he demoted whomever he wanted to demote. ²⁰ But when he became so arrogant and conceited that he became overconfident, he was removed from the royal throne.

His honor was taken away from him. ²¹ He was chased away from people, and his mind was changed into an animal's mind. He lived with wild donkeys, ate grass like cattle, and his body became wet with dew from the sky. This happened until he realized that the Most High God has power over human kingdoms. God puts whomever he wishes in charge of them.

²² "Belshazzar, you are one of Nebuchadnezzar's successors. You didn't remain humble, even though you knew all this. ²³ But you made yourself greater than the Lord of heaven. You had the utensils from his temple brought to you. You, your nobles, wives, and concubines drank wine from them. You praised your gods made of silver, gold, bronze, iron, wood, or stone. These gods can't see, hear, or know anything. You didn't honor God, who has power over your life and everything you do. ²⁴ So he sent the hand to write this inscription. ²⁵ This is what has been written: Numbered, Numbered, Weighed, and Divided. ²⁶ This is its meaning: Numbered—God has numbered the days of your kingdom and will bring it to an end. ²⁷ Weighed—you have been weighed on a scale and found to be too light. ²⁸ Divided—your kingdom will be divided and given to the Medes and Persians."

²⁹ Then Belshazzar ordered that Daniel be dressed in purple and wear a gold chain on his neck. He made Daniel the third-highest ruler in the kingdom. ³⁰ That night King Belshazzar of Babylon was killed. ³¹ Darius the Mede took over the kingdom. He was 62 years old.

DANIEL IS THROWN INTO THE LION'S DEN

Daniel 6:1-28

¹Darius decided it would be good to appoint 120 satraps to rule throughout the kingdom. ²Over these satraps were three officials. Daniel was one of these officials. The satraps were to report to these three officials so that the king wouldn't be cheated.

³This man, Daniel, distinguished himself among the other officials and satraps because there was an extraordinary spirit in him. The king thought about putting him in charge of the whole kingdom. ⁴So the other officials and satraps tried to find something to accuse Daniel of in his duties for the kingdom. But they couldn't find anything wrong because he was trustworthy. No error or fault could be found. ⁵These men said, "We won't find anything to accuse this man, Daniel, unless we find it in his religious practices."

⁶So these officials and satraps went to the king as a group. They said to him, "May King Darius live forever! All the officials, governors, satraps, advisers, and mayors agree that the king should make a statute and enforce a decree. The decree should state that for the next 30 days whoever asks for anything from any god or person except you, Your Majesty, will be thrown into a lions' den. ⁸Your Majesty, issue this decree, and sign it. According to the law of the Medes and Persians no one could change it or repeal it." ⁹So Darius signed the written decree.

¹⁰When Daniel learned that the document had been signed, he went to his house. An upper room in his house had windows that opened in the direction of Jerusalem. Three times each day he got down on his knees and prayed to his God. He had always praised God this way.

¹¹One of those times the men came in as a group and found Daniel praying and pleading to his God. ¹²Then they went and spoke to the king about his decree. ⌊They asked,⌋ "Didn't you sign a decree which stated that for 30 days whoever asks for anything from any god or person except you, Your Majesty, will be thrown into a lions' den?"

The king answered, "That's true. According to the law of the Medes and Persians the decree can't be repealed."

¹³They replied, "Your Majesty, Daniel, one of the captives from Judah, refuses to obey your order or the decree that you signed. He prays three times each day."

¹⁴The king was very displeased when he heard this. He tried every way he could think of to save Daniel. Until sundown he did everything he could to rescue him.

¹⁵Then Daniel's accusers gathered in front of the king. They said to him, "Remember, Your Majesty, the Medes and Persians have a law that no decree or statute the king makes can be changed."

So the king gave the order, and Daniel was brought to him and thrown into the lions' den. The king told Daniel, "May your God, whom you always worship, save you!"

A stone was brought and placed over the opening of the den. The king put his seal on the stone, using his ring and the rings of his nobles, so that Daniel's situation could not be changed.

Then the king went to his palace and spent the night without food or company. He couldn't get to sleep. At dawn, as soon as it was light, the king got up and quickly went to the lions' den. As he came near the den where Daniel was, the king called to Daniel with anguish in his voice, "Daniel, servant of the living God! Was God, whom you always worship, able to save you from the lions?"

Daniel said to the king, "Your Majesty, may you live forever! My God sent his angel and shut the lions' mouths so that they couldn't hurt me. He did this because he considered me innocent. Your Majesty, I haven't committed any crime."

The king was overjoyed and had Daniel taken out of the den. When Daniel was taken out of the den, people saw that he was completely unharmed because he trusted his God.

The king ordered those men who had brought charges against Daniel to be brought to him. They, their wives, and their children were thrown into the lions' den. Before they reached the bottom of the den, the lions attacked them and crushed all their bones.

Then King Darius wrote to the people of every province, nation, and language all over the world:

I wish you peace and prosperity.

I decree that in every part of my kingdom people should tremble with terror in front of Daniel's God, the living God who continues forever. His kingdom will never be destroyed. His power lasts to the end ⌊of time⌋. He saves, rescues, and does miraculous signs and amazing things in heaven and on earth. He saved Daniel from the lions.

This man, Daniel, prospered during the reign of Darius and the reign of Cyrus the Persian.

THE PROUD KING

Esther 1:1-7

In the days of Xerxes the following events took place. This was the same Xerxes who ruled over 127 provinces from India to Sudan. At the time when King Xerxes sat on the royal throne in the fortress of Susa, he held a banquet in the third year of his reign. The banquet was for all his officials and advisers, that is, the military officers of the Persians and Medes, the nobles and officials of the provinces who had access to him. He showed them the enormous wealth of his kingdom and the costly splendor of his greatness for many days, 180 to be exact. When those days were over, the king held a banquet lasting seven days. This banquet was held in the enclosed garden of the king's palace for all people in the fortress of Susa, whatever their rank.

The garden had white and violet linen curtains. These curtains were attached to silver rods and marble pillars by cords made of white and purple fine linen. Gold and silver couches were on a mosaic pavement of purple rock, white marble, pearl-like stone, and black marble. People drank from golden cups. No two cups were alike. The king also provided plenty of royal wine out of his royal generosity.

QUEEN VASHTI'S REFUSAL

Esther 1:10-21

On the seventh day when the king was drunk on wine, he ordered Mehuman, Biztha, Harbona, Bigtha, Abagtha, Zethar, and Carcas, the seven eunuchs who served under King Xerxes, to bring Queen Vashti in front of the king, wearing her royal crown. He wanted to show the people, especially the officials, her beauty, because she was very attractive. But Queen Vashti refused the king's command that the eunuchs delivered to her. As a result, the king became very angry, and his rage burned inside him.

Now, the king usually asked for advice from all the experts in royal decrees and decisions, from those closest to him—Carshena, Shethar, Admatha, Tarshish, Meres, Marsena, and Memucan. These seven officials of the Persians and Medes had access to the king and held the highest rank in the kingdom. The king asked these wise men who knew the times, "According to the royal decrees, what must we do with Queen Vashti since she did not obey King Xerxes' command, which the eunuchs delivered?"

¹⁶ Then Memucan spoke up in the presence of
the king and the officials, "Queen Vashti has done
wrong, not only against the king but also against all
the officials and all the people in every province of
King Xerxes. ¹⁷ The news of what the queen has done
will spread to all women, and they will despise their
husbands. They will say, 'King Xerxes ordered Queen
Vashti to be brought to him, but she would not come.'
Today the wives of the officials in Persia and Media
who have heard what the queen did will talk back
to all the king's officials. There will be contempt and
short tempers. ¹⁹ If it pleases you, Your Majesty, issue
a royal decree. It should be recorded in the decrees
of the Persians and Medes, never to be repealed, that
Vashti may never again appear in front of King Xerxes.
Furthermore, Your Majesty, you should give her royal
position to another woman who is more worthy
than she. ²⁰ When you issue your decree, your whole
kingdom, great as it is, will hear it. Then all the wives
will honor their husbands, regardless of their status."
²¹ The king and his officials approved of this, and
the king did as Memucan suggested.

A NEW QUEEN IS CHOSEN

Esther 2:1-17

[1] Later, when King Xerxes got over his raging anger, he remembered Vashti, what she had done, and what had been decided against her.

[2] So the king's personal staff said to him, "Search for attractive young virgins for the king. [3] And appoint scouts in all the provinces of your kingdom to gather all the attractive young virgins and bring them to the fortress of Susa, to the women's quarters. There, in the care of the king's eunuch Hegai, the guardian of the women, they will have their beauty treatment. [4] Then the young woman who pleases you, Your Majesty, will become queen instead of Vashti."

The king liked the suggestion, and so he did just that.

[5] In the fortress of Susa there was a Jew from the tribe of Benjamin named Mordecai. He was the son of Jair, the grandson of Shimei, and the great-grandson of Kish. [6] (Kish had been taken captive from Jerusalem together with the others who had gone into exile along with Judah's King Jehoiakin, whom King Nebuchadnezzar of Babylon had carried away.)

[7] Mordecai had raised Hadassah, also known as Esthe[r], his uncle's daughter, because she was an orphan. The young woman had a beautiful figure and was very attractive. When her father and mother died, Morde[cai] adopted her as his own daughter.

[8] When the king's announcement and decree wer[e] heard, many young women were gathered together and brought to the fortress of Susa. They were place[d] in the care of Hegai. Esther also was taken to the kin[g's] palace and placed in the care of Hegai, the guardian [of] the women. [9] The young woman pleased him and wo[n] his affection. So he immediately provided her with t[he] beauty treatment, a daily supply of food, and seven suitable female servants from the king's palace. The[n] he moved her and her servants to the best place in t[he] women's quarters.

[10] Esther did not reveal her nationality or her fam[ily] background, because Mordecai had ordered her not [to.] [11] Every day Mordecai would walk back and forth in front of the courtyard of the women's quarters to fin[d] out how Esther was and what was happening to her.

[12] Each young woman had her turn to go to King Xerxes after she had completed the required

12-month treatment for women. The time of beauty treatment was spent as follows: six months using oil of myrrh and six months using perfumes and other treatments for women.

13 After that, the young woman would go to the king. Anything she wanted to take with her from the women's quarters to the king's palace was given to her. **14** She would go in the evening and come back in the morning to the other quarters for women. There she would be in the care of the king's eunuch Shaashgaz, the guardian of the concubines. She never went to the king again unless the king desired her and requested her by name.

¹⁵ (Esther was the daughter of Abihail, Mordecai's uncle. Mordecai had adopted her as his own daughter.)

When Esther's turn came to go to the king, she asked only for what the king's eunuch Hegai, the guardian of the women, advised. Everyone who saw Esther liked her. ¹⁶ So Esther was taken to King Xerxes in his royal palace in the month of Tebeth, the tenth month, in the seventh year of his reign.

¹⁷ Now, the king loved Esther more than all the other women and favored her over all the other virgins. So he put the royal crown on her head and made her queen instead of Vashti.

THE JEWISH PEOPLE MUST DIE

Esther 2:19-3:15

¹⁹ When the virgins were gathered a second time, Mordecai was sitting at the king's gate. ²⁰ Esther still had not revealed her family background or nationality, as Mordecai had ordered her. Esther always did whatever Mordecai told her, as she did when she was a child.

²¹ In those days, while Mordecai was sitting at the king's gate, Bigthan and Teresh, two of the king's eunuchs who guarded the entrance, became angry and planned to kill King Xerxes. ²² But Mordecai found out about it and informed Queen Esther. Then Esther told the king, on behalf of Mordecai. ²³ When the report was investigated and found to be true, the dead bodies of Bigthan and Teresh were hung on a pole. The matter was written up in the king's presence in his official record of daily events.

Later, King Xerxes promoted Haman. (Haman was the son of Hammedatha and was from Agag.) He gave Haman a position higher in authority than all the other officials who were with him. ² All the king's advisers were at the king's gate, kneeling and bowing to Haman with their faces touching the ground, because the king had commanded it. But Mordecai would not kneel and bow to him.

³ Then the king's advisers at the king's gate asked Mordecai, "Why do you ignore the king's command?" ⁴ Although they asked him day after day, he paid no attention to them. So they informed Haman to see if Mordecai's actions would be tolerated, since Mordecai had told them that he was a Jew.

⁵ When Haman saw that Mordecai did not kneel and bow to him, Haman was infuriated. ⁶ Because the king's advisers had informed him about Mordecai's nationality, he thought it beneath himself to kill only Mordecai. So Haman planned to wipe out Mordecai's people—all the Jews in the entire kingdom of Xerxes.

⁷In Xerxes' twelfth year as king, *Pur* (which means *the lot*) was thrown in front of Haman for every day of every month, from Nisan, the first month, until Adar, the twelfth month.

⁸Now, Haman told King Xerxes, "Your Majesty, there is a certain nationality scattered among—but separate from—the nationalities in all the provinces of your kingdom. Their laws differ from those of all other nationalities. They do not obey your decrees. So it is not in your interest to tolerate them, Your Majesty. ⁹If you approve, have the orders for their destruction be written. For this I will pay 750,000 pounds of silver to your treasurers to be put in your treasury."

¹⁰At that, the king removed his signet ring and gave it to Haman, the enemy of the Jews. (Haman was the son of Hammedatha and was from Agag.) ¹¹The king told Haman, "You can keep your silver and do with the people whatever you like."

¹²On the thirteenth day of the first month the king's scribes were summoned. All Haman's orders were written to the king's satraps, the governors of every province, and the officials of every people. They wrote to each province in its own script and to the people in each province in their own language. The orders were signed in the name of King Xerxes and sealed with the king's ring. ¹³Messengers were sent with official documents to all the king's provinces. ⌊The people were ordered⌋ to wipe out, kill, and destroy all the Jews—young and old, women and children—on a single day, the thirteenth day of the twelfth month, the month of Adar. Their possessions were also to be seized. ¹⁴A copy of the document was made public in a decree to every province. All the people were to be ready for this day.

¹⁵The messengers hurried out as the king told them. The decree was also issued at the fortress of Susa. So the king and Haman sat down to drink a toast, but the city of Susa was in turmoil.

ESTHER HAS A PLAN

Esther 4:8-5:9

⁸He also gave him a copy of the decree that was issued in Susa. The decree gave permission to exterminate the Jews. Hathach was supposed to show it to Esther, inform and command her to go to the king, beg him for mercy, and appeal to him for her people. ⁹So Hathach returned and told Esther what Mordecai had said.

¹⁰Esther spoke to Hathach and commanded him to say to Mordecai, ¹¹"All the king's advisers and the people in the king's provinces know that no one approaches the king in the throne room without being summoned. By law that person must be put to death

Only if the king holds out the golden scepter to him will he live. I, myself, have not been summoned to enter the king's presence for 30 days now." [12] So Esther's servants told Mordecai what Esther said.

[13] Mordecai sent this answer back to Esther, "Do not imagine that just because you are in the king's palace you will be any safer than all the rest of the Jews. [14] The fact is, even if you remain silent now, someone else will help and rescue the Jews, but you and your relatives will die. And who knows, you may have gained your royal position for a time like this."

[15] Esther sent this reply back to Mordecai, [16] "Assemble all the Jews in Susa. Fast for me: Do not eat or drink at all for three entire days. My servants and I will also fast. After that, I will go to the king, even if it is against a royal decree. If I die, I die."

[17] Mordecai did just as Esther had commanded him.

[1] On the third day Esther put on her royal robes. She stood in the courtyard of the king's palace, facing the king's throne room. The king was sitting on the royal throne inside the palace, facing the entrance.

[2] When the king saw Queen Esther standing in the entrance, she won his favor. So the king held out the golden scepter that was in his hand to Esther. Esther went up to him and touched the top of the scepter.

[3] Then the king asked her, "What is troubling you, Queen Esther? What would you like? Even if it is up to half of the kingdom, it will be granted to you."

[4] So Esther answered, "If it pleases you, Your Majesty, come today with Haman to a dinner I have prepared for you."

[5] The king replied, "Bring Haman right away, and do whatever Esther asks." So the king and Haman came to the dinner that Esther had prepared.

[6] While they were drinking wine, the king asked Esther, "What is your request? It will be granted to you. What would you like? Even if it is up to half of the kingdom, it will be granted."

[7] Esther answered, "My request? What would I like? [8] Your Majesty, come with Haman to a dinner I will prepare for you. And tomorrow I will answer you, Your Majesty. If I have found favor with you, Your Majesty, and if it pleases you, Your Majesty, may you ˪then˨ grant my request and do what I would like."

[9] When Haman left that day, he was happy and feeling good. But when Haman saw Mordecai at the king's gate, neither getting up nor trembling in his presence, Haman was furious with Mordecai.

E LORD USES ESTHER TO SAVE HIS PEOPLE

her 7:1-6

the king and Haman came to have dinner with
een Esther. ² On the second day, while they were
nking wine, the king asked Esther, "What is your
uest, Queen Esther? It will be granted to you. And
at would you like? Even if it is up to half of the
gdom, it will be granted."

³ Then Queen Esther answered, "If I have found
or with you, Your Majesty, and if it pleases you,
ır Majesty, spare my life. That is my request. And
ıre the life of my people. That is what I ask for.
ıu see, we—my people and I—have been sold
that we can be wiped out, killed, and destroyed.
ıur men and women had only been sold as slaves,
ould have kept silent because the enemy is not
rth troubling you about, Your Majesty."

⁵ Then King Xerxes interrupted Queen Esther and
d, "Who is this person? Where is the person who
s dared to do this?"

⁶ Esther answered, "Our vicious enemy is this
:ked man Haman!" Then Haman became panic-
icken in the presence of the king and queen.

MAN IS HUNG

her 7:7-8:2

ıe king was furious as he got up from dinner and
 nt into the palace garden. But Haman stayed to
Queen Esther for his life, because he saw that the
ıg had a terrible end in mind for him. ⁸ When the
ıg returned from the palace garden to the palace
ıing room, Haman was falling on the couch where
her was lying. The king thought, "Is he even going
ape the queen while I'm in the palace?" Then the
ıg passed sentence on him, and servants covered
man's face.

⁹ Harbona, one of the eunuchs present with the
ıg, said, "What a coincidence! The 75-foot pole
man made for Mordecai, who spoke up for the well-
ng of the king, is still standing at Haman's house."

The king responded, "Hang him on it!" ¹⁰ So
vants hung Haman's ⌞dead body⌟ on the very pole
had prepared for Mordecai. Then the king got over
raging anger.

ı that same day King Xerxes gave the property
Haman, the enemy of the Jews, to Queen Esther.
o, Mordecai came to the king because Esther had
d him how Mordecai was related to her. ² Then the
ıg took off his signet ring, which he had taken
m Haman, and gave it to Mordecai. And Esther
Mordecai in charge of Haman's property.

THE JEWISH PEOPLE ARE GIVEN A CHANCE TO SURVIVE

Esther 8:3-17

³Esther spoke again to the king. She fell down at his feet crying and begged him to have mercy and to undo the evil plot of Haman, who was from Agag, and his conspiracy against the Jews. ⁴The king held out his golden scepter to Esther, and Esther got up and stood in front of the king. ⁵She said, "Your Majesty, if it pleases you, and if I have found favor with you, if you consider my cause to be reasonable and if I am pleasing to you, cancel the official orders ⌊concerning⌋ the plot of Haman (who was the son of Hammedatha and was from Agag). He signed ⌊the order⌋ to destroy the Jews in all your provinces, Your Majesty. ⁶I cannot bear to see my people suffer such evil. And I simply cannot bear to see the destruction of my relatives."

⁷King Xerxes said to Queen Esther and Mordecai the Jew, "I have given Haman's property to Esther, an Haman's ⌊dead body⌋ was hung on the pole because he tried to kill the Jews. ⁸You write what you think i best for the Jews in the king's name. Seal it also with the king's signet ring, because whatever is written i the king's name and sealed with the king's signet ri cannot be canceled."

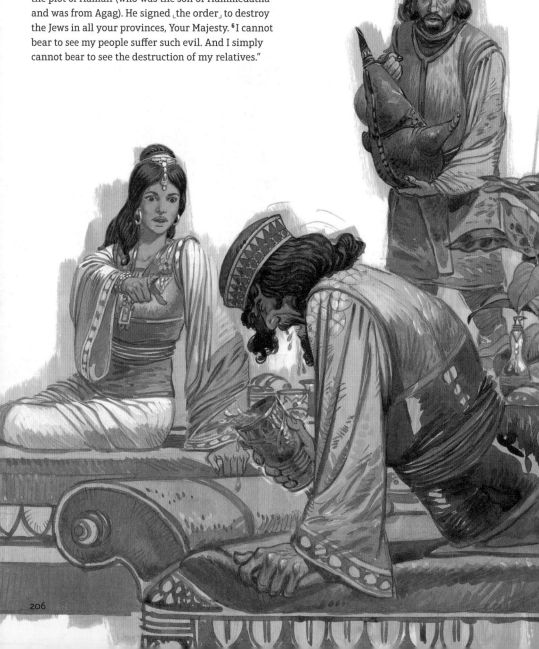

⁹At that time on the twenty-third day of Sivan, the third month, the king's scribes were summoned. What Mordecai had ordered was written to the Jews and to the satraps, governors, and officers of the 127 provinces from India to Sudan. It was written to each province in its own script, to each people in their own language, and to the Jews in their own script and their own language.

¹⁰Mordecai wrote in King Xerxes' name and sealed the official documents with the king's signet ring. Then he sent them by messengers who rode special horses bred for speed. ⌐He wrote¬ ¹¹that the king had given permission for the Jews in every city to assemble, to defend themselves, to wipe out, to kill, and to destroy every armed force of the people and province that is hostile to them, even women and children, and to seize their goods.

¹²⌐This was permitted¬ on one day in all the provinces of King Xerxes, on the thirteenth day of Adar, the twelfth month. ¹³The copy of the document was made public in a decree to every province for all people. On that day the Jews were to be ready to take revenge on their enemies.

¹⁴The messengers rode the king's fastest horses. They left quickly, in keeping with the king's command. The decree was issued also in the fortress of Susa.

¹⁵Mordecai went out from the presence of the king wearing the royal violet and white robe, a large gold crown, and a purple outer robe of fine linen. And the city of Susa cheered and rejoiced.

¹⁶So the Jews were cheerful, happy, joyful, and successful. ¹⁷In every province and every city where the king's message and decree arrived, the Jews were happy and joyful, feasting and enjoying a holiday. Then many common people pretended to be Jews because they were terrified of the Jews.

THE JEWISH PEOPLE FIGHT BACK

Esther 9:1-28

[1] On the thirteenth day of Adar, the twelfth month, the king's command and decree were to be carried out. On that very day, when the enemies of the Jews expected to overpower them, the exact opposite happened: The Jews overpowered those who hated them.

[2] The Jews assembled in their cities throughout all the provinces of King Xerxes to kill those who were planning to harm them. No one could stand up against them, because all the people were terrified of them. [3] All the officials of the provinces, the satraps, the governors, and the king's treasurers assisted the Jews because they were terrified of Mordecai. [4] Mordecai was an important man in the king's palace. Moreover, his reputation was spreading to all the provinces, since Mordecai was becoming more and more powerful.

[5] Then with their swords, the Jews attacked all their enemies, killing them, destroying them, and doing whatever they pleased to those who hated them. [6] In the fortress of Susa the Jews killed and wiped out 500 men. [7] They also killed Parshandatha, Dalphon, Aspatha, [8] Poratha, Adalia, Aridatha, [9] Parmashta, Arisai, Aridai, and Vaizatha. [10] These were the ten sons of Haman, who was the son of Hammedatha and the enemy of the Jews. But the Jews did not seize any of their possessions.

[11] On that day the number of those killed in the fortress of Susa was reported to the king. [12] So the king said to Queen Esther, "In the fortress of Susa the Jews have killed and wiped out 500 men and Haman's 10 sons. What must they have done in the rest of the king's provinces! Now, what is your request? It will be granted to you. And what else would you like? It, too, will be granted."

[13] Esther said, "If it pleases you, Your Majesty, allow the Jews in Susa to do tomorrow what was decreed for today. Let them hang Haman's ten sons on poles."

[14] The king commanded this, issuing a decree in Susa. And so they hung Haman's ten sons ⌐on poles⌐.

[15] The Jews in Susa also assembled on the fourteenth day of the month of Adar and killed 300 men in Susa, but they did not seize any of their possessions. [16] The other Jews who were in the king's provinces had also assembled to defend and free themselves from their enemies. They killed 75,000 of those who hated them, but they did not seize any of their possessions. [17] This was on the thirteenth day of the month of Adar. On the fourteenth they rested and made it a day of feasting and celebration. [18] But the Jews in Susa had assembled on the thirteenth and fourteenth. They rested on the fifteenth and made it a day of feasting and celebration.

[19] That is why the Jews who live in the villages and in the unwalled towns make the fourteenth day of the month of Adar a holiday for feasting and celebration. They also send gifts of food to one another.

[20] Now, Mordecai wrote these things down and sent official letters to all the Jews in all the provinces of King Xerxes, near and far. [21] He established the fourteenth and fifteenth days of the month of Adar as days they must observe every year. [22] They were to observe them just like the days when the Jews freed themselves from their enemies. In that month their grief turned to joy and their mourning into a holiday. He declared that these days are to be days for feasting and celebrating and for sending gifts of food to one another, especially gifts to the poor.

[23] So the Jews accepted as tradition what they had begun, as Mordecai had written to them. [24] It was because Haman, the enemy of all the Jews, had plotted against the Jews to destroy them. (Haman was the son of Hammedatha and was from Agag.) Haman had the *Pur* (which means *the lot*) thrown ⌐in order to determine when⌐ to crush and destroy them. [25] But when this came to the king's attention, he ordered, in the well-known letter, that the evil plan Haman had plotted against the Jews should turn back on his own head. As a result, they hung Haman and his sons on poles.

[26] So the Jews called these days Purim, based on the word *Pur*. Therefore, because of everything that was said in this letter—both what they had seen and what had happened to them—[27] the Jews established a tradition for themselves and their descendants and for anyone who would join them. The tradition was that a person should never fail to observe these two days every year, as they were described and at their appointed time. [28] So these days must be remembered and observed in every age, family, province, and city. These days of Purim must not be ignored among the Jews, and the importance of these days must never be forgotten by the generations to come.

AN ANGEL VISITS MARY

Luke 1:5-38

⁵ When Herod was king of Judea, there was a priest named Zechariah, who belonged to the division of priests named after Abijah. Zechariah's wife Elizabeth was a descendant of Aaron. ⁶ Zechariah and Elizabeth had God's approval. They followed all the Lord's commands and regulations perfectly. ⁷ Yet, they never had any children because Elizabeth couldn't become pregnant. Both of them were too old to have children.

⁸ Zechariah was on duty with his division of priests. As he served in God's presence, ⁹ he was chosen by priestly custom to go into the Lord's temple to burn incense. ¹⁰ All the people were praying outside while he was burning incense.

Testament

¹¹ Then, to the right of the incense altar, an angel of the Lord appeared to him. ¹² Zechariah was troubled and overcome with fear.

¹³ The angel said to him, "Don't be afraid, Zechariah! God has heard your prayer. Your wife Elizabeth will have a son, and you will name him John. ¹⁴ He will be your pride and joy, and many people will be glad that he was born. ¹⁵ As far as the Lord is concerned, he will be a great man. He will never drink wine or any other liquor. He will be filled with the Holy Spirit even before he is born. ¹⁶ He will bring many people in Israel back to the Lord their God. ¹⁷ He will go ahead of the Lord with the spirit and power that Elijah had. He will change parents' attitudes toward their children. He will change disobedient people so that they will accept the wisdom of those who have God's approval. In this way he will prepare the people for their Lord."

¹⁸ Zechariah said to the angel, "What proof is there for this? I'm an old man, and my wife is beyond her childbearing years."

¹⁹ The angel answered him, "I'm Gabriel! I stand in God's presence. God sent me to tell you this good news. ²⁰ But because you didn't believe what I said, you will be unable to talk until the day this happens. Everything will come true at the right time."

²¹ Meanwhile, the people were waiting for Zechariah. They were amazed that he was staying in the temple so long. ²² When he did come out, he was unable to speak to them. So they realized that he had seen a vision in the temple. He motioned to them but remained unable to talk.

²³ When the days of his service were over, he went home. ²⁴ Later, his wife Elizabeth became pregnant and didn't go out in public for five months. She said, "The Lord has done this for me now. He has removed my public disgrace."

²⁶ Six months after Elizabeth had become pregnant, God sent the angel Gabriel to Nazareth, a city in Galilee. ²⁷ The angel went to a virgin promised in marriage to a descendant of David named Joseph. The virgin's name was Mary.

²⁸ When the angel entered her home, he greeted her and said, "You are favored by the Lord! The Lord is with you."

²⁹ She was startled by what the angel said and tried to figure out what this greeting meant.

³⁰ The angel told her,

"Don't be afraid, Mary. You have
        found favor with God.
³¹ You will become pregnant, give birth to a son,
        and name him Jesus.
³² He will be a great man
        and will be called the Son of the Most High.
    The Lord God will give him
        the throne of his ancestor David.
³³ Your son will be king of Jacob's people forever,
        and his kingdom will never end."

³⁴ Mary asked the angel, "How can this be? I'm a virgin."

³⁵ The angel answered her, "The Holy Spirit will come to you, and the power of the Most High will overshadow you. Therefore, the holy child developing inside you will be called the Son of God.

³⁶ "Elizabeth, your relative, is six months pregnant with a son in her old age. People said she couldn't have a child. ³⁷ But nothing is impossible for God."

³⁸ Mary answered, "I am the Lord's servant. Let everything you've said happen to me." Then the angel left her.

A TRIP OVER THE MOUNTAINS

Luke 1:39-45

³⁹ Soon afterward, Mary hurried to a city in the mountain region of Judah. ⁴⁰ She entered Zechariah's home and greeted Elizabeth.

⁴¹ When Elizabeth heard the greeting, she felt the baby kick. Elizabeth was filled with the Holy Spirit. ⁴² She said in a loud voice, "You are the most blessed of all women, and blessed is the child that you will have. ⁴³ I feel blessed that the mother of my Lord is visiting me. ⁴⁴ As soon as I heard your greeting, I felt the baby jump for joy. ⁴⁵ You are blessed for believing that the Lord would keep his promise to you."

JOSEPH'S DREAM

Matthew 1:18-24

¹⁸ The birth of Jesus Christ took place in this way. His mother Mary had been promised to Joseph in marriage. But before they were married, Mary realized that she was pregnant by the Holy Spirit. ¹⁹ Her husband Joseph was an honorable man and did not want to disgrace her publicly. So he decided to break the marriage agreement with her secretly.

²⁰ Joseph had this in mind when an angel of the Lord appeared to him in a dream. The angel said to him, "Joseph, descendant of David, don't be afraid to take Mary as your wife. She is pregnant by the Holy Spirit. ²¹ She will give birth to a son, and you will name him Jesus [He Saves], because he will save his people from their sins." ²² All this happened so that what the Lord had spoken through the prophet came true: ²³ "The virgin will become pregnant and give birth to a son, and they will name him Immanuel," which means "God is with us."

²⁴ When Joseph woke up, he did what the angel of the Lord had commanded him to do. He took Mary to be his wife. ²⁵ He did not have marital relations with her before she gave birth to a son. Joseph named the child Jesus.

ESUS IS BORN

Luke 2:1-7

At that time the Emperor Augustus ordered a census of the Roman Empire. ²This was the first census taken while Quirinius was governor of Syria. ³All the people went to register in the cities where their ancestors had lived.

⁴So Joseph went from Nazareth, a city in Galilee, to a Judean city called Bethlehem. Joseph, a descendant of King David, went to Bethlehem because David had been born there. ⁵Joseph went there to register with Mary. She had been promised to him in marriage and was pregnant.

⁶While they were in Bethlehem, the time came for Mary to have her child. ⁷She gave birth to her firstborn son. She wrapped him in strips of cloth and laid him in a manger because there wasn't any room for them in the inn.

THE SHEPHERDS

Luke 2:8-20

⁸Shepherds were in the fields near Bethlehem. They were taking turns watching their flock during the night. ⁹An angel from the Lord suddenly appeared to them. The glory of the Lord filled the area with light, and they were terrified. ¹⁰The angel said to them, "Don't be afraid! I have good news for you, a message that will fill everyone with joy. ¹¹Today your Savior, Christ the Lord, was born in David's city. ¹²This is how you will recognize him: You will find an infant wrapped in strips of cloth and lying in a manger."

¹³Suddenly, a large army of angels appeared with the angel. They were praising God by saying,

¹⁴"Glory to God in the highest heaven,
and on earth peace to those
who have his good will!"

¹⁵The angels left them and went back to heaven. The shepherds said to each other, "Let's go to Bethlehem and see what the Lord has told us about."

¹⁶They went quickly and found Mary and Joseph with the baby, who was lying in a manger. ¹⁷When they saw the child, they repeated what they had been told about him. ¹⁸Everyone who heard the shepherds' story was amazed.

¹⁹Mary treasured all these things in her heart and always thought about them.

²⁰As the shepherds returned to their flock, they glorified and praised God for everything they had seen and heard. Everything happened the way the angel had told them.

E STAR THAT LED TO THE BABY'S CRADLE

tthew 2:1-12

sus was born in Bethlehem in Judea when Herod
s king. After Jesus' birth wise men from the east
rived in Jerusalem. ² They asked, "Where is the one
o was born to be the king of the Jews? We saw his
r rising and have come to worship him."

³ When King Herod and all Jerusalem heard about
s, they became disturbed. ⁴ He called together all
e chief priests and the experts in the Scriptures and
ed to find out from them where the Messiah was
pposed to be born.

⁵ They told him, "In Bethlehem in Judea. The
ophet wrote about this:

⁶ Bethlehem in the land of Judah,
    you are by no means least
        among the leaders of Judah.
    A leader will come from you.
        He will shepherd my people Israel."

⁷ Then Herod secretly called the wise men and
found out from them exactly when the star had
appeared. ⁸ As he sent them to Bethlehem, he said,
"Go and search carefully for the child. When you have
found him, report to me so that I may go and worship
him too."

⁹ After they had heard the king, they started out.
The star they had seen rising led them until it stopped
over the place where the child was. ¹⁰ They were
overwhelmed with joy to see the star. ¹¹ When they
entered the house, they saw the child with his mother
Mary. So they bowed down and worshiped him. Then
they opened their treasure chests and offered him
gifts of gold, frankincense, and myrrh.

¹² God warned them in a dream not to go back to
Herod. So they left for their country by another road.

HE WILL BE CALLED A NAZARENE

Matthew 2:13-23

13 After they had left, an angel of the Lord appeared to Joseph in a dream. The angel said to him, "Get up, take the child and his mother, and flee to Egypt. Stay there until I tell you, because Herod intends to search for the child and kill him."

14 Joseph got up, took the child and his mother, and left for Egypt that night. **15** He stayed there until Herod died. What the Lord had spoken through the prophet came true: "I have called my son out of Egypt."

16 When Herod saw that the wise men had tricked him, he became furious. He sent soldiers to kill all the boys two years old and younger in or near Bethlehem. This matched the exact time he had learned from the wise men. **17** Then the words spoken through the prophet Jeremiah came true:

18 "A sound was heard in Ramah,
the sound of crying in bitter grief.
Rachel was crying for her children.
She refused to be comforted
because they were dead."

19 After Herod was dead, an angel of the Lord appeared in a dream to Joseph in Egypt. **20** The angel said to him, "Get up, take the child and his mother, and go to Israel. Those who tried to kill the child are dead."

21 Joseph got up, took the child and his mother, and went to Israel. **22** But when he heard that Archelaus had succeeded his father Herod as king of Judea, Joseph was afraid to go there. Warned in a dream, he left for Galilee **23** and made his home in a city called Nazareth. So what the prophets had said came true: "He will be called a Nazarene."

Luke 2:40

40 The child grew and became strong. He was filled with wisdom, and God's favor was with him.

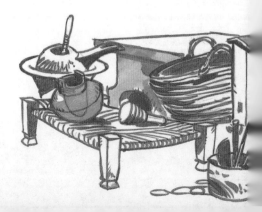

JOSEPH AND MARY LOSE JESUS

Luke 2:41-52

[41] Every year Jesus' parents would go to Jerusalem for the Passover festival. [42] When he was 12 years old, they went as usual.

[43] When the festival was over, they left for home. The boy Jesus stayed behind in Jerusalem, but his parents didn't know it. [44] They thought that he was with the others who were traveling with them. After traveling for a day, they started to look for him among their relatives and friends. [45] When they didn't find him, they went back to Jerusalem to look for him.

[46] Three days later, they found him in the temple courtyard. He was sitting among the teachers, listening to them, and asking them questions. [47] His understanding and his answers stunned everyone who heard him.

[48] When his parents saw him, they were shocked. His mother asked him, "Son, why have you done this to us? Your father and I have been worried sick looking for you!"

[49] Jesus said to them, "Why were you looking for me? Didn't you realize that I had to be in my Father's house?" [50] But they didn't understand what he meant.

[51] Then he returned with them to Nazareth and was obedient to them.

His mother treasured all these things in her heart. [52] Jesus grew in wisdom and maturity. He gained favor from God and people.

223

JESUS IS BAPTIZED

Matthew 3:1-17

[1]Later, John the Baptizer appeared in the desert of Judea. His message was, [2]"Turn to God and change the way you think and act, because the kingdom of heaven is near." [3]Isaiah the prophet spoke about this man when he said,

> "A voice cries out in the desert:
>> 'Prepare the way for the Lord!
>>> Make his paths straight!'"

[4]John wore clothes made from camel's hair and had a leather belt around his waist. His diet consisted of locusts and wild honey.

[5]Jerusalem, all Judea, and the whole Jordan Valley went to him. [6]As they confessed their sins, he baptized them in the Jordan River.

[7]But when he saw many Pharisees and Sadducees coming to be baptized, he said to them, "You poisonous snakes! Who showed you how to flee from God's coming anger? [8]Do those things that prove you have turned to God and have changed the way you think and act. [9]Don't think you can say, 'Abraham is our ancestor.' I can guarantee that God can raise up descendants for Abraham from these stones. [10]The ax is now ready to cut the roots of the trees. Any tree that doesn't produce good fruit will be cut down and thrown into a fire. [11]I baptize you with water so that you will change the way you think and act. But the one who comes after me is more powerful than I. I am not worthy to remove his sandals. He will baptize you with the Holy Spirit and fire. [12]His winnowing shovel is in his hand, and he will clean up his threshing floor. He will gather his wheat into a barn, but he will burn the husks in a fire that can never be put out."

[13]Then Jesus appeared. He came from Galilee to the Jordan River to be baptized by John. [14]But John tried to stop him and said, "I need to be baptized by you. Why are you coming to me?"

[15]Jesus answered him, "This is the way it has to be now. This is the proper way to do everything that God requires of us."

Then John gave in to him. [16]After Jesus was baptized, he immediately came up from the water. Suddenly, the heavens were opened, and he saw the Spirit of God coming down as a dove to him. [17]Then a voice from heaven said, "This is my Son, whom I love—my Son with whom I am pleased."

JESUS AND HIS FRIEND

John 1:19-34

¹⁹ This was John's answer when the Jews sent priests and Levites from Jerusalem to ask him, "Who are you?" ²⁰ John didn't refuse to answer. He told them clearly, "I'm not the Messiah."

²¹ They asked him, "Well, are you Elijah?"

John answered, "No, I'm not."

Then they asked, "Are you the prophet?"

John replied, "No."

²² So they asked him, "Who are you? Tell us so that we can take an answer back to those who sent us. What do you say about yourself?"

²³ John said, "I'm a voice crying out in the desert, 'Make the way for the Lord straight,' as the prophet Isaiah said."

²⁴ Some of those who had been sent were Pharisees. ²⁵ They asked John, "Why do you baptize if you're not the Messiah or Elijah or the prophet?"

²⁶ John answered them, "I baptize with water. Someone you don't know is standing among you. ²⁷ He's the one who comes after me. I am not worthy to untie his sandal strap."

²⁸ This happened in Bethany on the east side of the Jordan River, where John was baptizing.

²⁹ John saw Jesus coming toward him the next day and said, "Look! This is the Lamb of God who takes away the sin of the world. ³⁰ He is the one I spoke about when I said, 'A man who comes after me was before me because he existed before I did.' ³¹ I didn't know who he was. However, I came to baptize with water to show him to the people of Israel."

³² John said, "I saw the Spirit come down as a dove from heaven and stay on him. ³³ I didn't know who he was. But God, who sent me to baptize with water, had told me, 'When you see the Spirit come down and stay on someone, you'll know that person is the one who baptizes with the Holy Spirit.' ³⁴ I have seen this and have declared that this is the Son of God."

THE ENEMY OF GOD TEMPTS JESUS

Luke 4:1-15

¹ Jesus was filled with the Holy Spirit as he left the Jordan River. The Spirit led him while he was in the desert, ² where he was tempted by the devil for 40 days. During those days Jesus ate nothing, so when they were over, he was hungry.

³ The devil said to him, "If you are the Son of God, tell this stone to become a loaf of bread."

⁴ Jesus answered him, "Scripture says, 'A person cannot live on bread alone.'"

⁵ The devil took him to a high place and showed him all the kingdoms of the world in an instant. ⁶ The devil said to him, "I will give you all the power and glory of these kingdoms. All of it has been given to me, and I give it to anyone I please. ⁷ So if you will worship me, all this will be yours."

⁸ Jesus answered him, "Scripture says, 'Worship the Lord your God and serve only him.'"

⁹ Then the devil took him into Jerusalem and had him stand on the highest part of the temple. He said to Jesus, "If you are the Son of God, jump from here! ¹⁰ Scripture says, 'He will put his angels in charge of you to watch over you carefully. ¹¹ They will carry you in their hands so that you never hit your foot against a rock.'"

¹² Jesus answered him, "It has been said, 'Never tempt the Lord your God.'"

¹³ After the devil had finished tempting Jesus in every possible way, the devil left him until another time.

¹⁴ Jesus returned to Galilee. The power of the Spirit was with him, and the news about him spread throughout the surrounding country. ¹⁵ He taught in the synagogues, and everyone praised him.

THE FIRST DISCIPLES

John 1:35-51

[35] The next day John was standing with two of his disciples. [36] John saw Jesus walk by. John said, "Look! This is the Lamb of God." [37] When the two disciples heard John say this, they followed Jesus.

[38] Jesus turned around and saw them following him. He asked them, "What are you looking for?"

They said to him, "Rabbi" (which means "teacher"), "where are you staying?"

[39] Jesus told them, "Come, and you will see." So they went to see where he was staying and spent the rest of that day with him. It was about ten o'clock in the morning.

[40] Andrew, Simon Peter's brother, was one of the two disciples who heard John and followed Jesus. [41] Andrew at once found his brother Simon and told him, "We have found the Messiah" (which means "Christ"). [42] Andrew brought Simon to Jesus.

Jesus looked at Simon and said, "You are Simon, son of John. Your name will be Cephas" (which means "Peter").

[43] The next day Jesus wanted to go to Galilee. He found Philip and told him, "Follow me!" [44] (Philip was from Bethsaida, the hometown of Andrew and Peter.)

[45] Philip found Nathanael and told him, "We have found the man whom Moses wrote about in his teachings and whom the prophets wrote about. He is Jesus, son of Joseph, from the city of Nazareth."

[46] Nathanael said to Philip, "Can anything good come from Nazareth?"

Philip told him, "Come and see!"

[47] Jesus saw Nathanael coming toward him and remarked, "Here is a true Israelite who is sincere."

[48] Nathanael asked Jesus, "How do you know anything about me?"

Jesus answered him, "I saw you under the fig tree before Philip called you."

[49] Nathanael said to Jesus, "Rabbi, you are the Son of God! You are the king of Israel!"

[50] Jesus replied, "You believe because I told you that I saw you under the fig tree. You will see greater things than that." [51] Jesus said to Nathanael, "I can guarantee this truth: You will see the sky open and God's angels going up and coming down to the Son of Man."

IS IS HOW TO CATCH FISH

e 5:1-11

e day Jesus was standing by the Sea of Galilee. people crowded around him as they listened to l's word. ²Jesus saw two boats on the shore. The ermen had stepped out of them and were washing ir nets. ³So Jesus got into the boat that belonged imon and asked him to push off a little from the re. Then Jesus sat down and taught the crowd from boat.

⁴When he finished speaking, he told Simon, e the boat into deep water, and lower your nets atch some fish."

⁵Simon answered, "Teacher, we worked hard all night and caught nothing. But if you say so, I'll lower the nets."

⁶After the men had done this, they caught such a large number of fish that their nets began to tear. ⁷So they signaled to their partners in the other boat to come and help them. Their partners came and filled both boats until the boats nearly sank.

⁸When Simon Peter saw this, he knelt in front of Jesus and said, "Leave me, Lord! I'm a sinful person!" ⁹Simon and everyone who was with him were amazed to see the large number of fish they had caught. ¹⁰James and John, who were Zebedee's sons and Simon's partners, were also amazed.

Jesus told Simon, "Don't be afraid. From now on you will catch people instead of fish."

¹¹Simon and his partners brought the boats to shore, left everything, and followed Jesus.

JESUS PERFORMS HIS FIRST MIRACLE — TURNING WATER INTO WINE

John 2:1-11

¹ Three days later a wedding took place in the city of Cana in Galilee. Jesus' mother was there. ² Jesus and his disciples had been invited too.

³ When the wine was gone, Jesus' mother said to him, "They're out of wine."

⁴ Jesus said to her, "Why did you come to me? My time has not yet come."

⁵ His mother told the servers, "Do whatever he tells you."

⁶ Six stone water jars were there. They were used for Jewish purification rituals. Each jar held 18 to 27 gallons.

⁷ Jesus told the servers, "Fill the jars with water." The servers filled the jars to the brim. ⁸ Jesus said to them, "Pour some, and take it to the person in charge." The servers did as they were told.

⁹ The person in charge tasted the water that had become wine. He didn't know where it had come fro although the servers who had poured the water kne The person in charge called the groom ¹⁰ and said to him, "Everyone serves the best wine first. When people are drunk, the host serves cheap wine. But y have saved the best wine for now."

¹¹ Cana in Galilee was the place where Jesus begar perform miracles. He made his glory public there, a his disciples believed in him.

THE UNHOLY TEMPLE

John 2:13-22

[13] The Jewish Passover was near, so Jesus went to Jerusalem. [14] He found those who were selling cattle, sheep, and pigeons in the temple courtyard. He also found moneychangers sitting there. [15] He made a whip from small ropes and threw everyone with their sheep and cattle out of the temple courtyard. He dumped the moneychangers' coins and knocked over their tables.

[16] He told those who sold pigeons, "Pick up this stuff, and get it out of here! Stop making my Father's house a marketplace!"

¹⁷ His disciples remembered that Scripture said, "Devotion for your house will consume me."

¹⁸ The Jews reacted by asking Jesus, "What miracle can you show us to justify what you're doing?"

¹⁹ Jesus replied, "Tear down this temple, and I'll rebuild it in three days."

²⁰ The Jews said, "It took forty-six years to build this temple. Do you really think you're going to rebuild it in three days?"

²¹ But the temple Jesus spoke about was his own body. ²² After he came back to life, his disciples remembered that he had said this. So they believed the Scripture and this statement that Jesus had made.

JESUS IS THE WATER OF LIFE

John 4:4-26

[1] Jesus knew that the Pharisees had heard that he was making and baptizing more disciples than John. [2] (Actually, Jesus was not baptizing people. His disciples were.) [3] So he left the Judean countryside and went back to Galilee.

[4] Jesus had to go through Samaria. [5] He arrived at a city in Samaria called Sychar. Sychar was near the piece of land that Jacob had given to his son Joseph. [6] Jacob's Well was there. Jesus sat down by the well because he was tired from traveling. The time was about six o'clock in the evening.

[7] A Samaritan woman went to get some water. Jesus said to her, "Give me a drink of water." [8] (His disciples had gone into the city to buy some food.)

[9] The Samaritan woman asked him, "How can a Jewish man like you ask a Samaritan woman like me for a drink of water?" (Jews, of course, don't associate with Samaritans.)

[10] Jesus replied to her, "If you only knew what God's gift is and who is asking you for a drink, you would have asked him for a drink. He would have given you living water."

[11] The woman said to him, "Sir, you don't have anything to use to get water, and the well is deep. So where are you going to get this living water? [12] You're not more important than our ancestor Jacob, are you? He gave us this well. He and his sons and his animals drank water from it."

[13] Jesus answered her, "Everyone who drinks this water will become thirsty again. [14] But those who drink the water that I will give them will never become thirsty again. In fact, the water I will give them will become in them a spring that gushes up to eternal life.

[15] The woman told Jesus, "Sir, give me this water! Then I won't get thirsty or have to come here to get water."

[16] Jesus told her, "Go to your husband, and bring him here."

[17] The woman replied, "I don't have a husband."

Jesus told her, "You're right when you say that you don't have a husband. [18] You've had five husbands, and the man you have now isn't your husband. You've told the truth."

[19] The woman said to Jesus, "I see that you're a prophet! [20] Our ancestors worshiped on this mountain. But you Jews say that people must worship in Jerusalem."

[21] Jesus told her, "Believe me. A time is coming when you Samaritans won't be worshiping the Father on this mountain or in Jerusalem. [22] You don't know what you're worshiping. We ⌞Jews⌟ know what we're worshiping, because salvation comes from the Jews. [23] Indeed, the time is coming, and it is now here, when the true worshipers will worship the Father in spirit and truth. The Father is looking for people like that to worship him. [24] God is a spirit. Those who worship him must worship in spirit and truth."

[25] The woman said to him, "I know that the Messiah is coming. When he comes, he will tell us everything." (Messiah is the one called *Christ*.)

[26] Jesus told her, "I am he, and I am speaking to you now."

THE WOMAN AT THE WELL

John 4:27-42

[27] At that time his disciples returned. They were surprised that he was talking to a woman. But none of them asked him, "What do you want from her?" or "Why are you talking to her?"

[28] Then the woman left her water jar and went back into the city. She told the people, [29] "Come with me, and meet a man who told me everything I've ever done. Could he be the Messiah?" [30] The people left the city and went to meet Jesus.

[31] Meanwhile, the disciples were urging him, "Rabbi, have something to eat."

[32] Jesus told them, "I have food to eat that you don't know about."

[33] The disciples asked each other, "Did someone bring him something to eat?"

[34] Jesus told them, "My food is to do what the one who sent me wants me to do and to finish the work he has given me.

[35] "Don't you say, 'In four more months the harvest will be here'? I'm telling you to look and see that the fields are ready to be harvested. [36] The person who harvests the crop is already getting paid. He is gathering grain for eternal life. So the person who plants the grain and the person who harvests it are happy together. [37] In this respect the saying is true: 'One person plants, and another person harvests.' [38] I have sent you to harvest a crop you have not worked for. Other people have done the hard work, and you have followed them in their work."

[39] Many Samaritans in that city believed in Jesus because of the woman who said, "He told me everything I've ever done." [40] So when the Samaritans went to Jesus, they asked him to stay with them. He stayed in Samaria for two days. [41] Many more Samaritans believed because of what Jesus said. [42] They told the woman, "Our faith is no longer based on what you've said. We have heard him ourselves, and we know that he really is the savior of the world."

FOUR MEN ON THE ROOF

Luke 5:17-26

[17] One day when Jesus was teaching, some Pharisees and experts in Moses' Teachings were present. They had come from every village in Galilee and Judea and from Jerusalem. Jesus had the power of the Lord to heal.

[18] Some men brought a paralyzed man on a stretcher. They tried to take him into the house and put him in front of Jesus. [19] But they could not find a way to get him into the house because of the crowd. So they went up on the roof. They made an opening in the tiles and let the man down on his stretcher among the people. (They lowered him in front of Jesus.)

[20] When Jesus saw their faith, he said, "Sir, your sins are forgiven." [21] The experts in Moses' Teachings and the Pharisees thought, "Who is this man? He's dishonoring God! Who besides God can forgive sins?"

[22] Jesus knew what they were thinking. So he said to them, "What are you thinking? [23] Is it easier to say, 'Your sins are forgiven,' or to say, 'Get up and walk'? [24] I want you to know that the Son of Man has authority on earth to forgive sins." Then he said to the paralyzed man, "Get up, pick up your stretcher, and go home."

[25] The man immediately stood up in front of them and picked up the stretcher he had been lying on. Praising God, he went home.

[26] Everyone was amazed and praised God. They were filled with awe and said, "We've seen things today we can hardly believe!"

THE TAX COLLECTOR SAYS YES TO JESUS

Mark 2:13-17

[13] Jesus went to the seashore again. Large crowds came to him, and he taught them.

[14] When Jesus was leaving, he saw Levi, son of Alphaeus, sitting in a tax office. Jesus said to him, "Follow me!" So Levi got up and followed him.

[15] Later Jesus was having dinner at Levi's house. Many tax collectors and sinners who were followers of Jesus were eating with him and his disciples. [16] When the experts in Moses' Teachings who were Pharisees saw him eating with sinners and tax collectors, they asked his disciples, "Why does he eat with tax collectors and sinners?"

[17] When Jesus heard that, he said to them, "Healthy people don't need a doctor; those who are sick do. I've come to call sinners, not people who think they have God's approval."

ter, Jesus went to Jerusalem for a Jewish festival.
ear Sheep Gate in Jerusalem was a pool called
hesda in Hebrew. It had five porches. ³Under these
rches a large number of sick people—people who
re blind, lame, or paralyzed—used to lie. ⁵One
n, who had been sick for 38 years, was lying there.

⁶Jesus saw the man lying there and knew that he
had been sick for a long time. So Jesus asked the man,
"Would you like to get well?"

⁷The sick man answered Jesus, "Sir, I don't have
anyone to put me into the pool when the water is
stirred. While I'm trying to get there, someone else
steps into the pool ahead of me."

⁸Jesus told the man, "Get up, pick up your cot, and
walk." ⁹The man immediately became well, picked up
his cot, and walked.

That happened on a day of rest—a holy day.

TWELVE MEN SET APART AS APOSTLES

Luke 6:12-16

¹² At that time Jesus went to a mountain to pray. He spent the whole night in prayer to God.

¹³ When it was day, he called his disciples. He chose twelve of them and called them apostles. ¹⁴ They were Simon (whom Jesus named Peter) and Simon's brother Andrew, James, John, Philip, Bartholomew, ¹⁵ Matthew, Thomas, James (son of Alphaeus), Simon (who was called the Zealot), ¹⁶ Judas (son of James), and Judas Iscariot (who became a traitor).

Luke 9:2-6

² He sent them to spread the message about God's kingdom and to cure the sick.

³ He told them, "Don't take anything along on the trip. Don't take a walking stick, traveling bag, any food, money, or a change of clothes. ⁴ When you go into a home, stay there until you're ready to leave. ⁵ If people don't welcome you, leave that city, and shake its dust off your feet as a warning to them."

⁶ The apostles went from village to village, told the Good News, and cured the sick everywhere.

TRUE HAPPINESS

Matthew 4:23-25

²³ Jesus went all over Galilee. He taught in the synagogues and spread the Good News of the kingdom. He also cured every disease and sickness among the people.

²⁴ The news about Jesus spread throughout Syria. People brought him everyone who was sick, those who suffered from any kind of disease or pain. They also brought epileptics, those who were paralyzed, and people possessed by demons, and he cured them all. ²⁵ Large crowds followed him. They came from Galilee, the Ten Cities, Jerusalem, Judea, and from across the Jordan River.

Matthew 5:1-12

¹ When Jesus saw the crowds, he went up a mountain and sat down. His disciples came to him, ² and he began to teach them:

³ "Blessed are those who recognize
    they are spiritually helpless.
  The kingdom of heaven belongs to them.
⁴ Blessed are those who mourn.
    They will be comforted.
⁵ Blessed are those who are gentle.
    They will inherit the earth.
⁶ Blessed are those who hunger and thirst
    for God's approval.
    They will be satisfied.
⁷ Blessed are those who show mercy.
    They will be treated mercifully.
⁸ Blessed are those whose thoughts are pure.
    They will see God.
⁹ Blessed are those who make peace.
    They will be called God's children.
¹⁰ Blessed are those who are persecuted
    for doing what God approves of.
  The kingdom of heaven belongs to them.

¹¹ "Blessed are you when people insult you,
    persecute you,
      lie, and say all kinds of evil things
        about you because of me.
¹² Rejoice and be glad because you have
    a great reward in heaven!
  The prophets who lived before you
      were persecuted in these ways.

DO YOU KNOW HOW TO BE SALT?

Matthew 5:13-16

¹³ "You are salt for the earth. But if salt loses its taste, how will it be made salty again? It is no longer good for anything except to be thrown out and trampled on by people.

¹⁴ "You are light for the world. A city cannot be hidden when it is located on a hill. ¹⁵ No one lights a lamp and puts it under a basket. Instead, everyone who lights a lamp puts it on a lamp stand. Then its light shines on everyone in the house. ¹⁶ In the same way let your light shine in front of people. Then they will see the good that you do and praise your Father in heaven.

THE TREASURE HUNT

Matthew 6:19-30

[19] "Stop storing up treasures for yourselves on earth, where moths and rust destroy and thieves break in and steal. [20] Instead, store up treasures for yourselves in heaven, where moths and rust don't destroy and thieves don't break in and steal. [21] Your heart will be where your treasure is.

[22] "The eye is the lamp of the body. So if your eye is unclouded, your whole body will be full of light. [23] But if your eye is evil, your whole body will be full of darkness. If the light in you is darkness, how dark it will be!

[24] "No one can serve two masters. He will hate the first master and love the second, or he will be devoted to the first and despise the second. You cannot serve God and wealth.

[25] "So I tell you to stop worrying about what you will eat, drink, or wear. Isn't life more than food and the body more than clothes?

[26] "Look at the birds. They don't plant, harvest, or gather the harvest into barns. Yet, your heavenly Father feeds them. Aren't you worth more than they?

[27] "Can any of you add a single hour to your life by worrying?

28 "And why worry about clothes? Notice how the flowers grow in the field. They never work or spin yarn for clothes. 29 But I say that not even Solomon in all his majesty was dressed like one of these flowers. 30 That's the way God clothes the grass in the field. Today it's alive, and tomorrow it's thrown into an incinerator. So how much more will he clothe you people who have so little faith?

HOW TO BUILD A HOUSE

Matthew 7:24-29

24 "Therefore, everyone who hears what I say and obeys it will be like a wise person who built a house on rock. 25 Rain poured, and floods came. Winds blew and beat against that house. But it did not collapse, because its foundation was on rock.

26 "Everyone who hears what I say but doesn't obey it will be like a foolish person who built a house on sand. 27 Rain poured, and floods came. Winds blew and struck that house. It collapsed, and the result was a total disaster."

28 When Jesus finished this speech, the crowds were amazed at his teachings. 29 Unlike their experts in Moses' Teachings, he taught them with authority.

A SPECIAL ACT

Luke 7:36-50

³⁶ One of the Pharisees invited Jesus to eat with him. Jesus went to the Pharisee's house and was eating at the table.

³⁷ A woman who lived a sinful life in that city found out that Jesus was eating at the Pharisee's house. So she took a bottle of perfume ³⁸ and knelt at his feet. She was crying and washed his feet with her tears. Then she dried his feet with her hair, kissed them over and over again, and poured the perfume on them.

³⁹ The Pharisee who had invited Jesus saw this and thought, "If this man really were a prophet, he would know what sort of woman is touching him. She's a sinner."

⁴⁰ Jesus spoke up, "Simon, I have something to say to you."

Simon replied, "Teacher, you're free to speak."

⁴¹ ⌞So Jesus said,⌟ "Two men owed a moneylender some money. One owed him five hundred silver coins, and the other owed him fifty. ⁴² When they couldn't pay it back, he was kind enough to cancel their debts. Now, who do you think will love him the most?"

⁴³ Simon answered, "I suppose the one who had the largest debt canceled."

Jesus said to him, "You're right!" ⁴⁴ Then, turning to the woman, he said to Simon, "You see this woman, don't you? I came into your house. You didn't wash my feet. But she has washed my feet with her tears and dried them with her hair. ⁴⁵ You didn't give me a kiss. But ever since I came in, she has not stopped kissing my feet. ⁴⁶ You didn't put any olive oil on my head. But she has poured perfume on my feet. ⁴⁷ That's why I'm telling you that her many sins have been forgiven. Her great love proves that. But whoever receives little forgiveness loves very little."

⁴⁸ Then Jesus said to her, "Your sins have been forgiven." ⁴⁹ The other guests thought, "Who is this man who even forgives sins?"

⁵⁰ Jesus said to the woman, "Your faith has saved you. Go in peace!"

PLANTING SEEDS

Mark 4:1-9

[1] Jesus began to teach again by the Sea of Galilee. A very large crowd gathered around him, so he got into a boat and sat in it. The boat was in the water while the entire crowd lined the shore. [2] He used stories as illustrations to teach them many things.

While he was teaching them, he said, [3] "Listen! A farmer went to plant seed. [4] Some seeds were planted along the road, and birds came and devoured them. [5] Other seeds were planted on rocky ground, where there wasn't much soil. The plants sprouted quickly because the soil wasn't deep. [6] When the sun came up, they were scorched. They didn't have any roots, so they withered. [7] Other seeds were planted among thornbushes. The thornbushes grew up and choked them, and they didn't produce anything. [8] But other seeds were planted on good ground, sprouted, and produced thirty, sixty, or one hundred times as much as was planted." [9] He added, "Let the person who has ears listen!"

THE SEED IS GOD'S WORD

Mark 4:10-20

[10] When he was alone with his followers and the twelve apostles, they asked him about the stories.

[11] Jesus replied to them, "The mystery about God's kingdom has been given ⌊directly⌋ to you. To those on the outside, it is given in stories:

[12] 'They see clearly but don't perceive.
  They hear clearly but don't understand.
  They never return to me
    and are never forgiven.' "

¹³ Jesus asked them, "Don't you understand this story? How, then, will you understand any of the stories I use as illustrations?

¹⁴ "The farmer plants the word. ¹⁵ Some people are like seeds that were planted along the road. Whenever they hear the word, Satan comes at once and takes away the word that was planted in them. ¹⁶ Other people are like seeds that were planted on rocky ground. Whenever they hear the word, they accept it at once with joy. ¹⁷ But they don't develop any roots. They last for a short time. When suffering or persecution comes along because of the word, they immediately fall ⌊from faith⌋. ¹⁸ Other people are like seeds planted among thornbushes. They hear the word, ¹⁹ but the worries of life, the deceitful pleasures of riches, and the desires for other things take over. They choke the word so that it can't produce anything. ²⁰ Others are like seeds planted on good ground. They hear the word, accept it, and produce crops—thirty, sixty, or one hundred times as much as was planted."

THE DIFFERENCE BETWEEN WHEAT AND WEEDS

Matthew 13:24-30

[24] Jesus used another illustration. He said, "The kingdom of heaven is like a man who planted good seed in his field. [25] But while people were asleep, his enemy planted weeds in the wheat field and went away. [26] When the wheat came up and formed kernels, weeds appeared.

[27] "The owner's workers came to him and asked, 'Sir, didn't you plant good seed in your field? Where did the weeds come from?'

[28] "He told them, 'An enemy did this.'

"His workers asked him, 'Do you want us to pull out the weeds?'

[29] "He replied, 'No. If you pull out the weeds, you may pull out the wheat with them. [30] Let both grow together until the harvest. When the grain is cut, I will tell the workers to gather the weeds first and tie them in bundles to be burned. But I'll have them bring the wheat into my barn.'"

³⁶ When Jesus had sent the people away, he went into the house. His disciples came to him and said, "Explain what the illustration of the weeds in the field means."

³⁷ He answered, "The one who plants the good seeds is the Son of Man. ³⁸ The field is the world. The good seeds are those who belong to the kingdom. The weeds are those who belong to the evil one. ³⁹ The enemy who planted them is the devil. The harvest is the end of the world. The workers are angels. ⁴⁰ Just as weeds are gathered and burned, so it will be at the end of time. ⁴¹ The Son of Man will send his angels. They will gather everything in his kingdom that causes people to sin and everyone who does evil. ⁴² The angels will throw them into a blazing furnace. People will cry and be in extreme pain there. ⁴³ Then the people who have God's approval will shine like the sun in their Father's kingdom. Let the person who has ears listen!

MUSTARD SEED AND YEAST

Matthew 13:31-34

¹ Jesus used another illustration. He said, "The kingdom of heaven is like a mustard seed that someone planted in a field. ³² It's one of the smallest seeds. However, when it has grown, it is taller than the garden plants. It becomes a tree that is large enough for birds to nest in its branches."

³³ He used another illustration. "The kingdom of heaven is like yeast that a woman mixed into a large amount of flour until the yeast worked its way through all the dough."

³⁴ Jesus used illustrations to tell the crowds all these things. He did not tell them anything without illustrating it with a story.

THE STORM

Mark 4:35-38

³⁵ That evening, Jesus said to his disciples, "Let's cross to the other side."

³⁶ Leaving the crowd, they took Jesus along in a boat just as he was. Other boats were with him.

³⁷ A violent windstorm came up. The waves were breaking into the boat so that it was quickly filling up. ³⁸ But he was sleeping on a cushion in the back of the boat.

So they woke him up and said to him, "Teacher, don't you care that we're going to die?"

JESUS CALMS THE STORM

Mark 4:39-41

[39] Then he got up, ordered the wind to stop, and said to the sea, "Be still, absolutely still!" The wind stopped blowing, and the sea became very calm.

[40] He asked them, "Why are you such cowards? Don't you have any faith yet?"

[41] They were overcome with fear and asked each other, "Who is this man? Even the wind and the sea obey him!"

THE DEMON-POSSESSED MAN IN THE GRAVEYARD

Mark 5:1-20

[1] They arrived in the territory of the Gerasenes on the other side of the Sea of Galilee. [2] As Jesus stepped out of the boat, a man came out of the tombs and met him. The man was controlled by an evil spirit [3] and lived among the tombs. No one could restrain him any longer, not even with a chain. [4] He had often been chained hand and foot. However, he snapped the chains off his hands and broke the chains from his feet. No one could control him. [5] Night and day he was among the tombs and on the mountainsides screaming and cutting himself with stones.

[6] The man saw Jesus at a distance. So he ran ⌊to Jesus⌋, bowed down in front of him, [7] and shouted, "Why are you bothering me now, Jesus, Son of the Most High God? Swear to God that you won't torture me." [8] He shouted this because Jesus said, "You evil spirit, come out of the man."

[9] Jesus asked him, "What is your name?"

He told Jesus, "My name is Legion [Six Thousand], because there are many of us." [10] He begged Jesus not to send them out of the territory.

¹¹ A large herd of pigs was feeding on a mountainside nearby. ¹² The demons begged him, Send us into the pigs! Let us enter them!"

¹³ Jesus let them do this. The evil spirits came out of the man and went into the pigs. The herd of about two thousand pigs rushed down the cliff into the sea and drowned.

¹⁴ Those who took care of the pigs ran away. In the city and countryside they reported everything that had happened. So the people came to see what had happened. ¹⁵ They came to Jesus and saw the man who had been possessed by the legion of demons. The man was sitting there dressed and in his right mind. The people were frightened. ¹⁶ Those who saw this told what had happened to the demon-possessed man and the pigs. ¹⁷ Then the people began to beg Jesus to leave their territory.

¹⁸ As Jesus stepped into the boat, the man who had been demon-possessed begged him, "Let me stay with you." ¹⁹ But Jesus would not allow it. Instead, he told the man, "Go home to your family, and tell them how much the Lord has done for you and how merciful he has been to you."

²⁰ So the man left. He began to tell how much Jesus had done for him in the Ten Cities. Everyone was amazed.

JESUS HEALS MORE PEOPLE

Matthew 9:27-31

[27] When Jesus left that place, two blind men followed him. They shouted, "Have mercy on us, Son of David."

[28] Jesus went into a house, and the blind men followed him. He said to them, "Do you believe that I can do this?"

"Yes, Lord," they answered.

[29] He touched their eyes and said, "What you have believed will be done for you!" [30] Then they could see.

He warned them, "Don't let anyone know about this!" [31] But they went out and spread the news about him throughout that region.

THE WEAK KING

Mark 6:14-29

[14] King Herod heard about Jesus, because Jesus' name had become well-known. Some people were saying, "John the Baptizer has come back to life. That's why he has the power to perform these miracles." [15] Others said, "He is Elijah." Still others said, "He is a prophet like one of the other prophets." [16] But when Herod heard about it, he said, "I had John's head cut off, and he has come back to life!"

[17] Herod had sent men who had arrested John, tied him up, and put him in prison. Herod did that for Herodias, whom he had married. (She used to be his brother Philip's wife.) [18] John had been telling Herod, "It's not right for you to be married to your brother's wife."

[19] So Herodias held a grudge against John and wanted to kill him. But she wasn't allowed to do it [20] because Herod was afraid of John. Herod knew that John was a fair and holy man, so he protected him. When he listened to John, he would become very disturbed, and yet he liked to listen to him.

[21] An opportunity finally came on Herod's birthday. Herod gave a dinner for his top officials, army officers, and the most important people of Galilee. [22] His daughter, that is, Herodias' daughter, came in and danced. Herod and his guests were delighted with her. The king told the girl, "Ask me for anything you want, and I'll give it to you." [23] He swore an oath to her: "I'll give you anything you ask for, up to half of my kingdom."

[24] So she went out and asked her mother, "What should I ask for?"

Her mother said, "Ask for the head of John the Baptizer."

[25] So the girl hurried back to the king with her request. She said, "I want you to give me the head of John the Baptizer on a platter at once."

[26] The king deeply regretted his promise. But because of his oath and his guests, he didn't want to refuse her. [27] Immediately, the king sent a guard and ordered him to bring John's head. The guard cut off John's head in prison. [28] Then he brought the head on a platter and gave it to the girl, and the girl gave it to her mother.

[29] When John's disciples heard about this, they came for his body and laid it in a tomb.

TO A QUIET PLACE

Mark 6:30-33

³⁰ The apostles gathered around Jesus. They reported to him everything they had done and taught. ³¹ So he said to them, "Let's go to a place where we can be alone to rest for a while." Many people were coming and going, and Jesus and the apostles didn't even have a chance to eat.

³² So they went away in a boat to a place where they could be alone. ³³ But many people saw them leave and recognized them. The people ran from all the cities and arrived ahead of them.

TEACHING THOUSANDS

Mark 6:34-36

³⁴ When Jesus got out of the boat, he saw a large crowd and felt sorry for them. They were like sheep without a shepherd. So he spent a lot of time teaching them.

³⁵ When it was late, his disciples came to him. They said, "No one lives around here, and it's already late. ³⁶ Send the people to the closest farms and villages to buy themselves something to eat."

263

ANOTHER MIRACLE – FEEDING THOUSANDS OF HUNGRY PEOPLE

Mark 6:37

³⁷ Jesus replied, "You give them something to eat."

They said to him, "Should we go and spend about a year's wages on bread to feed them?"

John 6:8-14

⁶ Jesus asked this question to test him. He already knew what he was going to do.

⁷ Philip answered, "We would need about a year's wages to buy enough bread for each of them to have a piece."

⁸ One of Jesus' disciples, Andrew, who was Simon Peter's brother, told him, ⁹ "A boy who has five loaves of barley bread and two small fish is here. But they won't go very far for so many people."

¹⁰ Jesus said, "Have the people sit down."

The people had plenty of grass to sit on. (There were about 5,000 men in the crowd.)

¹¹ Jesus took the loaves, gave thanks, and distributed them to the people who were sitting there. He did the same thing with the fish. All the people ate as much as they wanted.

¹² When the people were full, Jesus told his disciples, "Gather the leftover pieces so that nothing will be wasted." ¹³ The disciples gathered the leftover pieces of bread and filled twelve baskets.

¹⁴ When the people saw the miracle Jesus performed, they said, "This man is certainly the prophet who is to come into the world."

JESUS WALKS ON WATER

Mark 6:45-50

⁴⁵ Jesus quickly made his disciples get into a boat and cross to Bethsaida ahead of him while he sent the people away. ⁴⁶ After saying goodbye to them, he went up a mountain to pray. ⁴⁷ When evening came, the boat was in the middle of the sea, and he was alone on the land.

⁴⁸ Jesus saw that they were in a lot of trouble as they rowed, because they were going against the wind. Between three and six o'clock in the morning, he came to them. He was walking on the sea. He wanted to pass by them. ⁴⁹ When they saw him walking on the sea, they thought, "It's a ghost!" and they began to scream. ⁵⁰ All of them saw him and were terrified.

Immediately, he said, "Calm down! It's me. Don't be afraid!"

PETER WALKS ON WATER

Matthew 14:28-33

[28] Peter answered, "Lord, if it is you, order me to come to you on the water."

[29] Jesus said, "Come!" So Peter got out of the boat and walked on the water toward Jesus. [30] But when he noticed how strong the wind was, he became afraid and started to sink. He shouted, "Lord, save me!"

[31] Immediately, Jesus reached out, caught hold of him, and said, "You have so little faith! Why did you doubt?"

[32] When they got into the boat, the wind stopped blowing. [33] The men in the boat bowed down in front of Jesus and said, "You are truly the Son of God."

THE FAITH OF A NON-JEWISH PERSON

Matthew 15:21-28

[21] Jesus left that place and went to the region of Tyre and Sidon.

[22] A Canaanite woman from that territory came ⌞to him⌟ and began to shout, "Have mercy on me, Lord, Son of David! My daughter is tormented by a demon."

[23] But he did not answer her at all. Then his disciples came to him and urged him, "Send her away. She keeps shouting behind us."

[24] Jesus responded, "I was sent only to the lost sheep of the nation of Israel."

[25] She came to him, bowed down, and said, "Lord, help me!"

[26] Jesus replied, "It's not right to take the children's food and throw it to the dogs."

[27] She said, "You're right, Lord. But even the dogs eat scraps that fall from their masters' tables."

[28] Then Jesus answered her, "Woman, you have strong faith! What you wanted will be done for you." At that moment her daughter was cured.

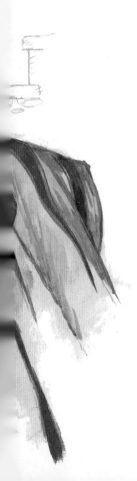

JESUS HEALS A BLIND MAN

Mark 8:22-26

²²As they came to Bethsaida, some people brought a blind man to Jesus. They begged Jesus to touch him. ²³Jesus took the blind man's hand and led him out of the village. He spit into the man's eyes and placed his hands on him. Jesus asked him, "Can you see anything?"

²⁴The man looked up and said, "I see people. They look like trees walking around."

²⁵Then Jesus placed his hands on the man's eyes a second time, and the man saw clearly. His sight was normal again. He could see everything clearly even at a distance. ²⁶Jesus told him when he sent him home, "Don't go into the village."

PETER DECLARES THAT JESUS IS GOD

Matthew 16:13-19

[13] When Jesus came to the region of Caesarea Philippi, he asked his disciples, "Who do people say the Son of Man is?"

[14] They answered, "Some say you are John the Baptizer, others Elijah, still others Jeremiah or one of the prophets."

[15] He asked them, "But who do you say I am?"

[16] Simon Peter answered, "You are the Messiah, the Son of the living God!"

[17] Jesus replied, "Simon, son of Jonah, you are blessed! No human revealed this to you, but my Father in heaven revealed it to you. [18] You are Peter, and I can guarantee that on this rock I will build my church. And the gates of hell will not overpower it. [19] I will give you the keys of the kingdom of heaven. Whatever you imprison, God will imprison. And whatever you set free, God will set free."

MOSES AND ELIJAH

Luke 9:28-36

[28] About eight days after he had said this, Jesus took Peter, John, and James with him and went up a mountain to pray. [29] While Jesus was praying, the appearance of his face changed, and his clothes became dazzling white. [30] Suddenly, both Moses and Elijah were talking with him. [31] They appeared in heavenly glory and were discussing Jesus' approaching death and what he was about to fulfill in Jerusalem.

[32] Peter and the men with him were sleeping soundly. When they woke up, they saw Jesus' glory and the two men standing with him. [33] As Moses and Elijah were leaving him, Peter said to Jesus, "Teacher, it's good that we're here. Let's put up three tents—one for you, one for Moses, and one for Elijah." Peter didn't know what he was saying.

[34] While he was saying this, a cloud overshadowed them. They were frightened as they went into the cloud. [35] A voice came out of the cloud and said, "This is my Son, whom I have chosen. Listen to him!"

[36] After the voice had spoken, they saw that Jesus was alone. The disciples said nothing, and for some time they told no one about what they had seen.

THE POWER OF CHILD-LIKE FAITH

Matthew 18:1-14

¹ At that time the disciples came to Jesus and asked, "Who is greatest in the kingdom of heaven?"

² He called a little child and had him stand among them. ³ Then he said to them, "I can guarantee this truth: Unless you change and become like little children, you will never enter the kingdom of heaven. ⁴ Whoever becomes like this little child is the greatest in the kingdom of heaven. ⁵ And whoever welcomes a child like this in my name welcomes me.

⁶ "These little ones believe in me. It would be best for the person who causes one of them to lose faith to be drowned in the sea with a large stone hung around his neck. ⁷ How horrible it will be for the world because it causes people to lose their faith. Situations that cause people to lose their faith will arise. How horrible it will be for the person who causes someone to lose his faith!

⁸ "If your hand or your foot causes you to lose your faith, cut it off and throw it away. It is better for you to enter life disabled or injured than to have two hands or two feet and be thrown into everlasting fire. ⁹ If your eye causes you to lose your faith, tear it out and throw it away. It is better for you to enter life with one eye than to have two eyes and be thrown into hellfire.

¹⁰ "Be careful not to despise these little ones. I can guarantee that their angels in heaven always see the face of my Father, who is in heaven.

¹² "What do you think? Suppose a man has 100 sheep and one of them strays. Won't he leave the 99 sheep in the hills to look for the one that has strayed? ¹³ I can guarantee this truth: If he finds it, he is happier about it than about the 99 that have not strayed. ¹⁴ In the same way, your Father in heaven does not want one of these little ones to be lost.

WE ARE NEVER ALONE

Matthew 18:15-20

[15] "If a believer does something wrong, go, confront him when the two of you are alone. If he listens to you, you have won back that believer. [16] But if he does not listen, take one or two others with you so that every accusation may be verified by two or three witnesses. [17] If he ignores these witnesses, tell it to the community of believers. If he also ignores the community, deal with him as you would a heathen or a tax collector. [18] I can guarantee this truth: Whatever you imprison, God will imprison. And whatever you set free, God will set free.

[19] "I can guarantee again that if two of you agree on anything here on earth, my Father in heaven will accept it. [20] Where two or three have come together in my name, I am there among them."

JESUS HEALS A LEPER

Luke 17:11-19

[11] Jesus traveled along the border between Samaria and Galilee on his way to Jerusalem. [12] As he went into a village, ten men with a skin disease met him. They stood at a distance [13] and shouted, "Jesus, Teacher, have mercy on us!"

[14] When he saw them, he told them, "Show yourselves to the priests." As they went, they were made clean. [15] When one of them saw that he was healed, he turned back and praised God in a loud voice. [16] He quickly bowed at Jesus' feet and thanked him. (The man was a Samaritan.)

[17] Jesus asked, "Weren't ten men made clean? Where are the other nine? [18] Only this foreigner came back to praise God."

[19] Jesus told the man, "Get up, and go home! Your faith has made you well."

A SECOND CHANCE

John 8:1-11

[1] Jesus went to the Mount of Olives. [2] Early the next morning he returned to the temple courtyard. All the people went to him, so he sat down and began to teach them.

[3] The experts in Moses' Teachings and the Pharisees brought a woman who had been caught committing adultery. They made her stand in front of everyone [4] and asked Jesus, "Teacher, we caught this woman in the act of adultery. [5] In his teachings, Moses ordered us to stone women like this to death. What do you say?" [6] They asked this to test him. They wanted to find a reason to bring charges against him.

Jesus bent down and used his finger to write on the ground. [7] When they persisted in asking him questions, he straightened up and said, "The person who is sinless should be the first to throw a stone at her." [8] Then he bent down again and continued writing on the ground.

[9] One by one, beginning with the older men, the experts in Moses' Teachings and Pharisees left. Jesus was left alone with the woman. [10] Then Jesus straightened up and asked her, "Where did they go? Has anyone condemned you?"

[11] The woman answered, "No one, sir."

Jesus said, "I don't condemn you either. Go! From now on don't sin."

THE GOOD SAMARITAN

Luke 10:25-37

²⁵ Then an expert in Moses' Teachings stood up to test Jesus. He asked, "Teacher, what must I do to inherit eternal life?"

²⁶ Jesus answered him, "What is written in Moses' Teachings? What do you read there?"

²⁷ He answered, "'Love the Lord your God with all your heart, with all your soul, with all your strength, and with all your mind. And love your neighbor as you love yourself.'"

²⁸ Jesus told him, "You're right! Do this, and life will be yours."

²⁹ But the man wanted to justify his question. So he asked Jesus, "Who is my neighbor?"

³⁰ Jesus replied, "A man went from Jerusalem to Jericho. On the way robbers stripped him, beat him, and left him for dead.

³¹ "By chance, a priest was traveling along that road. When he saw the man, he went around him and continued on his way. ³² Then a Levite came to that place. When he saw the man, he, too, went around him and continued on his way.

33 "But a Samaritan, as he was traveling along, came cross the man. When the Samaritan saw him, he felt rry for the man, **34** went to him, and cleaned and ndaged his wounds. Then he put him on his own imal, brought him to an inn, and took care of him. he next day the Samaritan took out two silver coins d gave them to the innkeeper. He told the innkeeper, ke care of him. If you spend more than that, I'll pay u on my return trip.'

36 "Of these three men, who do you think was a neighbor to the man who was attacked by robbers?"

37 The expert said, "The one who was kind enough to help him."

Jesus told him, "Go and imitate his example!"

MARTHA AND MARY

Luke 10:38-42

[38] As they were traveling along, Jesus went into a village. A woman named Martha welcomed him into her home. [39] She had a sister named Mary. Mary sat at the Lord's feet and listened to him talk.

[40] But Martha was upset about all the work she had to do. So she asked, "Lord, don't you care that my sister has left me to do the work all by myself? Tell her to help me."

[41] The Lord answered her, "Martha, Martha! You worry and fuss about a lot of things. [42] There's only one thing you need. Mary has made the right choice, and that one thing will not be taken away from her."

JESUS IS THE GOOD SHEPHERD

John 10:11-18

[11] "I am the good shepherd. The good shepherd gives his life for the sheep. [12] A hired hand isn't a shepherd and doesn't own the sheep. When he sees a wolf coming, he abandons the sheep and quickly runs away. So the wolf drags the sheep away and scatters the flock. [13] The hired hand is concerned about what he's going to get paid and not about the sheep.

[14] "I am the good shepherd. I know my sheep as the Father knows me. My sheep know me as I know the Father. [15] So I give my life for my sheep. [16] I also have other sheep that are not from this pen. I must lead them. They, too, will respond to my voice. So they will be one flock with one shepherd. [17] The Father loves me because I give my life in order to take it back again. [18] No one takes my life from me. I give my life of my own free will. I have the authority to give my life, and I have the authority to take my life back again. This is what my Father ordered me to do.

JESUS BRINGS LAZARUS BACK TO LIFE

John 11:1-44

¹Lazarus, who lived in Bethany, the village where Mary and her sister Martha lived, was sick. ²(Mary was the woman who poured perfume on the Lord and wiped his feet with her hair. Her brother Lazarus was the one who was sick.)

³So the sisters sent a messenger to tell Jesus, "Lord, your close friend is sick."

⁴When Jesus heard the message, he said, "His sickness won't result in death. Instead, this sickness will bring glory to God so that the Son of God will receive glory through it."

⁵Jesus loved Martha, her sister, and Lazarus. ⁶Yet, when Jesus heard that Lazarus was sick, he stayed where he was for two more days.

⁷Then, after the two days, Jesus said to his disciples, "Let's go back to Judea."

⁸The disciples said to him, "Rabbi, not long ago the Jews wanted to stone you to death. Do you really want to go back there?"

⁹Jesus answered, "Aren't there twelve hours of daylight? Those who walk during the day don't stumble, because they see the light of this world. ¹⁰However, those who walk at night stumble because they have no light in themselves."

¹¹After Jesus said this, he told his disciples, "Our friend Lazarus is sleeping, and I'm going to Bethany to wake him."

¹²His disciples said to him, "Lord, if he's sleeping, he'll get well."

¹³Jesus meant that Lazarus was dead, but the disciples thought Jesus meant that Lazarus was only sleeping. ¹⁴Then Jesus told them plainly, "Lazarus has died, ¹⁵but I'm glad that I wasn't there so that you can grow in faith. Let's go to Lazarus."

¹⁶Thomas, who was called Didymus, said to the rest of the disciples, "Let's go so that we, too, can die with Jesus."

¹⁷When Jesus arrived, he found that Lazarus had been in the tomb for four days. ¹⁸(Bethany was near Jerusalem, not quite two miles away.) ¹⁹Many Jews had come to Martha and Mary to comfort them about their brother.

²⁰When Martha heard that Jesus was coming, she went to meet him. Mary stayed at home. ²¹Martha told Jesus, "Lord, if you had been here, my brother would not have died. ²²But even now I know that God will give you whatever you ask him."

²³Jesus told Martha, "Your brother will come back to life."

²⁴Martha answered Jesus, "I know that he'll come back to life on the last day, when everyone will come back to life."

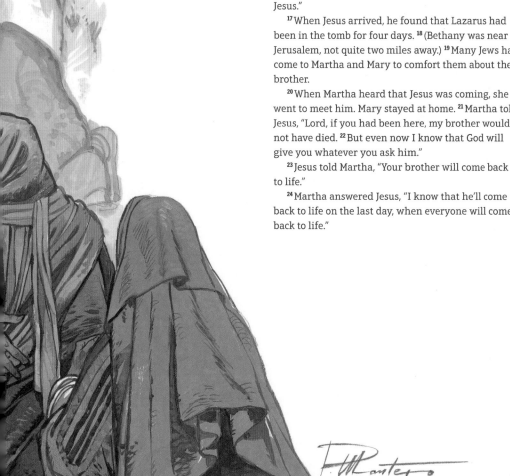

²⁵ Jesus said to her, "I am the one who brings people back to life, and I am life itself. Those who believe in me will live even if they die. ²⁶ Everyone who lives and believes in me will never die. Do you believe that?"

²⁷ Martha said to him, "Yes, Lord, I believe that you are the Messiah, the Son of God, the one who was expected to come into the world."

²⁸ After Martha had said this, she went back home and whispered to her sister Mary, "The teacher is here, and he is calling for you."

²⁹ When Mary heard this, she got up quickly and went to Jesus. ³⁰ (Jesus had not yet come into the village but was still where Martha had met him.) ³¹ The Jews who were comforting Mary in the house saw her get up quickly and leave. So they followed her. They thought that she was going to the tomb to cry. ³² When Mary arrived where Jesus was and saw him, she knelt at his feet and said, "Lord, if you had been here, my brother would not have died."

³³ When Jesus saw her crying, and the Jews who were crying with her, he was deeply moved and troubled.

³⁴ So Jesus asked, "Where did you put Lazarus?"

They answered him, "Lord, come and see."

³⁵ Jesus cried. ³⁶ The Jews said, "See how much Jesus loved him." ³⁷ But some of the Jews asked, "Couldn't this man who gave a blind man sight keep Lazarus from dying?"

³⁸ Deeply moved again, Jesus went to the tomb. It was a cave with a stone covering the entrance. ³⁹ Jesus said, "Take the stone away."

Martha, the dead man's sister, told Jesus, "Lord, there must already be a stench. He's been dead for four days."

⁴⁰ Jesus said to her, "Didn't I tell you that if you believe, you would see God's glory?" ⁴¹ So the stone was moved away from the entrance of the tomb.

Jesus looked up and said, "Father, I thank you for hearing me. ⁴² I've known that you always hear me. However, I've said this so that the crowd standing around me will believe that you sent me." ⁴³ After Jesus had said this, he shouted as loudly as he could, "Lazarus, come out!"

⁴⁴ The dead man came out. Strips of cloth were wound around his feet and hands, and his face was wrapped with a handkerchief. Jesus told them, "Free Lazarus, and let him go."

THE LOST SHEEP AND THE LOST COIN

Luke 15:1-10

¹ All the tax collectors and sinners came to listen to Jesus. ² But the Pharisees and the experts in Moses' Teachings complained, "This man welcomes sinners and eats with them."

³ Jesus spoke to them using this illustration: ⁴ "Suppose a man has 100 sheep and loses one of them. Doesn't he leave the 99 sheep grazing in the pasture and look for the lost sheep until he finds it? ⁵ When he finds it, he's happy. He puts that sheep on his shoulders and ⁶ goes home. Then he calls his friends and neighbors together and says to them, 'Let's celebrate! I've found my lost sheep!' ⁷ I can guarantee that there will be more happiness in heaven over one person who turns to God and changes the way he thinks and acts than over 99 people who already have turned to God and have his approval."

⁸ "Suppose a woman has ten coins and loses one. Doesn't she light a lamp, sweep the house, and look for the coin carefully until she finds it? ⁹ When she finds it, she calls her friends and neighbors together and says, 'Let's celebrate! I've found the coin that I lost.' ¹⁰ So I can guarantee that God's angels are happy about one person who turns to God and changes the way he thinks and acts."

THE LOVING FATHER

Luke 15:11-19

¹¹ Then Jesus said, "A man had two sons. ¹² The younger son said to his father, 'Father, give me my share of the property.' So the father divided his property between his two sons.

¹³ "After a few days, the younger son gathered his possessions and left for a country far away from home. There he wasted everything he had on a wild lifestyle. ¹⁴ He had nothing left when a severe famine spread throughout that country. He had nothing to live on. ¹⁵ So he got a job from someone in that country and was sent to feed pigs in the fields. ¹⁶ No one in the country would give him any food, and he was so hungry that he would have eaten what the pigs were eating.

¹⁷ "Finally, he came to his senses. He said, 'How many of my father's hired men have more food than they can eat, while I'm starving to death here? ¹⁸ I'll go at once to my father, and I'll say to him, "Father, I've sinned against heaven and you. ¹⁹ I don't deserve to be called your son anymore. Make me one of your hired men." '

HE LOVING FATHER WELCOMES HIS CHILD

ke 15:20-32

"So he went at once to his father. While he was still a distance, his father saw him and felt sorry for him. e ran to his son, put his arms around him, and kissed m. ²¹ Then his son said to him, 'Father, I've sinned gainst heaven and you. I don't deserve to be called ur son anymore.'

²² "The father said to his servants, 'Hurry! Bring t the best robe, and put it on him. Put a ring on his nger and sandals on his feet. ²³ Bring the fattened calf, ll it, and let's celebrate with a feast. ²⁴ My son was ad and has come back to life. He was lost but has en found.' Then they began to celebrate.

²⁵ "His older son was in the field. As he was coming ck to the house, he heard music and dancing. He called to one of the servants and asked what as happening.

²⁷ "The servant told him, 'Your brother has come me. So your father has killed the fattened calf to lebrate your brother's safe return.'

²⁸ "Then the older son became angry and wouldn't into the house. His father came out and begged m to come in. ²⁹ But he answered his father, 'All these ars I've worked like a slave for you. I've never sobeyed one of your commands. Yet, you've never ven me so much as a little goat for a celebration with y friends. ³⁰ But this son of yours spent your money prostitutes, and when he came home, you killed e fattened calf for him.'

³¹ "His father said to him, 'My child, you're ways with me. Everything I have is yours. ³² But have something to celebrate, something to be ppy about. This brother of yours was dead but has me back to life. He was lost but has been found.'"

293

MONEY LOVERS

Luke 16:10-14

[10] Whoever can be trusted with very little can also be trusted with a lot. Whoever is dishonest with very little is dishonest with a lot. [11] Therefore, if you can't be trusted with wealth that is often used dishonestly, who will trust you with wealth that is real? [12] If you can't be trusted with someone else's wealth, who will give you your own?

[13] "A servant cannot serve two masters. He will hate the first master and love the second, or he will be devoted to the first and despise the second. You cannot serve God and wealth."

[14] The Pharisees, who love money, heard all this and were making sarcastic remarks about him.

THE RICH MAN AND LAZARUS

Luke 16:19-31

[19] "There was a rich man who wore expensive clothes. Every day was like a party to him. [20] There was also a beggar named Lazarus who was regularly brought to the gate of the rich man's house. [21] Lazarus would have eaten any scraps that fell from the rich man's table. Lazarus was covered with sores, and dogs would lick them.

[22] "One day the beggar died, and the angels carried him to be with Abraham. The rich man also died and was buried. [23] He went to hell, where he was constantly tortured. As he looked up, in the distance he saw Abraham and Lazarus. [24] He yelled, 'Father Abraham! Have mercy on me! Send Lazarus to dip the tip of his finger in water to cool off my tongue. I am suffering in this fire.'

[25] "Abraham replied, 'Remember, my child, that you had a life filled with good times, while Lazarus' life was filled with misery. Now he has peace here, while you suffer. [26] Besides, a wide area separates us. People couldn't cross it in either direction even if they wanted to.'

[27] "The rich man responded, 'Then I ask you, Father, to send Lazarus back to my father's home. [28] I have five brothers. He can warn them so that they won't end up in this place of torture.'

[29] "Abraham replied, 'They have Moses' ⌊Teachings⌋ and the Prophets. Your brothers should listen to them.'

[30] "The rich man replied, 'No, Father Abraham! If someone comes back to them from the dead, they will turn to God and change the way they think and act.'

[31] "Abraham answered him, 'If they won't listen to Moses' ⌊Teachings⌋ and the Prophets, they won't be persuaded even if someone comes back to life.'"

MORE LESSONS ABOUT THE POWER OF PRAYER

Luke 18:1-8

[1] Jesus used this illustration with his disciples to show them that they need to pray all the time and never give up. [2] He said, "In a city there was a judge who didn't fear God or respect people. [3] In that city there was also a widow who kept coming to him and saying, 'Give me justice.'

[4] "For a while the judge refused to do anything. But then he thought, 'This widow really annoys me. Although I don't fear God or respect people, [5] I'll have to give her justice. Otherwise, she'll keep coming to me until she wears me out.'"

[6] The Lord added, "Pay attention to what the dishonest judge thought. [7] Won't God give his chosen people justice when they cry out to him for help day and night? Is he slow to help them? [8] I can guarantee that he will give them justice quickly. But when the Son of Man comes, will he find faith on earth?"

BROKEN HOMES

Mark 10:1-9

[1] Jesus left there and went into the territory of Judea along the other side of the Jordan River. Crowds gathered around him again, and he taught them as he usually did.

[2] Some Pharisees came to test him. They asked, "Can a husband divorce his wife?"

[3] Jesus answered them, "What command did Moses give you?"

[4] They said, "Moses allowed a man to give his wife a written notice to divorce her."

[5] Jesus said to them, "He wrote this command for you because you're heartless. [6] But God made them male and female in the beginning, at creation. [7] That's why a man will leave his father and mother and will remain united with his wife, [8] and the two will be one. So they are no longer two but one. [9] Therefore, don't let anyone separate what God has joined together."

CHILD-LIKE FAITH IS NECESSARY
TO ENTER GOD'S KINGDOM

Mark 10:13-16

¹³ Some people brought little children to Jesus to have him hold them. But the disciples told the people not to do that.

¹⁴ When Jesus saw this, he became irritated. He told them, "Don't stop the children from coming to me. Children like these are part of God's kingdom. ¹⁵ I can guarantee this truth: Whoever doesn't receive God's kingdom as a little child receives it will never enter it."

¹⁶ Jesus put his arms around the children and blessed them by placing his hands on them.

THE RICH YOUNG MAN FAILS THE TEST

Matthew 19:16-22

[16] Then a man came to Jesus and said, "Teacher, what good deed should I do to gain eternal life?"

[17] Jesus said to him, "Why do you ask me about what is good? There is only one who is good. If you want to enter into life, obey the commandments."

[18] "Which commandments?" the man asked.

Jesus said, "Never murder. Never commit adultery. Never steal. Never give false testimony. [19] Honor your father and mother. Love your neighbor as you love yourself."

[20] The young man replied, "I have obeyed all these commandments. What else do I need to do?"

[21] Jesus said to him, "If you want to be perfect, sell what you own. Give the money to the poor, and you will have treasure in heaven. Then follow me!"

[22] When the young man heard this, he went away sad because he owned a lot of property.

WHO COMES FIRST?

Mark 10:23-31

²³ Jesus looked around and said to his disciples, "How hard it will be for rich people to enter God's kingdom!"

²⁴ The disciples were stunned by his words. But Jesus said to them again, "Children, how hard it is to enter God's kingdom! ²⁵ It is easier for a camel to go through the eye of a needle than for a rich person to enter God's kingdom."

²⁶ This amazed his disciples more than ever. They asked each other, "Who, then, can be saved?"

²⁷ Jesus looked at them and said, "It's impossible for people ⌞to save themselves⌟, but it's not impossible for God to save them. Everything is possible for God."

²⁸ Then Peter spoke up, "We've given up everything to follow you."

²⁹ Jesus said, "I can guarantee this truth: Anyone who gave up his home, brothers, sisters, mother, father, children, or fields because of me and the Good News ³⁰ will certainly receive a hundred times as much here in this life. They will certainly receive homes, brothers, sisters, mothers, children and fields, along with persecutions. But in the world to come they will receive eternal life. ³¹ But many who are first will be last, and the last will be first."

THE WORKERS IN THE VINEYARD

Matthew 20:1-16

[1] "The kingdom of heaven is like a landowner who went out at daybreak to hire workers for his vineyard. [2] After agreeing to pay the workers the usual day's wages, he sent them to work in his vineyard. [3] About 9 a.m. he saw others standing in the marketplace without work. [4] He said to them, 'Work in my vineyard, and I'll give you whatever is right.' So they went.

[5] "He went out again about noon and 3 p.m. and did the same thing. [6] About 5 p.m. he went out and found some others standing around. He said to them, 'Why are you standing here all day long without work?'

[7] " 'No one has hired us,' they answered him.

"He said to them, 'Work in my vineyard.'

[8] "When evening came, the owner of the vineyard told the supervisor, 'Call the workers, and give them their wages. Start with the last, and end with the first.'

[9] "Those who started working about 5 p.m. came, and each received a day's wages. [10] When those who had been hired first came, they expected to receive more. But each of them received a day's wages. [11] Although they took it, they began to protest to the owner. [12] They said, 'These last workers have worked only one hour. Yet, you've treated us all the same, even though we worked hard all day under a blazing sun.'

[13] "The owner said to one of them, 'Friend, I'm not treating you unfairly. Didn't you agree with me on a day's wages? [14] Take your money and go! I want to give this last worker as much as I gave you. [15] Can't I do what I want with my own money? Or do you resent my generosity towards others?'

[16] "In this way the last will be first, and the first will be last."

THE FAITH OF THE LITTLE MAN IN THE TREE

Luke 19:1-10

[1] Jesus was passing through Jericho. [2] A man named Zacchaeus was there. He was the director of tax collectors, and he was rich. [3] He tried to see who Jesus was. But Zacchaeus was a small man, and he couldn't see Jesus because of the crowd. [4] So Zacchaeus ran ahead and climbed a fig tree to see Jesus, who was coming that way.

[5] When Jesus came to the tree, he looked up and said, "Zacchaeus, come down! I must stay at your house today."

[6] Zacchaeus came down and was glad to welcome Jesus into his home. [7] But the people who saw this began to express disapproval. They said, "He went to be the guest of a sinner."

[8] ⌊Later, at dinner,⌋ Zacchaeus stood up and said to the Lord, "Lord, I'll give half of my property to the poor. I'll pay four times as much as I owe to those I have cheated in any way."

[9] Then Jesus said to Zacchaeus, "You and your family have been saved today. You've shown that you, too, are one of Abraham's descendants. [10] Indeed, the Son of Man has come to seek and to save people who are lost."

THE MANAGEMENT OF THE GIFTS THAT GOD HAS GIVEN YOU

Luke 19:11-27

¹¹ Jesus was getting closer to Jerusalem, and the people thought that God's kingdom would appear suddenly. While Jesus had the people's attention, he used this illustration. ¹² He said, "A prince went to a distant country to be appointed king, and then he returned. ¹³ ⌐Before he left,⌐ he called ten of his servants and gave them ten coins. He said to his servants, 'Invest this money until I come back.'

¹⁴ "The citizens of his own country hated him. They sent representatives to follow him and say ⌐to the person who was going to appoint him⌐, 'We don't want this man to be our king.'

¹⁵ "After he was appointed king, he came back. Then he said, 'Call those servants to whom I gave money. I want to know how much each one has made by investing.'

¹⁶ "The first servant said, 'Sir, the coin you gave me has earned ten times as much.'

¹⁷ "The king said to him, 'Good job! You're a good servant. You proved that you could be trusted with a little money. Take charge of ten cities.'

¹⁸ "The second servant said, 'The coin you gave me, sir, has made five times as much.'

¹⁹ "The king said to this servant, 'You take charge of five cities.'

²⁰ "Then the other servant said, 'Sir, look! Here's your coin. I've kept it in a cloth for safekeeping because ²¹ I was afraid of you. You're a tough person to get along with. You take what isn't yours and harvest grain you haven't planted.'

²² "The king said to him, 'I'll judge you by what you've said, you evil servant! You knew that I was a tough person to get along with. You knew that I take what isn't mine and harvest grain I haven't planted. ²³ Then why didn't you put my money in the bank? When I came back, I could have collected it with interest.' ²⁴ The king told his men, 'Take his coin away, and give it to the man who has ten.'

²⁵ "They replied, 'Sir, he already has ten coins.'

²⁶ " 'I can guarantee that everyone who has something will be given more. But everything will be taken away from those who don't have much. ²⁷ Bring my enemies, who didn't want me to be their king. Kill them in front of me.' "

MARY'S ACT OF LOVE

John 12:1-8

[1] Six days before Passover, Jesus arrived in Bethany. Lazarus, whom Jesus had brought back to life, lived there. [2] Dinner was prepared for Jesus in Bethany. Martha served the dinner, and Lazarus was one of the people eating with Jesus.

[3] Mary took a bottle of very expensive perfume made from pure nard and poured it on Jesus' feet. Then she dried his feet with her hair. The fragrance of the perfume filled the house.

[4] One of his disciples, Judas Iscariot, who was going to betray him, asked, [5] "Why wasn't this perfume sold for a high price and the money given to the poor?" [6] (Judas didn't say this because he cared about the poor but because he was a thief. He was in charge of the moneybag and carried the contributions.) [7] Jesus said to Judas, "Leave her alone! She has done this to prepare me for the day I will be placed in a tomb. [8] You will always have the poor with you, but you will not always have me with you."

JESUS' TRIUMPHANT ENTRY INTO JERUSALEM

Luke 19:28-38

²⁸ After Jesus had given this illustration, he continued on his way to Jerusalem.

²⁹ When he came near Bethphage and Bethany at the Mount of Olives (as it was called), Jesus sent two of his disciples ahead of him. ³⁰ He said to them, "Go into the village ahead of you. As you enter, you will find a young donkey tied there. No one has ever sat on it. Untie it, and bring it. ³¹ If anyone asks you why you are untying it, say that the Lord needs it."

³² The men Jesus sent found it as he had told them. ³³ While they were untying the young donkey, its owners asked them, "Why are you untying the donkey?"

³⁴ The disciples answered, "The Lord needs it."

³⁵ They brought the donkey to Jesus, put their coats on it, and helped Jesus onto it. ³⁶ As he was riding along, people spread their coats on the road. ³⁷ By this time he was coming near the place where the road went down the Mount of Olives. Then the whole crowd of disciples began to praise God for all the miracles they had seen. ³⁸ They shouted joyfully,

> "Blessed is the king who comes
> in the name of the Lord!
> Peace in heaven, and glory
> in the highest heaven."

THE FATE OF JERUSALEM

Luke 19:39-44

³⁹ Some of the Pharisees in the crowd said to Jesus, "Teacher, tell your disciples to be quiet."

⁴⁰ Jesus replied, "I can guarantee that if they are quiet, the stones will cry out."

⁴¹ When he came closer and saw the city, he began to cry. ⁴² He said, "If you had only known today what would bring you peace! But now it is hidden, so you cannot see it. ⁴³ The time will come when enemy armies will build a wall to surround you and close you in on every side. ⁴⁴ They will level you to the ground and kill your people. One stone will not be left on top of another, because you didn't recognize the time when God came to help you."

309

JESUS CLEANS OUT THE TEMPLE

Mark 11:15-19

¹⁵ When they came to Jerusalem, Jesus went into the temple courtyard and began to throw out those who were buying and selling there. He overturned the moneychangers' tables and the chairs of those who sold pigeons. ¹⁶ He would not let anyone carry anything across the temple courtyard.

¹⁷ Then he taught them by saying, "Scripture says, 'My house will be called a house of prayer for all nations,' but you have turned it into a gathering place for thieves."

¹⁸ When the chief priests and the experts in Moses' Teachings heard him, they looked for a way to kill him. They were afraid of him because he amazed all the crowds with his teaching.

¹⁹ (Every evening Jesus and his disciples would leave the city.)

JESUS HEALS IN THE TEMPLE

Matthew 21:14-16

14 Blind and lame people came to him in the temple courtyard, and he healed them.

15 When the chief priests and the experts in Moses' teachings saw the amazing miracles he performed and the children shouting in the temple courtyard, "Hosanna to the Son of David!" they were irritated. They said to him, "Do you hear what these children are saying?"

Jesus replied, "Yes, I do. Have you never read, 'From the mouths of little children and infants, you have created praise'?"

17 He left them and went out of the city to Bethany and spent the night there.

JESUS REVEALS WHO GAVE THE MOST

Mark 12:41-44

⁴¹ As Jesus sat facing the temple offering box, he watched how ˌmuchˌ money people put into it. Many rich people put in large amounts. ⁴² A poor widow dropped in two small coins, worth less than a cent.

⁴³ He called his disciples and said to them, "I can guarantee this truth: This poor widow has given more than all the others. ⁴⁴ All of them have given what they could spare. But she, in her poverty, has given everything she had to live on."

THE FIVE CARELESS BRIDESMAIDS

Matthew 25:1-13

[1] "When the end comes, the kingdom of heaven will be like ten bridesmaids. They took their oil lamps and went to meet the groom. [2] Five of them were foolish, and five were wise. [3] The foolish bridesmaids took their lamps, but they didn't take any extra oil. [4] The wise bridesmaids, however, took along extra oil for their lamps. [5] Since the groom was late, all the bridesmaids became drowsy and fell asleep.

[6] "At midnight someone shouted, 'The groom is here! Come to meet him!' [7] Then all the bridesmaids woke up and got their lamps ready.

[8] "The foolish ones said to the wise ones, 'Give us some of your oil. Our lamps are going out.'

[9] "But the wise bridesmaids replied, 'We can't do that. There won't be enough for both of us. Go! Find someone to sell you some oil.'

[10] "While they were buying oil, the groom arrived. The bridesmaids who were ready went with him into the wedding hall, and the door was shut.

[11] "Later the other bridesmaids arrived and said, 'Sir, sir, open the door for us!'

[12] "But he answered them, 'I don't even know who you are!'

[13] "So stay awake, because you don't know the day or the hour.

315

JUDAS BETRAYS JESUS

Matthew 26:1-5

¹ When Jesus finished saying all these things, he told his disciples, ² "You know that the Passover will take place in two days. At that time the Son of Man will be handed over to be crucified."

³ Then the chief priests and the leaders of the people gathered in the palace of the chief priest Caiaphas. ⁴ They made plans to arrest Jesus in an underhanded way and to kill him. ⁵ But they said, "We shouldn't arrest him during the festival, or else there may be a riot among the people."

Matthew 26:14-16

¹⁴ Then one of the twelve apostles, the one named Judas Iscariot, went to the chief priests. ¹⁵ He asked, "What will you pay me if I hand him over to you?"

They offered him 30 silver coins. ¹⁶ From then on, he looked for a chance to betray Jesus.

PREPARING THE LAST PASSOVER

Luke 22:7-13

7 The day came during the Festival of Unleavened Bread when the Passover lamb had to be killed. **8** Jesus sent Peter and John and told them, "Go, prepare the Passover lamb for us to eat."

9 They asked him, "Where do you want us to prepare it?"

10 He told them, "Go into the city, and you will meet a man carrying a jug of water. Follow him into the house he enters. **11** Tell the owner of the house that the teacher asks, 'Where is the room where I can eat the Passover meal with my disciples?' **12** He will take you upstairs and show you a large furnished room. Get things ready there."

13 The disciples left. They found everything as Jesus had told them and prepared the Passover.

JESUS ASKS, WHO IS THE GREATEST?

Luke 22:14

14 When it was time to eat the Passover meal, Jesus and the apostles were at the table.

Luke 22:24-30

24 Then a quarrel broke out among the disciples. They argued about who should be considered the greatest.

25 Jesus said to them, "The kings of nations have power over their people, and those in authority call themselves friends of the people. **26** But you're not

oing to be that way! Rather, the greatest among you
ust be like the youngest, and your leader must be
ke a servant. ²⁷ Who's the greatest, the person who sits
t the table or the servant? Isn't it really the person
ho sits at the table? But I'm among you as a servant.

²⁸ "You have stood by me in the troubles that have
sted me. ²⁹ So as my Father has given me a kingdom,
m giving it to you. ³⁰ You will eat and drink at my
ble in my kingdom. You will also sit on thrones and
dge the twelve tribes of Israel."

JESUS – THE SERVANT KING

John 13:1-9

¹Before the Passover festival, Jesus knew that the time had come for him to leave this world and go back to the Father. Jesus loved his own who were in the world, and he loved them to the end.

²While supper was taking place, the devil had already put the idea of betraying Jesus into the mind of Judas, son of Simon Iscariot.

³The Father had put everything in Jesus' control. Jesus knew that. He also knew that he had come from God and was going back to God. ⁴So he got up from the table, removed his outer clothes, took a towel, and tied it around his waist. ⁵Then he poured water into a basin and began to wash the disciples' feet and dry them with the towel that he had tied around his waist.

⁶When Jesus came to Simon Peter, Peter asked him, "Lord, are you going to wash my feet?"

⁷Jesus answered Peter, "You don't know now what I'm doing. You will understand later."

⁸Peter told Jesus, "You will never wash my feet."

Jesus replied to Peter, "If I don't wash you, you don't belong to me."

⁹Simon Peter said to Jesus, "Lord, don't wash only my feet. Wash my hands and my head too!"

THE REASON WHY SERVICE IS SO IMPORTANT

John 13:12-17

¹² After Jesus had washed their feet and put on his outer clothes, he took his place at the table again. Then he asked his disciples, "Do you understand what I've done for you? ¹³ You call me teacher and Lord, and you're right because that's what I am. ¹⁴ So if I, your Lord and teacher, have washed your feet, you must wash each other's feet. ¹⁵ I've given you an example that you should follow. ¹⁶ I can guarantee this truth: Slaves are not superior to their owners, and messengers are not superior to the people who send them. ¹⁷ If you understand all of this, you are blessed whenever you follow my example.

JESUS INSTITUTES THE LORD'S SUPPER

Mark 14:18-25

[18] While they were at the table eating, Jesus said, "I can guarantee this truth: One of you is going to betray me, one who is eating with me!"

[19] Feeling hurt, they asked him one by one, "You don't mean me, do you?"

[20] He said to them, "It's one of you twelve, someone dipping his hand into the bowl with me. [21] The Son of Man is going to die as the Scriptures say he will. But how horrible it will be for that person who betrays the Son of Man! It would have been better for that person if he had never been born."

[22] While they were eating, Jesus took bread and blessed it. He broke the bread, gave it to them, and said, "Take this. This is my body."

[23] Then he took a cup, spoke a prayer of thanksgiving, and gave the cup to them. They all drank from it. [24] He said to them, "This is my blood, the blood of the promise. It is poured out for many people.

[25] "I can guarantee this truth: I won't drink this wine again until that day when I drink new wine in God's kingdom."

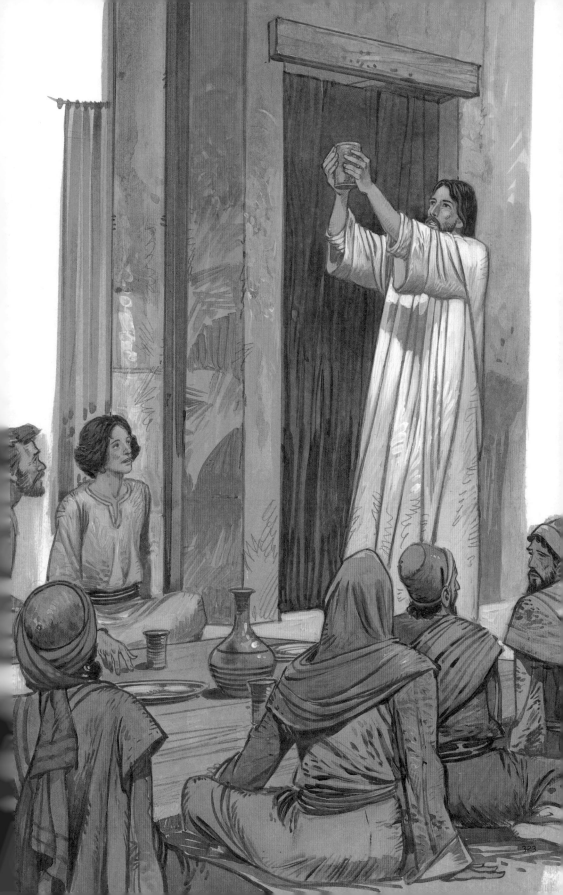

WHEN THE COCK CROWS

Mark 14:26-31

[26] After they sang a hymn, they went to the Mount of Olives.

[27] Then Jesus said to them, "All of you will abandon me. Scripture says,

'I will strike the shepherd,
  and the sheep will be scattered.'

[28] "But after I am brought back to life, I will go to Galilee ahead of you."

[29] Peter said to him, "Even if everyone else abandons you, I won't."

[30] Jesus said to Peter, "I can guarantee this truth: Tonight, before a rooster crows twice, you will say three times that you don't know me."

[31] But Peter said very strongly, "Even if I have to die with you, I will never say that I don't know you." All the other disciples said the same thing.

JESUS ASSURES HIS FOLLOWERS OF A HOME IN HEAVEN

John 14:1-6

[1] "Don't be troubled. Believe in God, and believe in me. [2] My Father's house has many rooms. If that were not true, would I have told you that I'm going to prepare a place for you? [3] If I go to prepare a place for you, I will come again. Then I will bring you into my presence so that you will be where I am. [4] You know the way to the place where I am going."

[5] Thomas said to him, "Lord, we don't know where you're going. So how can we know the way?"

[6] Jesus answered him, "I am the way, the truth, and the life. No one goes to the Father except through me.

JESUS PRAYS FOR HIS FOLLOWERS

John 17:1-18:1

¹ After saying this, Jesus looked up to heaven and said, "Father, the time is here. Give your Son glory so that your Son can give you glory. ² After all, you've given him authority over all humanity so that he can give eternal life to all those you gave to him. ³ This is eternal life: to know you, the only true God, and Jesus Christ, whom you sent. ⁴ On earth I have given you glory by finishing the work you gave me to do. ⁵ Now, Father, give me glory in your presence with the glory I had with you before the world existed.

⁶ "I made your name known to the people you gave me. They are from this world. They belonged to you, and you gave them to me. They did what you told them. ⁷ Now they know that everything you gave me comes from you, ⁸ because I gave them the message that you gave me. They have accepted this message, and they know for sure that I came from you. They have believed that you sent me.

⁹ "I pray for them. I'm not praying for the world but for those you gave me, because they are yours. ¹⁰ Everything I have is yours, and everything you have is mine. I have been given glory by the people you have given me. ¹¹ I won't be in the world much longer, but they are in the world, and I'm coming back to you. Holy Father, keep them safe by the power of your name, the name that you gave me, so that their unity may be like ours. ¹² While I was with them, I kept them safe by the power of your name, the name that you gave me. I watched over them, and none of them, except one person, became lost. So Scripture came true.

¹³ "But now, ⌊Father,⌋ I'm coming back to you. I say these things while I'm still in the world so that they will have the same joy that I have. ¹⁴ I have given them your message. But the world has hated them because they don't belong to the world any more than I belong to the world. ¹⁵ I'm not asking you to take them out of the world but to protect them from the evil one. ¹⁶ They don't belong to the world any more than I belong to the world.

¹⁷ "Use the truth to make them holy. Your words are truth. ¹⁸ I have sent them into the world the same way you sent me into the world. ¹⁹ I'm dedicating myself to this holy work I'm doing for them so that they, too, will use the truth to be holy.

²⁰ "I'm not praying only for them. I'm also praying for those who will believe in me through their message. ²¹ I pray that all of these people continue to have unity in the way that you, Father, are in me and I am in you. I pray that they may be united with us so that the world will believe that you have sent me. ²² I have given them the glory that you gave me. I did this so that they are united in the same way we are. ²³ I am in them, and you are in me. So they are completely united. In this way the world knows that you have sent me and that you have loved them in the same way you have loved me.

²⁴ "Father, I want those you have given to me to be with me, to be where I am. I want them to see my glory, which you gave me because you loved me before the world was made. ²⁵ Father, you have done what is right and the world didn't know you. Yet, I knew you, and these ˌdisciplesˌ have known that you sent me. ²⁶ I have made your name known to them, and I will make it known so that the love you have for me will be in them and I will be in them."

¹ After Jesus finished his prayer, he went with his disciples to the other side of the Kidron Valley. They entered the garden that was there.

Mark 14:33-42

³³ He took Peter, James, and John with him and began to feel distressed and anguished. ³⁴ He said to them, "My anguish is so great that I feel as if I'm dying. Wait here, and stay awake."

³⁵ After walking a little farther, he fell to the ground and prayed that if it were possible he might not have to suffer what was ahead of him. ³⁶ He said, "Abba! Father! You can do anything. Take this cup ˌof sufferingˌ away from me. But let your will be done rather than mine."

³⁷ He went back and found them asleep. He said to Peter, "Simon, are you sleeping? Couldn't you stay awake for one hour? ³⁸ Stay awake, and pray that you won't be tempted. You want to do what's right, but you're weak."

³⁹ He went away again and prayed the same prayer as before. ⁴⁰ He found them asleep because they couldn't keep their eyes open. They didn't even know what they should say to him.

⁴¹ He came back a third time and said to them, "You might as well sleep now. It's all over. The time has come for the Son of Man to be handed over to sinners. ⁴² Get up! Let's go! The one who is betraying me is near."

JESUS IS BETRAYED BY A KISS

John 18:2-8

² Judas, who betrayed him, knew the place because Jesus and his disciples often gathered there. ³ So Judas took a troop of soldiers and the guards from the chief priests and Pharisees and went to the garden. They were carrying lanterns, torches, and weapons.

⁴ Jesus knew everything that was going to happen to him. So he went to meet them and asked, "Who are you looking for?"

⁵ They answered him, "Jesus from Nazareth."

Jesus told them, "I am he."

Judas, who betrayed him, was standing with the crowd. ⁶ When Jesus told them, "I am he," the crowd backed away and fell to the ground.

⁷ Jesus asked them again, "Who are you looking for?"

They said, "Jesus from Nazareth."

⁸ Jesus replied, "I told you that I am he. So if you are looking for me, let these other men go."

Matthew 26:48-49

⁴⁸ Now, the traitor had given them a signal. He said, "The one I kiss is the man you want. Arrest him!"

⁴⁹ Then Judas quickly stepped up to Jesus and said, "Hello, Rabbi!" and kissed him.

329

PETER FIGHTS BACK

John 18:10-11

[10] Simon Peter had a sword. He drew it, attacked the chief priest's servant, and cut off the servant's right ear. (The servant's name was Malchus.)

[11] Jesus told Peter, "Put your sword away. Shouldn't I drink the cup ⌊of suffering⌋ that my Father has given me?"

Luke 22:51-53

[51] But Jesus said, "Stop! That's enough of this." Then he touched the servant's ear and healed him.

[52] Then Jesus said to the chief priests, temple guards, and leaders who had come for him, "Have you come out with swords and clubs as if I were a criminal? [53] I was with you in the temple courtyard every day and you didn't try to arrest me. But this is your time, when darkness rules."

JESUS IS TAKEN PRISONER

John 18:12-14

¹² Then the army officer and the Jewish guards arrested Jesus. They tied Jesus up ¹³ and took him first to Annas, the father-in-law of Caiaphas. Caiaphas, the chief priest that year, ¹⁴ was the person who had advised the Jews that it was better to have one man die for the people.

PETER'S LACK OF FAITH

Luke 22:54-62

⁵⁴ So they arrested Jesus and led him away to the chief priest's house.

Peter followed at a distance.

⁵⁵ Some men had lit a fire in the middle of the courtyard. As they sat together, Peter sat among them. ⁵⁶ A female servant saw him as he sat facing the glow of the fire. She stared at him and said, "This man was with Jesus."

⁵⁷ But Peter denied it by saying, "I don't know him, woman."

⁵⁸ A little later someone else saw Peter and said, "You are one of them."

But Peter said, "Not me!"

⁵⁹ About an hour later another person insisted, "It's obvious that this man was with him. He's a Galilean!"

⁶⁰ But Peter said, "I don't know what you're talking about!"

Just then, while he was still speaking, a rooster crowed. ⁶¹ Then the Lord turned and looked directly at Peter. Peter remembered what the Lord had said: "Before a rooster crows today, you will say three times that you don't know me." ⁶² Then Peter went outside and cried bitterly.

JESUS' TRIAL BEFORE THE JEWISH CHIEF PRIEST

Mark 14:53-65

⁵³ The men took Jesus to the chief priest. All the chief priests, the leaders, and the experts in Moses' Teachings had gathered together. ⁵⁴ Peter followed him at a distance and went into the chief priest's courtyard. He sat with the guards and warmed himself facing the glow of a fire.

⁵⁵ The chief priests and the whole Jewish council were searching for some testimony against Jesus in order to execute him. But they couldn't find any. ⁵⁶ Many gave false testimony against him, but their statements did not agree.

57 Then some men stood up and gave false testimony against him. They said, **58** "We heard him say, 'I'll tear down this temple made by humans, and in three days I'll build another temple, one not made by human hands.'" **59** But their testimony did not agree even on this point.

60 So the chief priest stood up in the center and asked Jesus, "Don't you have any answer to what these men testify against you?"

61 But he was silent.

The chief priest asked him again, "Are you the Messiah, the Son of the Blessed One?"

62 Jesus answered, "Yes, I am, and you will see the Son of Man in the honored position—the one next to God the Father on the heavenly throne. He will be coming with the clouds of heaven."

63 The chief priest tore his clothes in horror and said, "Why do we need any more witnesses? **64** You've heard him dishonor God! What's your verdict?"

All of them condemned him with the death sentence. **65** Some of them began to spit on him. They covered his face and hit him with their fists. They said to him, "Prophesy!" Even the guards took him and slapped him.

Mark 15:1

1 Early in the morning the chief priests immediately came to a decision with the leaders and the experts in Moses' Teachings. The whole Jewish council decided to tie Jesus up, lead him away, and hand him over to Pilate.

JESUS' CONFRONTATION WITH HEROD

Luke 23:7-12

[7] When Pilate found out that he was, he sent Jesus to Herod. Herod ruled Galilee and was in Jerusalem at that time.

[8] Herod was very pleased to see Jesus. For a long time he had wanted to see him. He had heard about Jesus and hoped to see him perform some kind of miracle. [9] Herod asked Jesus many questions, but Jesus wouldn't answer him. [10] Meanwhile, the chief priests and the experts in Moses' Teachings stood there and shouted their accusations against Jesus.

[11] Herod and his soldiers treated Jesus with contempt and made fun of him. They put a colorful robe on him and sent him back to Pilate. [12] So Herod and Pilate became friends that day. They had been enemies before this.

337

THE ROMAN GOVERNOR, PILATE, TRIES TO FREE JESUS

John 18:28-40

²⁸ Early in the morning, Jesus was taken from Caiaphas' house to the governor's palace.

The Jews wouldn't go into the palace. They didn't want to become unclean, since they wanted to eat the Passover. ²⁹ So Pilate came out to them and asked, "What accusation are you making against this man?"

³⁰ The Jews answered Pilate, "If he weren't a criminal, we wouldn't have handed him over to you."

³¹ Pilate told the Jews, "Take him, and try him by your law."

The Jews answered him, "We're not allowed to execute anyone." ³² In this way what Jesus had predicted about how he would die came true.

³³ Pilate went back into the palace, called for Jesus, and asked him, "Are you the king of the Jews?"

³⁴ Jesus replied, "Did you think of that yourself, or did others tell you about me?"

³⁵ Pilate answered, "Am I a Jew? Your own people and the chief priests handed you over to me. What have you done?"

³⁶ Jesus answered, "My kingdom doesn't belong to this world. If my kingdom belonged to this world, my followers would fight to keep me from being handed over to the Jews. My kingdom doesn't have its origin on earth."

³⁷ Pilate asked him, "So you are a king?"

Jesus replied, "You're correct in saying that I'm a king. I have been born and have come into the world for this reason: to testify to the truth. Everyone who belongs to the truth listens to me."

³⁸ Pilate said to him, "What is truth?"

After Pilate said this, he went out to the Jews again and told them, "I don't find this man guilty of anything. ³⁹ You have a custom that I should free one person for you at Passover. Would you like me to free the king of the Jews for you?"

⁴⁰ The Jews shouted again, "Don't free this man! Free Barabbas!" (Barabbas was a political revolutionary.)

JESUS IS GIVEN THE DEATH SENTENCE

John 19:1-16

¹Then Pilate had Jesus taken away and whipped. ²The soldiers twisted some thorny branches into a crown, placed it on his head, and put a purple cape on him. ³They went up to him, said, "Long live the king of the Jews!" and slapped his face.

⁴Pilate went outside again and told the Jews, "I'm bringing him out to you to let you know that I don't find this man guilty of anything." ⁵Jesus went outside. He was wearing the crown of thorns and the purple cape. Pilate said to the Jews, "Look, here's the man!"

⁶When the chief priests and the guards saw Jesus, they shouted, "Crucify him! Crucify him!"

Pilate told them, "You take him and crucify him. I don't find this man guilty of anything."

⁷The Jews answered Pilate, "We have a law, and by that law he must die because he claimed to be the Son of God."

⁸When Pilate heard them say that, he became more afraid than ever. ⁹He went into the palace again and asked Jesus, "Where are you from?" But Jesus didn't answer him.

¹⁰So Pilate said to Jesus, "Aren't you going to answer me? Don't you know that I have the authority to free you or to crucify you?"

¹¹Jesus answered Pilate, "You wouldn't have any authority over me if it hadn't been given to you from above. That's why the man who handed me over to you is guilty of a greater sin."

¹²When Pilate heard what Jesus said, he wanted to free him. But the Jews shouted, "If you free this man, you're not a friend of the emperor. Anyone who claims to be a king is defying the emperor."

¹³When Pilate heard what they said, he took Jesus outside and sat on the judge's seat in a place called Stone Pavement. (In Hebrew it is called *Gabbatha*.) ¹⁴The time was about six o'clock in the morning on the Friday of the Passover festival.

Pilate said to the Jews, "Look, here's your king!"

¹⁵Then the Jews shouted, "Kill him! Kill him! Crucify him!"

Pilate asked them, "Should I crucify your king?"

The chief priests responded, "The emperor is the only king we have!"

¹⁶Then Pilate handed Jesus over to them to be crucified.

THE WEEPING WOMEN

Luke 23:26-31

[26] As the soldiers led Jesus away, they grabbed a man named Simon, who was from the city of Cyrene. Simon was coming into Jerusalem. They laid the cross on him and made him carry it behind Jesus.

[27] A large crowd followed Jesus. The women in the crowd cried and sang funeral songs for him. [28] Jesus turned to them and said, "You women of Jerusalem, don't cry for me! Rather, cry for yourselves and your children! [29] The time is coming when people will say, 'Blessed are the women who couldn't get pregnant, who couldn't give birth, and who couldn't nurse a child.' [30] Then people will say to the mountains, 'Fall on us!' and to the hills, 'Cover us!' [31] If people do this to a green tree, what will happen to a dry one?"

343

JESUS ON THE CROSS

Luke 23:32-38

³² Two others, who were criminals, were led away to be executed with him.

³³ When they came to the place called The Skull, they crucified him. The criminals were also crucified, one on his right and the other on his left.

³⁴ Then Jesus said, "Father, forgive them. They don't know what they're doing."

Meanwhile, the soldiers divided his clothes among themselves by throwing dice.

³⁵ The people stood there watching. But the rulers were making sarcastic remarks. They said, "He saved others. If he's the Messiah that God has chosen, let him save himself!" ³⁶ The soldiers also made fun of him. They would go up to him, offer him some vinegar, ³⁷ and say, "If you're the king of the Jews, save yourself!"

³⁸ A written notice was placed above him. It said, "This is the king of the Jews."

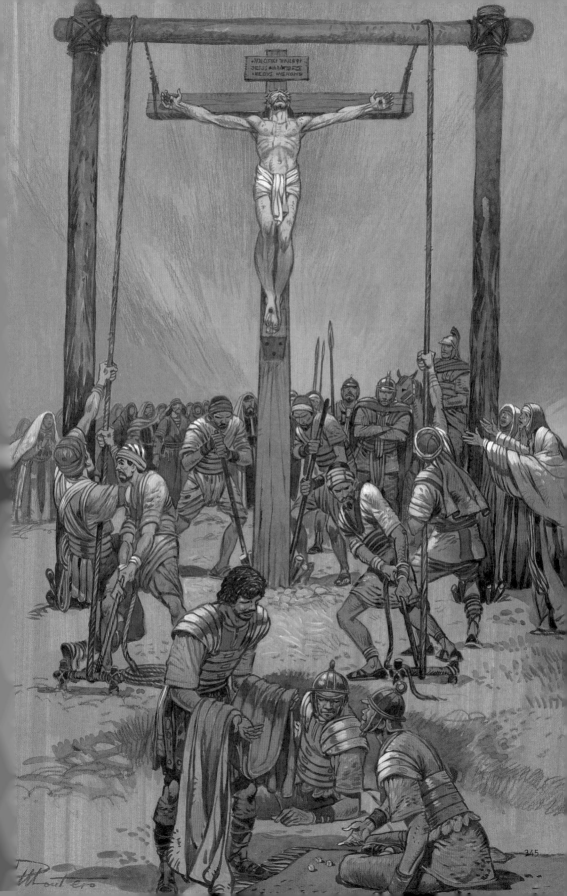

345

THE DEATH OF JESUS

Luke 23:39-44

39 One of the criminals hanging there insulted Jesus by saying, "So you're really the Messiah, are you? Well, save yourself and us!"

40 But the other criminal scolded him: "Don't you fear God at all? Can't you see that you're condemned in the same way that he is? **41** Our punishment is fair. We're getting what we deserve. But this man hasn't done anything wrong."

42 Then he said, "Jesus, remember me when you enter your kingdom."

43 Jesus said to him, "I can guarantee this truth: Today you will be with me in paradise."

44 Around noon darkness came over the entire land and lasted until three in the afternoon.

²⁸ After this, when Jesus knew that everything had now been finished, he said, "I'm thirsty." He said this so that Scripture could finally be concluded.

²⁹ A jar filled with vinegar was there. So the soldiers put a sponge soaked in the vinegar on a hyssop stick and held it to his mouth.

³⁰ After Jesus had taken the vinegar, he said, "It is finished!"

Then he bowed his head and died.

AMONG OTHER MIRACULOUS EVENTS, THE TEMPLE CURTAIN SPLITS IN TWO WHEN JESUS DIES

Matthew 27:51-54

⁵¹ Suddenly, the curtain in the temple was split in two from top to bottom. The earth shook, and the rocks were split open. ⁵² The tombs were opened, and the bodies of many holy people who had died came back to life. ⁵³ They came out of the tombs after he had come back to life, and they went into the holy city where they appeared to many people.

⁵⁴ An army officer and those watching Jesus with him saw the earthquake and the other things happening. They were terrified and said, "Certainly, this was the Son of God!"

JESUS' BODY IS PLACED IN A TOMB

John 19:31-34

31 Since it was Friday and the next day was an especially important day of rest—a holy day, the Jews didn't want the bodies to stay on the crosses. So they asked Pilate to have the men's legs broken and their bodies removed. **32** The soldiers broke the legs of the first man and then of the other man who had been crucified with Jesus.

33 When the soldiers came to Jesus and saw that he was already dead, they didn't break his legs. **34** However, one of the soldiers stabbed Jesus' side with his spear, and blood and water immediately came out.

Matthew 27:57-61

57 In the evening a rich man named Joseph arrived. He was from the city of Arimathea and had become a disciple of Jesus. **58** He went to Pilate and asked for the body of Jesus. Pilate ordered that it be given to him.

59 Joseph took the body and wrapped it in a clean linen cloth. **60** Then he laid it in his own new tomb, which had been cut in a rock. After rolling a large stone against the door of the tomb, he went away. **61** Mary from Magdala and the other Mary were sitting there, facing the tomb.

351

352

GUARDS AT THE TOMB

Matthew 27:62-66

[62] The next day, which was the day of rest—a holy day, the chief priests and Pharisees gathered together and went to Pilate. [63] They said, "Sir, we remember how that deceiver said while he was still alive, 'After three days I will be brought back to life.' [64] Therefore, give the order to make the tomb secure until the third day. Otherwise, his disciples may steal him and say to the people, 'He has been brought back to life.' Then the last deception will be worse than the first."

[65] Pilate told them, "You have the soldiers you want for guard duty. Go and make the tomb as secure as you know how."

[66] So they went to secure the tomb. They placed a seal on the stone and posted the soldiers on guard duty.

AN EMPTY TOMB – JESUS DEFEATS DEATH

Matthew 28:1-10

[1] After the day of rest—a holy day, as the sun rose Sunday morning, Mary from Magdala and the other Mary went to look at the tomb.

[2] Suddenly, there was a powerful earthquake. An angel of the Lord had come down from heaven, rolled the stone away, and was sitting on it. [3] He was as bright as lightning, and his clothes were as white as snow. [4] The guards were so deathly afraid of him that they shook.

[5] The angel said to the women, "Don't be afraid! I know you're looking for Jesus, who was crucified.

[6] He's not here. He has been brought back to life as he said. Come, see the place where he was lying. [7] Then go quickly, and tell his disciples that he has been brought back to life. He's going ahead of them into Galilee. There they will see him. Take note that I have told you."

[8] They hurried away from the tomb with fear and great joy and ran to tell his disciples.

[9] Suddenly, Jesus met them and greeted them. They went up to him, bowed down to worship him, and took hold of his feet.

[10] Then Jesus said to them, "Don't be afraid! Go, tell my followers to go to Galilee. There they will see me."

355

MARY MAGDALENE SEES JESUS AFTER HE COMES BACK TO LIFE

John 20:2-18

²So she ran to Simon Peter and the other disciple, whom Jesus loved. She told them, "They have removed the Lord from the tomb, and we don't know where they've put him."

³So Peter and the other disciple headed for the tomb. ⁴The two were running side by side, but the other disciple ran faster than Peter and came to the tomb first. ⁵He bent over and looked inside the tomb. He saw the strips of linen lying there but didn't go inside.

⁶Simon Peter arrived after him and went into the tomb. He saw the strips of linen lying there. ⁷He also saw the cloth that had been on Jesus' head. It wasn't lying with the strips of linen but was rolled up separately. ⁸Then the other disciple, who arrived at the tomb first, went inside. He saw and believed. ⁹They didn't know yet what Scripture meant when it said that Jesus had to come back to life. ¹⁰So the disciples went back home.

¹¹Mary, however, stood there and cried as she looked at the tomb. As she cried, she bent over and looked inside. ¹²She saw two angels in white clothes. They were sitting where the body of Jesus had been lying. One angel was where Jesus' head had been, and the other was where his feet had been. ¹³The angels asked her why she was crying.

Mary told them, "They have removed my Lord, and I don't know where they've put him."

¹⁴After she said this, she turned around and saw Jesus standing there. However, she didn't know that it was Jesus. ¹⁵Jesus asked her, "Why are you crying? Who are you looking for?"

Mary thought it was the gardener speaking to her. So she said to him, "Sir, if you carried him away, tell me where you have put him, and I'll remove him."

¹⁶ Jesus said to her, "Mary!"

Mary turned around and said to him in Hebrew, "Rabboni!" (This word means "teacher.")

¹⁷ Jesus told her, "Don't hold on to me. I have not yet gone to the Father. But go to my brothers and sisters and tell them, 'I am going to my Father and your Father, to my God and your God.'"

¹⁸ Mary from Magdala went to the disciples and told them, "I have seen the Lord." She also told them what he had said to her.

JESUS APPEARS TO HIS DISCIPLES

John 20:19

19 That Sunday evening, the disciples were together behind locked doors because they were afraid of the Jews. Jesus stood among them and said to them, "Peace be with you!"

Luke 24:37-45

37 They were terrified, and thought they were seeing a ghost.

38 He asked them, "Why are you afraid? Why do you have doubts? **39** Look at my hands and feet, and see that it's really me. Touch me, and see for yourselves. Ghosts don't have flesh and bones, but you can see that I do." **40** As he said this, he showed them his hands and feet.

41 The disciples were overcome with joy and amazement because this seemed too good to be true. Then Jesus asked them, "Do you have anything to eat?" **42** They gave him a piece of broiled fish. **43** He took it and ate it while they watched him.

44 Then he said to them, "These are the words I spoke to you while I was still with you. I told you that everything written about me in Moses' Teachings, the Prophets, and the Psalms had to come true." **45** Then he opened their minds to understand the Scriptures.

John 20:21-23

21 Jesus said to them again, "Peace be with you! As the Father has sent me, so I am sending you." **22** After he had said this, he breathed on the disciples and said, "Receive the Holy Spirit. **23** Whenever you forgive sins, they are forgiven. Whenever you don't forgive them, they are not forgiven."

359

THE STORY OF THOMAS AND HIS FAITH

John 20:24-29

²⁴ Thomas, one of the twelve apostles, who was called Didymus, wasn't with them when Jesus came. ²⁵ The other disciples told him, "We've seen the Lord."

Thomas told them, "I refuse to believe this unless I see the nail marks in his hands, put my fingers into them, and put my hand into his side."

²⁶ A week later Jesus' disciples were again in the house, and Thomas was with them. Even though the doors were locked, Jesus stood among them and said, "Peace be with you!" ²⁷ Then Jesus said to Thomas, "Put your finger here, and look at my hands. Take your hand, and put it into my side. Stop doubting, and believe."

²⁸ Thomas responded to Jesus, "My Lord and my God!"

²⁹ Jesus said to Thomas, "You believe because you've seen me. Blessed are those who haven't seen me but believe."

BREAKFAST BY THE SEA

John 21:1-14

¹ Later, by the Sea of Tiberias, Jesus showed himself again to the disciples. This is what happened. ² Simon Peter, Thomas (called Didymus), Nathanael from Cana in Galilee, Zebedee's sons, and two other disciples of Jesus were together. ³ Simon Peter said to the others, "I'm going fishing."

They told him, "We're going with you."

They went out in a boat but didn't catch a thing that night. ⁴ As the sun was rising, Jesus stood on the shore. The disciples didn't realize that it was Jesus.

⁵ Jesus asked them, "Friends, haven't you caught any fish?"

They answered him, "No, we haven't."

⁶ He told them, "Throw the net out on the right side of the boat, and you'll catch some." So they threw the net out and were unable to pull it in because so many fish were in it.

⁷ The disciple whom Jesus loved said to Peter, "It's the Lord." When Simon Peter heard that it was the Lord, he put back on the clothes that he had taken off and jumped into the sea. ⁸ The other disciples came with the boat and dragged the net full of fish. They weren't far from the shore, only about 100 yards.

⁹When they went ashore, they saw a fire with a fish lying on the coals, and they saw a loaf of bread.

¹⁰Jesus told them, "Bring some of the fish you've just caught." ¹¹Simon Peter got into the boat and pulled the net ashore. Though the net was filled with 153 large fish, it was not torn.

¹²Jesus told them, "Come, have breakfast." None of the disciples dared to ask him who he was. They knew he was the Lord. ¹³Jesus took the bread, gave it to them, and did the same with the fish.

¹⁴This was the third time that Jesus showed himself to the disciples after he had come back to life.

DO YOU REALLY LOVE ME?

John 21:15-19

¹⁵ After they had eaten breakfast, Jesus asked Simon Peter, "Simon, son of John, do you love me more than the other disciples do?"

Peter answered him, "Yes, Lord, you know that I love you."

Jesus told him, "Feed my lambs."

¹⁶ Jesus asked him again, a second time, "Simon, son of John, do you love me?"

Peter answered him, "Yes, Lord, you know that I love you."

Jesus told him, "Take care of my sheep."

¹⁷ Jesus asked him a third time, "Simon, son of John, do you love me?"

Peter felt sad because Jesus had asked him a third time, "Do you love me?" So Peter said to him, "Lord, you know everything. You know that I love you."

Jesus told him, "Feed my sheep. ¹⁸ I can guarantee this truth: When you were young, you would get ready to go where you wanted. But when you're old, you will stretch out your hands, and someone else will get you ready to take you where you don't want to go." ¹⁹ Jesus said this to show by what kind of death Peter would bring glory to God. After saying this, Jesus told Peter, "Follow me!"

JESUS ASCENDS INTO HEAVEN AND GOES HOME TO THE FATHER

Acts 1:3-11

³After his death Jesus showed the apostles a lot of convincing evidence that he was alive. For 40 days he appeared to them and talked with them about God's kingdom.

⁴Once, while he was meeting with them, he ordered them not to leave Jerusalem but to wait there for what the Father had promised. Jesus said to them, "I've told you what the Father promises: ⁵John baptized with water, but in a few days you will be baptized with the Holy Spirit."

⁶So when the apostles came together, they asked him, "Lord, is this the time when you're going to restore the kingdom to Israel?"

⁷Jesus told them, "You don't need to know about times or periods that the Father has determined by his own authority. ⁸But you will receive power when the Holy Spirit comes to you. Then you will be my witnesses to testify about me in Jerusalem, throughout Judea and Samaria, and to the ends of the earth."

⁹After he had said this, he was taken to heaven. A cloud hid him so that they could no longer see him.

¹⁰They were staring into the sky as he departed. Suddenly, two men in white clothes stood near them. ¹¹They asked, "Why are you men from Galilee standing here looking at the sky? Jesus, who was taken from you to heaven, will come back in the same way that you saw him go to heaven."

JESUS WILL SEND THE HOLY SPIRIT –
THE HELPER – TO EVERYONE
WHO BELIEVES IN HIM

Acts 2:1-17

[1] When Pentecost, the fiftieth day after Passover, came, all the believers were together in one place. [2] Suddenly, a sound like a violently blowing wind came from the sky and filled the whole house where they were staying. [3] Tongues that looked like fire appeared to them. The tongues arranged themselves so that one came to rest on each believer. [4] All the believers were filled with the Holy Spirit and began to speak in other languages as the Spirit gave them the ability to speak.

[5] Devout Jewish men from every nation were living in Jerusalem. [6] They gathered when they heard the wind. Each person was startled to recognize his own dialect when the disciples spoke.

[7] Stunned and amazed, the people in the crowd said, "All of these men who are speaking are Galileans. [8] Why do we hear them speaking in our native dialects? [9] We're Parthians, Medes, and Elamites. We're people from Mesopotamia, Judea, Cappadocia, Pontus, the province of Asia, [10] Phrygia, Pamphylia, Egypt, and the country near Cyrene in Libya. We're Jewish people, converts to Judaism, and visitors from Rome, [11] Crete, and Arabia. We hear these men in our own languages as they tell about the miracles that God has done."

[12] All of these devout men were stunned and puzzled. They asked each other, "What can this mean?" [13] Others said jokingly, "They're drunk on sweet wine."

[14] Then Peter stood up with the eleven apostles. In a loud voice he said to them, "Men of Judea and everyone living in Jerusalem! You must understand this, so pay attention to what I say. [15] These men are not drunk as you suppose. It's only nine in the morning. [16] Rather, this is what the prophet Joel spoke about:

[17] 'In the last days, God says,
    I will pour my Spirit on everyone.
      Your sons and daughters
         will speak what God
         has revealed.
      Your young men will see visions.
      Your old men will dream dreams.

THE APOSTLES HEAL AND TEACH

Acts 2:43-47; 3:1-8

⁴³ A feeling of fear came over everyone as many amazing things and miraculous signs happened through the apostles. ⁴⁴ All the believers kept meeting together, and they shared everything with each other. ⁴⁵ From time to time, they sold their property and other possessions and distributed the money to anyone who needed it. ⁴⁶ The believers had a single purpose and went to the temple every day. They were joyful and humble as they ate at each other's homes and shared their food. ⁴⁷ At the same time, they praised God and had the good will of all the people. Every day the Lord saved people, and they were added to the group.

Acts 3:1-8

¹ Peter and John were going to the temple courtyard for the three o'clock prayer. ² At the same time, a man who had been lame from birth was being carried by some men. Every day these men would put the lame man at a gate in the temple courtyard. The gate was called Beautiful Gate. There he would beg for handouts from people going into the courtyard. ³ When the man saw that Peter and John were about to go into the courtyard, he asked them for a handout.

⁴ Peter and John stared at him. "Look at us!" Peter said. ⁵ So the man watched them closely. He expected to receive something from them. ⁶ However, Peter said to him, "I don't have any money, but I'll give you what I do have. Through the power of Jesus Christ from Nazareth, walk!" ⁷ Peter took hold of the man's right hand and began to help him up. Immediately, the man's feet and ankles became strong. ⁸ Springing to his feet, he stood up and started to walk. He went with Peter and John into the temple courtyard. The man was walking, jumping, and praising God.

PETER AND JOHN IN TROUBLE

Acts 3:11-4:22

[11] They were excited, and everyone ran to see them at the place called Solomon's Porch. The man wouldn't let go of Peter and John.

[12] When Peter saw this, he said to the people, "Men of Israel, why are you amazed about this man? Why are you staring at us as though we have made him walk by our own power or godly life? [13] The God of our ancestors Abraham, Isaac, and Jacob has glorified his servant Jesus. You handed Jesus over to Pilate. You rejected him in Pilate's presence, even though Pilate had decided to let him go free. [14] You rejected the man who was holy and innocent. You asked to have a murderer given to you, [15] and you killed the source of life. But God brought him back to life, and we are witnesses to that. [16] We believe in the one named Jesus. Through his power alone this man, whom you know, was healed, as all of you saw.

[17] "And now, brothers, I know that like your rulers you didn't know what you were doing. [18] But in this way God made the sufferings of his Messiah come true. God had predicted these sufferings through all the prophets. [19] So change the way you think and act, and turn ⸢to God⸥ to have your sins removed. [20] Then times will come when the Lord will refresh you. He will send you Jesus, whom he has appointed to be the Christ. [21] Heaven must receive Jesus until the time when everything will be restored as God promised through his holy prophets long ago.

[22] "Moses said, 'The Lord your God will send you a prophet, an Israelite like me. Listen to everything he tells you. [23] Those who won't listen to that prophet will be excluded from the people.' [24] Samuel and all the prophets who followed him spoke about these days. [25] You are the descendants of the prophets and the heirs of the promise that God made to our ancestors when he said to Abraham, 'Through your descendant all people on earth will be blessed.' [26] God has brought his servant back to life and has sent him to you first. God did this to bless you by turning every one of you from your evil ways."

¹Some priests, the officer in charge of the temple guards, and some Sadducees approached Peter and John while they were speaking to the people. ²These religious authorities were greatly annoyed. Peter and John were teaching the people and spreading the message that the dead will come back to life through Jesus. ³So the temple guards arrested them. Since it was already evening, they put Peter and John in jail until the next day.

⁴But many of those who had heard the message became believers, so the number of men who believed grew to about 5,000.

⁵The next day the Jewish rulers, the leaders, and the experts in Moses' Teachings met in Jerusalem. ⁶The chief priest Annas, Caiaphas, John, Alexander, and the rest of the chief priest's family were present. ⁷They made Peter and John stand in front of them and then asked, "By what power or in whose name did you do this?"

⁸Then Peter, because he was filled with the Holy Spirit, said to them, "Rulers and leaders of the people, ⁹today you are cross-examining us about the good we did for a crippled man. You want to know how he was made well. ¹⁰You and all the people of Israel must understand that this man stands in your presence with a healthy body because of the power of Jesus Christ from Nazareth. You crucified Jesus Christ, but God has brought him back to life. ¹¹He is the stone that the builders rejected, the stone that has become the cornerstone. ¹²No one else can save us. Indeed, we can be saved only by the power of the one named Jesus and not by any other person."

¹³After they found out that Peter and John had no education or special training, they were surprised to see how boldly they spoke. They realized that these men had been with Jesus. ¹⁴When they saw the man who was healed standing with Peter and John, they couldn't say anything against the two apostles. ¹⁵So they ordered Peter and John to leave the council room and began to discuss the matter among themselves. ¹⁶They said, "What should we do to these men? Clearly, they've performed a miracle that everyone in Jerusalem knows about. We can't deny that. ¹⁷So let's threaten them. Let's tell them that they must never speak to anyone about the one named Jesus. Then the news about the miracle that they have performed will not spread any further among the people."

¹⁸They called Peter and John and ordered them never to teach about Jesus or even mention his name.

¹⁹Peter and John answered them, "Decide for yourselves whether God wants people to listen to you rather than to him. ²⁰We cannot stop talking about what we've seen and heard."

²¹The authorities threatened them even more and then let them go. Since all the people were praising God for what had happened, the authorities couldn't find any way to punish Peter and John. ²²(The man who was healed by this miracle was over 40 years old.)

AN ANGEL FREES THE APOSTLES

Acts 5:12-20

[12] The people saw the apostles perform many miracles and do amazing things. The believers had a common faith in Jesus as they met on Solomon's Porch. [13] None of the other people dared to join them, although everyone spoke highly of them. [14] More men and women than ever began to believe in the Lord. [15] As a result, people carried their sick into the streets. They placed them on stretchers and cots so that at least Peter's shadow might fall on some sick people as he went by. [16] Crowds from the cities around Jerusalem would gather. They would bring their sick and those who were troubled by evil spirits, and each person was cured.

[17] The chief priest and the whole party of the Sadducees who were with him were extremely jealous. So they took action [18] by arresting the apostles and putting them in the city jail. [19] But at night an angel from the Lord opened the doors to their cell and led them out of the prison. [20] The angel told them, "Stand in the temple courtyard, and tell the people everything about life ⌊in Christ⌋."

THE APOSTLES ARE QUESTIONED

Acts 5:21-42

[21] Early in the morning, after they had listened to the angel, the apostles went into the temple courtyard and began to teach.

The chief priest and those who were with him called together the Jewish council, that is, all the leaders of Israel. They also sent men to the prison to get the apostles. [22] When the temple guards arrived at the prison, they didn't find the apostles. The guards came back and reported, [23] "We found the prison securely locked and the guards standing at the doors. However, when we opened the doors, we found no one inside." [24] When the officer of the temple guards and the chief priests heard this, they were puzzled about what could have happened.

[25] Then someone told them, "The men you put in prison are standing in the temple courtyard. They're teaching the people."

[26] Then the officer of the temple guards went with some of his men to bring back the apostles without using force. After all, the officer and his guards were afraid that the people would stone them to death for using force. [27] When they brought back the apostles, they made them stand in front of the council. The chief priest questioned them. [28] He said, "We gave you strict orders not to mention Jesus' name when you teach. Yet, you've filled Jerusalem with your teachings.

You want to take revenge on us for putting that man to death."

²⁹ Peter and the other apostles answered, "We must obey God rather than people. ³⁰ You murdered Jesus by hanging him on a cross. But the God of our ancestors brought him back to life. ³¹ God used his power to give Jesus the honored position—the one next to him on the heavenly throne as leader and savior. He did this to lead the people of Israel to him, to change the way they think and act, and to forgive their sins. ³² We are witnesses to these things, and so is the Holy Spirit, whom God has given to those who obey him."

³³ When the men on the council heard this, they became furious and wanted to execute the apostles. ³⁴ But a Pharisee named Gamaliel stood up. He was a highly respected expert in Moses' Teachings. He ordered that the apostles should be taken outside for a little while.

³⁵ Then he said to the council, "Men of Israel, consider carefully what you do with these men. ³⁶ Some time ago Theudas appeared. He claimed that he was important, and about four hundred men joined him. He was killed, and all his followers were scattered. The whole movement was a failure.

³⁷ "After that man, at the time of the census, Judas from Galilee appeared and led people in a revolt. He, too, died, and all his followers were scattered.

³⁸ "We should keep away from these men for now. We should leave them alone. I can guarantee that if the plan they put into action is of human origin, it will fail. ³⁹ However, if it's from God, you won't be able to stop them. You may even discover that you're fighting against God."

⁴⁰ The council took his advice. They called the apostles, beat them, ordered them not to speak about the one named Jesus, and let them go.

⁴¹ The apostles left the council room. They were happy to have been considered worthy to suffer dishonor for speaking about Jesus. ⁴² Every day in the temple courtyard and from house to house, they refused to stop teaching and telling the Good News that Jesus is the Messiah.

STEPHEN IS NOT AFRAID OF DEATH

Acts 6:8-7:60

8 Stephen was a man filled with God's favor and power. He did amazing things and performed miracles. **9** ⌊One day⌋ some men from the cities of Cyrene and Alexandria and the provinces of Cilicia and Asia started an argument with Stephen. They belonged to a synagogue called Freedmen's Synagogue. **10** They couldn't argue with Stephen because he spoke with the wisdom that the Spirit had given him. **11** Then they bribed some men to lie.

These men said, "We heard him slander Moses and God." **12** The liars stirred up trouble among the people, the leaders, and the experts in Moses' Teachings. So they went to Stephen, took him by force, and brought him in front of the Jewish council. **13** Some witnesses stood up and lied about Stephen. They said, "This man never stops saying bad things about the holy place and Moses' Teachings. **14** We heard him say that Jesus from Nazareth will destroy the temple and change the customs that Moses gave us."

15 Everyone who sat in the council stared at him and saw that his face looked like an angel's face.

1 Then the chief priest asked Stephen, "Is this true?" **2** Stephen answered, "Brothers and fathers, listen to me. The God who reveals his glory appeared to our ancestor Abraham in Mesopotamia. This happened before Abraham lived in Haran. **3** God told him, 'Leave your land and your relatives. Go to the land that I will show you.'

4 "Then Abraham left the country of Chaldea and lived in the city of Haran. After his father died, God made him move from there to this land where we now live.

5 "Yet, God didn't give Abraham anything in this land to call his own, not even a place to rest his feet. But God promised to give this land to him and to his descendants, even though Abraham didn't have a child. **6** God told Abraham that his descendants would be foreigners living in another country and that the people there would make them slaves and mistreat them for 400 years. **7** God also told him, 'I will punish the people whom they will serve. After that, they will leave that country and worship me here.'

"God gave Abraham circumcision to confirm his promise. So when Abraham's son Isaac was born, Abraham circumcised him on the eighth day. Isaac did the same to his son Jacob, and Jacob did the same to his twelve sons (the ancestors of our tribes).

⁹ "Jacob's sons were jealous of their brother Joseph. They sold him into slavery, and he was taken to Egypt. But God was with Joseph ¹⁰ and rescued him from all his suffering. When Joseph stood in the presence of Pharaoh (the king of Egypt), God gave Joseph divine favor and wisdom so that he became ruler of Egypt and of Pharaoh's whole palace. ¹¹ Then a famine throughout Egypt and Canaan brought a lot of suffering. Our ancestors couldn't find any food. ¹² When Jacob heard that Egypt had food, he sent our ancestors there. That was their first trip. ¹³ On the second trip, Joseph told his brothers who he was, and Pharaoh learned about Joseph's family. ¹⁴ Joseph sent for his father Jacob and his relatives, 75 people in all. ¹⁵ So Jacob went to Egypt, and he and our ancestors died there. ¹⁶ They were taken to Shechem for burial in the tomb that Abraham purchased in Shechem from Hamor's sons.

¹⁷ "When the time that God had promised to Abraham had almost come, the number of our people in Egypt had grown very large. ¹⁸ Then a different king, who knew nothing about Joseph, began to rule in Egypt. ¹⁹ This king was shrewd in the way he took advantage of our people. He mistreated our ancestors. He made them abandon their newborn babies outdoors, where they would die.

²⁰ "At that time Moses was born, and he was a very beautiful child. His parents took care of him for three months. ²¹ When Moses was abandoned outdoors, Pharaoh's daughter adopted him and raised him as her son. ²² So Moses was educated in all the wisdom of the Egyptians and became a great man in what he said and did. ²³ When he was 40 years old, he decided to visit his own people, the Israelites. ²⁴ When he saw an Israelite man being treated unfairly by an Egyptian, he defended the Israelite. He took revenge by killing the Egyptian. ²⁵ Moses thought his own people would understand that God was going to use him to give them freedom. But they didn't understand. ²⁶ The next day Moses saw two Israelites fighting, and he tried to make peace between them. He said to them, 'Men, you are brothers. Why are you treating each other unfairly?'

²⁷ "But one of the men pushed Moses aside. He asked Moses, 'Who made you our ruler and judge? ²⁸ Do you want to kill me as you killed the Egyptian yesterday?' ²⁹ After he said that, Moses quickly left Egypt and lived in Midian as a foreigner. In Midian he fathered two sons.

³⁰ "Forty years later, a Messenger appeared to him in the flames of a burning bush in the desert of Mount Sinai. ³¹ Moses was surprised when he saw this. As he went closer to look at the bush, the voice of the Lord said to him, ³² 'I am the God of your ancestors—the God of Abraham, Isaac, and Jacob.' Moses began to tremble and didn't dare to look at the bush. ³³ The Lord told him, 'Take off your sandals. The place where you're standing is holy ground. ³⁴ I've seen how my people are mistreated in Egypt. I've heard their groaning and have come to rescue them. So now I'm sending you to Egypt.'

³⁵ "This is the Moses whom the Israelites rejected by saying, 'Who made you our ruler and judge?' This is the one God sent to free them and to rule them with the help of the Messenger who appeared to him in the bush. ³⁶ This is the man who led our ancestors out of Egypt. He is the person who did amazing things and worked miracles in Egypt, at the Red Sea, and in the desert for 40 years. ³⁷ This is the same Moses who told the Israelites, 'God will send you a prophet, an Israelite

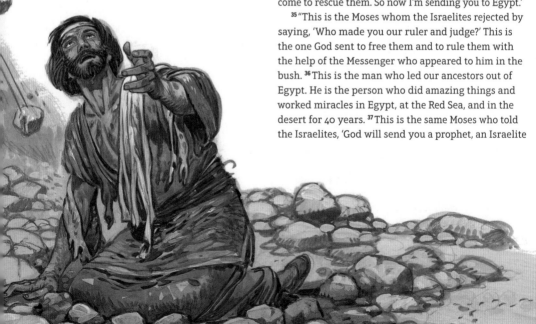

like me.' [38] This is the Moses who was in the assembly in the desert. Our ancestors and the Messenger who spoke to him on Mount Sinai were there with him. Moses received life-giving messages to give to us, [39] but our ancestors were not willing to obey him. Instead, they pushed him aside, and in their hearts they turned back to Egypt. [40] They told Aaron, 'We don't know what has happened to this Moses, who led us out of Egypt. So make gods who will lead us.' [41] That was the time they made a calf. They offered a sacrifice to that false god and delighted in what they had made.

[42] "So God turned away from them and let them worship the sun, moon, and stars. This is written in the book of the prophets: 'Did you bring me sacrifices and grain offerings in the desert for 40 years, nation of Israel? [43] You carried along the shrine of Moloch, the star of the god Rephan, and the statues you made for yourselves to worship. I will send you into exile beyond the city of Babylon.'

[44] "In the desert our ancestors had the tent of God's promise. Moses built this tent exactly as God had told him. He used the model he had seen. [45] After our ancestors received the tent, they brought it into this land. They did this with Joshua's help when they took possession of the land from the nations that God forced out of our ancestors' way. This tent remained here until the time of David, [46] who won God's favor. David asked that he might provide a permanent place for the family of Jacob. [47] But Solomon was the one who built a house for God.

[48] "However, the Most High doesn't live in a house built by humans, as the prophet says:

[49] 'The Lord says,
  "Heaven is my throne.
  The earth is my footstool.
    What kind of house are you going
        to build for me?
    Where will I rest?
[50] Didn't I make all these things?"'

[51] "How stubborn can you be? How can you be so heartless and disobedient? You're just like your ancestors. They always opposed the Holy Spirit, and so do you! [52] Was there ever a prophet your ancestors didn't persecute? They killed those who predicted that a man with God's approval would come. You have now become the people who betrayed and murdered that man. [53] You are the people who received Moses' Teachings, which were put into effect by angels. But you haven't obeyed those teachings."

[54] As council members listened to Stephen, they became noticeably furious. [55] But Stephen was full of the Holy Spirit. He looked into heaven, saw God's glory, and Jesus in the honored position—the one next to God the Father on the heavenly throne. [56] So Stephen said, "Look, I see heaven opened and the Son of Man in the honored position—the one next to God the Father on the throne!"

[57] But the council members shouted and refused to listen. Then they rushed at Stephen with one purpose in mind, [58] and after they had thrown him out of the city, they began to stone him to death. The witnesses left their coats with a young man named Saul.

[59] While council members were executing Stephen, he called out, "Lord Jesus, welcome my spirit." [60] Then he knelt down and shouted, "Lord, don't hold this sin against them." After he had said this, he died

SAUL ON THE ROAD TO DAMASCUS

Acts 8:1-3

[1] Saul approved of putting Stephen to death.

On that day widespread persecution broke out against the church in Jerusalem. Most believers, except the apostles, were scattered throughout Judea and Samaria.

[2] Devout men buried Stephen as they mourned loudly for him.

[3] Saul tried to destroy the church. He dragged men and women out of one home after another and threw them into prison.

Acts 9:1-18

[1] Saul kept threatening to murder the Lord's disciples. He went to the chief priest [2] and asked him to write letters of authorization to the synagogue leaders in the city of Damascus. Saul wanted to arrest any man or woman who followed the way ⌐of Christ⌐ and imprison them in Jerusalem.

[3] As Saul was coming near the city of Damascus, a light from heaven suddenly flashed around him. [4] He fell to the ground and heard a voice say to him, "Saul! Saul! Why are you persecuting me?"

[5] Saul asked, "Who are you, sir?"

The person replied, "I'm Jesus, the one you're persecuting. [6] Get up! Go into the city, and you'll be told what you should do."

[7] Meanwhile, the men traveling with him were speechless. They heard the voice but didn't see anyone.

[8] Saul was helped up from the ground. When he opened his eyes, he was blind. So his companions led him into Damascus. [9] For three days he couldn't see and didn't eat or drink.

375

[10] A disciple named Ananias lived in the city of Damascus. The Lord said to him in a vision, "Ananias!"

Ananias answered, "Yes, Lord."

[11] The Lord told him, "Get up! Go to Judas' house on Straight Street, and ask for a man named Saul from the city of Tarsus. He's praying. [12] In a vision he has seen a man named Ananias place his hands on him to restore his sight."

[13] Ananias replied, "Lord, I've heard a lot of people tell about the many evil things this man has done to your people in Jerusalem. [14] Saul has come here to Damascus with authority from the chief priests to put anyone who calls on your name in prison."

[15] The Lord told Ananias, "Go! I've chosen this man to bring my name to nations, to kings, and to the people of Israel. [16] I'll show him how much he has to suffer for the sake of my name."

[17] Ananias left and entered Judas' house. After he placed his hands on Saul, Ananias said, "Brother Saul, the Lord Jesus, who appeared to you on your way to Damascus, sent me to you. He wants you to see again and to be filled with the Holy Spirit."

[18] Immediately, something like fish scales fell from Saul's eyes, and he could see again. Then Saul stood up and was baptized.

PETER AND CORNELIUS ARE GIVEN DIVINE VISIONS

Acts 10:1-16

[1] A man named Cornelius lived in the city of Caesarea. He was a Roman army officer in the Italian Regiment. [2] He and everyone in his home were devout and respected God. Cornelius gave many gifts to poor Jewish people and always prayed to God.

[3] One day, about three in the afternoon, he had a vision. He clearly saw an angel from God come to him and say, "Cornelius!"

[4] He stared at the angel and was terrified. Cornelius asked the angel, "What do you want, sir?"

The angel answered him, "God is aware of your prayers and your gifts to the poor, and he has remembered you. [5] Send messengers now to the city of Joppa, and summon a man whose name is Simon Peter. [6] He is a guest of Simon, a leatherworker, whose house is by the sea."

[7] After saying this, the angel left. Cornelius called two of his household servants and a devout soldier, one of those who served him regularly. [8] Cornelius explained everything to them and sent them to Joppa.

⁹ Around noon the next day, while Cornelius' men were on their way and coming close to Joppa, Peter went on the roof to pray. ¹⁰ He became hungry and wanted to eat. While the food was being prepared, he fell into a trance. ¹¹ He saw the sky open and something like a large linen sheet being lowered by its four corners to the ground. ¹² In the sheet were all kinds of four-footed animals, reptiles, and birds.

¹³ A voice told him, "Get up, Peter! Kill these animals, and eat them."

¹⁴ Peter answered, "I can't do that, Lord! I've never eaten anything that is impure or unclean."

¹⁵ A voice spoke to him a second time, "Don't say that the things which God has made clean are impure."

¹⁶ This happened three times. Then the sheet was quickly taken into the sky

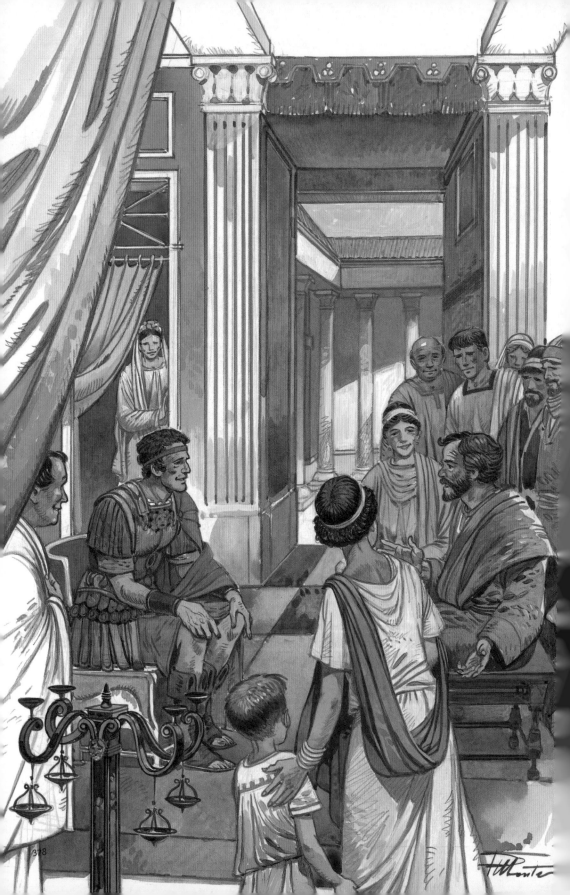

PETER VISITS AN ARMY OFFICER

Acts 10:19-45

¹⁹ Peter was still thinking about the vision when the Spirit said to him, "Three men are looking for you. ²⁰ Get up, and go downstairs. Don't hesitate to go with these men. I have sent them."

²¹ So Peter went to the men. He said, "I'm the man you're looking for. Why are you here?"

²² The men replied, "Cornelius, a Roman army officer, sent us. He's a man who has God's approval and who respects God. Also, the Jewish people respect him. A holy angel told him to summon you to his home to hear what you have to say."

²³ Peter asked the men to come into the house and had them stay overnight.

The next day Peter left with them. Some disciples from Joppa went along. ²⁴ The following day they arrived in Caesarea. Cornelius was expecting them and had called his relatives and close friends together.

²⁵ When Peter was about to enter Cornelius' house, Cornelius met him, bowed down, and worshiped Peter. ²⁶ But Peter made him get up. He told him, "Stand up! I'm only a man."

²⁷ As Peter talked, he entered Cornelius' house and found that many people had gathered. ²⁸ He said to them, "You understand how wrong it is for a Jewish man to associate or visit with anyone of another race. But God has shown me that I should no longer call anyone impure or unclean. ²⁹ That is why I didn't object to coming here when you sent for me. I want to know why you sent for me."

³⁰ Cornelius answered, "Four days ago I was praying at home. It was at this same time, three o'clock in the afternoon. Suddenly, a man dressed in radiant clothes stood in front of me. ³¹ He said to me, 'Cornelius, God has heard your prayer and has remembered your gifts to the poor. ³² So send messengers to Joppa, and summon a man whose name is Simon Peter. He's a guest in the home of Simon, a leatherworker who lives by the sea.' ³³ So I sent for you immediately. Thank you for coming. All of us are here now in the presence of God to listen to everything the Lord has ordered you to say."

³⁴ Then Peter said, "Now I understand that God doesn't play favorites. ³⁵ Rather, whoever respects God and does what is right is acceptable to him in any nation. ³⁶ God sent his word to the people of Israel and brought them the Good News of peace through Jesus Christ. This Jesus Christ is everyone's Lord. ³⁷ You know what happened throughout Judea. Everything began in Galilee after John spread the news about baptism. ³⁸ You know that God anointed Jesus from Nazareth with the Holy Spirit and with power. Jesus went everywhere and did good things, such as healing everyone who was under the devil's power. Jesus did these things because God was with him. ³⁹ We can testify to everything Jesus did in the land of the Jews and in Jerusalem. People hung him on a cross and killed him, ⁴⁰ but God brought him back to life on the third day. God didn't show him ⁴¹ to all the people. He showed Jesus to witnesses, apostles he had already chosen. We apostles are those men who ate and drank with Jesus after he came back to life. ⁴² He ordered us to warn the people, 'God has appointed Jesus to judge the living and the dead.' ⁴³ In addition, all the prophets testify that people who believe in the one named Jesus receive forgiveness for their sins through him."

⁴⁴ While Peter was still speaking, the Holy Spirit came to everyone who heard his message. ⁴⁵ All the believers who were circumcised and who had come with Peter were amazed that the gift of the Holy Spirit had been poured on people who were not Jewish.

JESUS ANNOUNCES THAT THE GOOD NEWS IS FOR EVERYONE

Acts 11:1-4

¹ The apostles and the believers throughout Judea heard that people who were not Jewish had accepted God's word. ² However, when Peter went to Jerusalem, the believers who insisted on circumcision began to argue with him. ³ They said, "You went to visit men who were uncircumcised, and you even ate with them."

⁴ Then Peter began to explain to them point by point what had happened. He said,

Acts 11:18

¹⁸ When the others heard this, they had no further objections. They praised God by saying, "Then God has also led people who are not Jewish to turn to him so that they can change the way they think and act and have eternal life."

PETER ESCAPES FROM PRISON

Acts 12:1-17

[1] About that time King Herod devoted his attention to mistreating certain members of the church. [2] He had James, the brother of John, executed. [3] When he saw how this pleased the Jews, he arrested Peter too. This happened during the days of Unleavened Bread. [4] After capturing Peter, Herod had him thrown into prison with sixteen soldiers in squads of four to guard him. Herod wanted to bring Peter to trial in front of the people after Passover. [5] So Peter was kept in prison, but the church was praying very hard to God for him.

[6] The night before Herod was going to bring Peter to trial, Peter was sleeping between two soldiers. His hands were bound with two chains, and guards were in front of the door. They were watching the prison.

[7] Suddenly, an angel from the Lord stood near Peter, and his cell was filled with light. The angel nudged Peter's side, woke him up, and said, "Hurry! Get up!" At that moment the chains fell from Peter's hands.

[8] The angel told him, "Put your shoes on, and get ready to go!" Peter did this. Then the angel told him, "Put your coat on, and follow me."

[9] Peter followed the angel out of the cell. He didn't realize that what the angel was doing was actually happening. He thought he was seeing a vision. [10] They passed the first and second guardposts and came to the iron gate that led into the city. This gate opened by itself for them, so they went outside and up the street. The angel suddenly left Peter.

[11] When Peter came to his senses, he said, "Now I'm sure that the Lord sent his angel to rescue me from Herod and from everything the Jewish people are expecting to happen to me."

[12] When Peter realized what had happened, he went to the home of Mary, the mother of John Mark. Many people had gathered at her home and were praying. [13] Peter knocked on the door of the entryway, and a servant named Rhoda came to answer. [14] When she recognized Peter's voice, she was so happy that instead of opening the door, she ran back inside and reported, "Peter is standing at the door!"

[15] The people told her, "You're crazy!" But she insisted that Peter was at the door. They said, "It has to be his angel."

[16] But Peter kept knocking. When they opened the door, they were shocked to see him. [17] Peter motioned with his hand to quiet them down and told them how the Lord had taken him out of prison. He added, "Tell James and the other believers about this." Then he left and went somewhere else.

PAUL BECOMES A PREACHER AND DEFENDER OF THE GOOD NEWS

Acts 14:8-20

⁸ A man who was born lame was in Lystra. He was always sitting because he had never been able to walk. ⁹ He listened to what Paul was saying. Paul observed him closely and saw that the man believed he could be made well. ¹⁰ So Paul said in a loud voice, "Stand up." The man jumped up and began to walk.

¹¹ The crowds who saw what Paul had done shouted in the Lycaonian language, "The gods have come to us, and they look human." ¹² They addressed Barnabas as Zeus and Paul as Hermes because Paul did most of the talking. ¹³ Zeus' temple was at the entrance to the city. The priest of the god Zeus brought bulls with flowery wreaths around their necks to the temple gates. The priest and the crowd wanted to offer a sacrifice ⌊to Paul and Barnabas⌋.

¹⁴ When the apostles Barnabas and Paul heard what was happening, they were very upset. They rushed into the crowd ¹⁵ and said, "Men, what are you doing? We're human beings like you. We're spreading the Good News to you to turn you away from these worthless gods to the living God. The living God made the sky, the land, the sea, and everything in them. ¹⁶ In the past God allowed all people to live as they pleased. ¹⁷ Yet, by doing good, he has given evidence of his existence. He gives you rain from heaven and crops in their seasons. He fills you with food and your lives with happiness." ¹⁸ Although Paul and Barnabas said these things, they hardly kept the crowd from sacrificing to them.

¹⁹ However, Jews from the cities of Antioch and Iconium arrived in Lystra and won the people over. They tried to stone Paul to death and dragged him out of the city when they thought that he was dead. ²⁰ But when the disciples gathered around him, he got up and went back into the city.

PAUL AND SILAS PREACH AND PERFORM MIRACLES IN THE ROMAN PRISON

Acts 16:16-34

¹⁶ One day when we were going to the place of prayer, a female servant met us. She was possessed by an evil spirit that told fortunes. She made a lot of money for her owners by telling fortunes. ¹⁷ She used to follow Paul and shout, "These men are servants of the Most High God. They're telling you how you can be saved." ¹⁸ She kept doing this for many days. Paul became annoyed, turned to the evil spirit, and said, "I command you in the name of Jesus Christ to come out of her!"

As Paul said this, the evil spirit left her. ¹⁹ When her owners realized that their hope of making money was gone, they grabbed Paul and Silas and dragged them to the authorities in the public square. ²⁰ In front of the Roman officials, they said, "These men are stirring up a lot of trouble in our city. They're Jews, ²¹ and they're advocating customs that we can't accept or practice as Roman citizens."

²² The crowd joined in the attack against Paul and Silas. Then the officials tore the clothes off Paul and Silas and ordered ⌞the guards⌟ to beat them with sticks. ²³ After they had hit Paul and Silas many times, they threw them in jail and ordered the jailer to keep them under tight security. ²⁴ So the jailer followed these orders and put Paul and Silas into solitary confinement with their feet in leg irons.

²⁵ Around midnight Paul and Silas were praying and singing hymns of praise to God. The other prisoners were listening to them. ²⁶ Suddenly, a violent earthquake shook the foundations of the jail. All the doors immediately flew open, and all the prisoners' chains came loose.

²⁷ The jailer woke up and saw the prison doors open. Thinking the prisoners had escaped, he drew his sword and was about to kill himself. ²⁸ But Paul shouted as loudly as he could, "Don't hurt yourself! We're all here!"

²⁹ The jailer asked for torches and rushed into the jail. He was trembling as he knelt in front of Paul and Silas. ³⁰ Then he took Paul and Silas outside and asked, "Sirs, what do I have to do to be saved?"

³¹ They answered, "Believe in the Lord Jesus, and you and your family will be saved." ³² They spoke the Lord's word to the jailer and everyone in his home.

³³ At that hour of the night, the jailer washed Paul and Silas' wounds. The jailer and his entire family were baptized immediately. ³⁴ He took Paul and Silas upstairs into his home and gave them something to eat. He and his family were thrilled to be believers in God.

PAUL IS WARNED

Acts 20:17-38

¹⁷ From Miletus Paul sent messengers to the city of Ephesus and called the spiritual leaders of the church to meet with him ⌊in Miletus⌋. ¹⁸ When they were with him, he said to them, "You know how I spent all my time with you from the first day I arrived in the province of Asia. ¹⁹ I humbly served the Lord, often with tears in my eyes. I served the Lord during the difficult times I went through when the Jews plotted against me. ²⁰ I didn't avoid telling you anything that would help you, and I didn't avoid teaching you publicly and from house to house. ²¹ I warned Jews and Greeks to change the way they think and act and to believe in our Lord Jesus.

²² "I am determined to go to Jerusalem now. I don't know what will happen to me there. ²³ However, the Holy Spirit warns me in every city that imprisonment and suffering are waiting for me. ²⁴ But I don't place any value on my own life. I want to finish the race I'm running. I want to carry out the mission I received from the Lord Jesus—the mission of testifying to the Good News of God's kindness.

²⁵ "Now I know that none of you whom I told about God's kingdom will see me again. ²⁶ Therefore, I declare to you today that I am not responsible for the ⌊spiritual⌋ death of any of you. ²⁷ I didn't avoid telling you the whole plan of God. ²⁸ Pay attention to yourselves and to the entire flock in which the Holy Spirit has placed you as bishops to be shepherds for God's church which he acquired with his own blood. ²⁹ I know that fierce wolves will come to you after I leave, and they won't spare the flock. ³⁰ Some of your own men will come forward and say things that distort the truth. They will do this to lure disciples into following them. ³¹ So be alert! Remember that I instructed each of you for three years, day and night, at times with tears in my eyes.

³² "I am now entrusting you to God and to his message that tells how kind he is. That message can help you grow and can give you the inheritance that is shared by all of God's holy people.

³³ "I never wanted anyone's silver, gold, or clothes. ³⁴ You know that I worked to support myself and those who were with me. ³⁵ I have given you an example that by working hard like this we should help the weak. We should remember the words that the Lord Jesus said, 'Giving gifts is more satisfying than receiving them.' "

³⁶ When Paul had finished speaking, he knelt down and prayed with all of them. ³⁷ Everyone cried a lot as they put their arms around Paul and kissed him. ³⁸ The thought of not seeing Paul again hurt them most of all. Then they took Paul to the ship.

PAUL SPEAKS TO THE MOB

Acts 21:27-36

²⁷ When the seven days were almost over, the Jews from the province of Asia saw Paul in the temple courtyard. They stirred up the whole crowd and grabbed Paul. ²⁸ Then they began shouting, "Men of Israel, help! This is the man who teaches everyone everywhere to turn against the Jewish people, Moses' Teachings, and this temple. He has even brought Greeks into the temple courtyard and has made this holy place unclean." ²⁹ They had seen Trophimus from Ephesus with him in the city earlier and thought Paul had taken him into the temple courtyard.

³⁰ The whole city was in chaos, and a mob formed. The mob grabbed Paul and dragged him out of the temple courtyard. The courtyard doors were immediately shut.

³¹ As the people were trying to kill Paul, the officer in charge of the Roman soldiers received a report that all Jerusalem was rioting. ³² Immediately, he took some soldiers and officers and charged the crowd. When the crowd saw the officer and the soldiers, they stopped beating Paul. ³³ Then the officer went to Paul, grabbed him, and ordered him to be tied up with two chains.

The officer asked who Paul was and what he had done. ³⁴ Some of the crowd shouted one thing, while others shouted something else. The officer couldn't get any facts because of the noise and confusion, so he ordered Paul to be taken into the barracks. ³⁵ When Paul came to the stairs of the barracks, the crowd was so violent that the soldiers had to carry him. ³⁶ The mob was behind them shouting, "Kill him!"

Acts 22:23-24

²³ The mob was yelling, taking off their coats, and throwing dirt into the air. ²⁴ So the officer ordered the soldiers to take Paul into the barracks and told them to question Paul as they whipped him. The officer wanted to find out why the people were yelling at Paul like this.

PAUL MUST DIE!

Acts 24:24-27

²⁴ Some days later Felix arrived with his wife Drusilla, who was Jewish. He sent for Paul and listened to him talk about faith in Christ Jesus. ²⁵ As Paul discussed the subjects of God's approval, self-control, and the coming judgment, Felix became afraid and said, "That's enough for now. You can go. When I find time, I'll send for you again." ²⁶ At the same time, Felix was hoping that Paul would give him some money. For that reason, Felix would send for Paul rather often to have friendly conversations with him.

²⁷ Two years passed. Then Porcius Festus took Felix's place. (Since Felix wanted to do the Jews a favor, he left Paul in prison.)

8 Paul defended himself by saying, "I haven't broken any Jewish law or done anything against the temple or the emperor."

9 But Festus wanted to do the Jews a favor. So he asked Paul, "Are you willing to go to Jerusalem to be tried there on these charges with me as your judge?"

10 Paul said, "I am standing in the emperor's court where I must be tried. I haven't done anything wrong to the Jews, as you know very well. 11 If I am guilty and have done something wrong for which I deserve the death penalty, I don't reject the idea of dying. But if their accusations are untrue, no one can hand me over to them as a favor. I appeal my case to the emperor!"

12 Festus discussed the appeal with his advisers and then replied to Paul, "You have appealed your case to the emperor, so you'll go to the emperor!"

PAUL IS SHIPWRECKED ON HIS WAY TO ROME

Acts 27:1-44

1 When it was decided that we should sail to Italy, Paul and some other prisoners were turned over to an army officer. His name was Julius, and he belonged to the emperor's division. 2 We set sail on a ship from the city of Adramyttium. The ship was going to stop at ports on the coast of the province of Asia. Aristarchus, a Macedonian from the city of Thessalonica, went with us.

3 The next day we arrived at the city of Sidon. Julius treated Paul kindly and allowed him to visit his friends and receive any care he needed. 4 Leaving Sidon, we sailed on the northern side of the island of Cyprus because we were traveling against the wind. 5 We sailed along the coast of the provinces of Cilicia and Pamphylia and arrived at the city of Myra in the province of Lycia. 6 In Myra the officer found a ship from Alexandria that was on its way to Italy and put us on it. 7 We were sailing slowly for a number of days. Our difficulties began along the coast of the city of Cnidus because the wind would not let us go further. So at Cape Salmone, we started to sail for the south side of the island of Crete. 8 We had difficulty sailing along the shore of Crete. We finally came to a port called Fair Harbors. The port was near the city of Lasea.

9 We had lost so much time that the day of fasting had already past. Sailing was now dangerous, so Paul advised them, 10 "Men, we're going to face a disaster and heavy losses on this voyage. This disaster will cause damage to the cargo and the ship, and it will affect our lives." 11 However, the officer was persuaded by what the pilot and the owner of the ship said and not by what Paul said. 12 Since the harbor was not a good place to spend the winter, most of the men decided to sail from there. They hoped to reach the city of Phoenix somehow and spend the winter there. (Phoenix is a harbor that faces the southwest and northwest winds and is located on the island of Crete.)

¹³ When a gentle breeze began to blow from the south, the men thought their plan would work. They raised the anchor and sailed close to the shore of Crete.

¹⁴ Soon a powerful wind (called a northeaster) blew from the island. ¹⁵ The wind carried the ship away, and we couldn't sail against the wind. We couldn't do anything, so we were carried along by the wind. ¹⁶ As we drifted to the sheltered side of a small island called Cauda, we barely got control of the ship's lifeboat. ¹⁷ The men pulled it up on deck. Then they passed ropes under the ship to reinforce it. Fearing that they would hit the large sandbank off the shores of Libya, they lowered the sail and were carried along by the wind. ¹⁸ We continued to be tossed so violently by the storm that the next day the men began to throw the cargo overboard. ¹⁹ On the third day they threw the ship's equipment overboard. ²⁰ For a number of days we couldn't see the sun or the stars. The storm wouldn't let up. It was so severe that we finally began to lose any hope of coming out of it alive.

²¹ Since hardly anyone wanted to eat, Paul stood among them and said, "Men, you should have followed my advice not to sail from Crete. You would have avoided this disaster and loss. ²² Now I advise you to have courage. No one will lose his life. Only the ship will be destroyed. ²³ I know this because an angel from the God to whom I belong and whom I serve stood by me last night. ²⁴ The angel told me, 'Don't be afraid, Paul! You must present your case to the emperor. God has granted safety to everyone who is sailing with you.' ²⁵ So have courage, men! I trust God that everything will turn out as he told me. ²⁶ However, we will run aground on some island."

²⁷ On the fourteenth night we were still drifting through the Mediterranean Sea. About midnight the sailors suspected that we were approaching land. ²⁸ So they threw a line with a weight on it into the water. It sank 120 feet. They waited a little while and did the same thing again. This time the line sank 90 feet. ²⁹ Fearing we might hit rocks, they dropped four anchors from the back of the ship and prayed for morning to come.

³⁰ The sailors tried to escape from the ship. They let the lifeboat down into the sea and pretended they were going to lay out the anchors from the front of the ship. ³¹ Paul told the officer and the soldiers, "If these sailors don't stay on the ship, you have no hope of staying alive." ³² Then the soldiers cut the ropes that held the lifeboat and let it drift away.

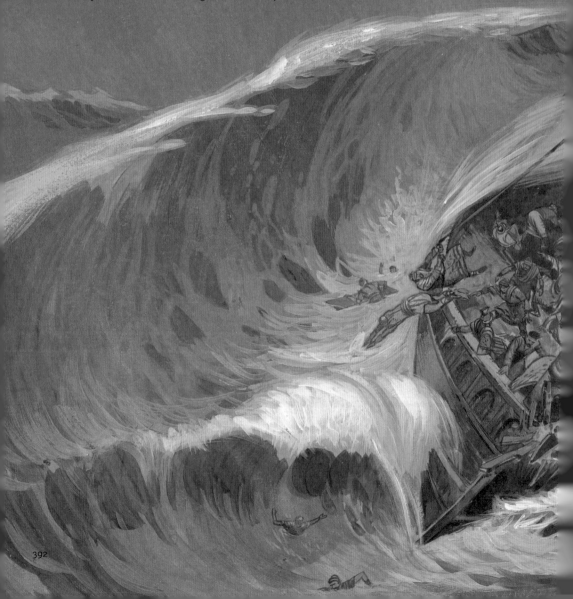

³³ Just before daybreak Paul was encouraging everyone to have something to eat. "This is the fourteenth day you have waited and have had nothing to eat. ³⁴ So I'm encouraging you to eat something. Eating will help you survive, since not a hair from anyone's head will be lost." ³⁵ After Paul said this, he took some bread, thanked God in front of everyone, broke it, and began to eat. ³⁶ Everyone was encouraged and had something to eat. ³⁷ (There were 276 of us on the ship.) ³⁸ After the people had eaten all they wanted, they lightened the ship by dumping the wheat into the sea.

³⁹ In the morning they couldn't recognize the land, but they could see a bay with a beach. So they decided to try to run the ship ashore. ⁴⁰ They cut the anchors free and left them in the sea. At the same time they untied the ropes that held the steering oars. Then they raised the top sail to catch the wind and steered the ship to the shore. ⁴¹ They struck a sandbar in the water and ran the ship aground. The front of the ship stuck and couldn't be moved, while the back of the ship was broken to pieces by the force of the waves.

⁴² The soldiers had a plan to kill the prisoners to keep them from swimming away and escaping. ⁴³ However, the officer wanted to save Paul, so he stopped the soldiers from carrying out their plan. He ordered those who could swim to jump overboard first and swim ashore. ⁴⁴ Then he ordered the rest to follow on planks or some other pieces ₍of wood₎ from the ship. In this way everyone got to shore safely.

PAUL REACHES ROME AT LAST

Acts 28:11-31

[11] After three months we sailed on an Alexandrian ship that had spent the winter at the island. The ship had the gods Castor and Pollux carved on its front. [12] We stopped at the city of Syracuse and stayed there for three days. [13] We sailed from Syracuse and arrived at the city of Rhegium. The next day a south wind began to blow, and two days later we arrived at the city of Puteoli. [14] In Puteoli we discovered some believers who begged us to spend a week with them.

[15] Believers in Rome heard that we were coming, so they came as far as the cities of Appius' Market and Three Taverns to meet us. When Paul saw

them, he thanked God and felt encouraged. So we finally arrived in the city of Rome. [16] After our arrival, Paul was allowed to live by himself, but he had a soldier who guarded him.

[17] After three days Paul invited the most influential Jews in Rome to meet with him. When they assembled, he said to them, "Brothers, I haven't done anything against the Jewish people or violated the customs handed down by our ancestors. Yet, I'm a prisoner from Jerusalem, and I've been handed over to the Roman authorities. [18] The Roman authorities cross-examined me and wanted to let me go because I was accused of nothing for which I deserved to die. [19] But when the Jews objected, I was forced to appeal my case to the emperor. That doesn't mean I have any charges to bring against my own people. [20] That's why I asked to see you and speak with you. I'm wearing these chains because of what Israel hopes for."

[21] The Jewish leaders told Paul, "We haven't received any letters from Judea about you, and no Jewish person who has come to Rome has reported or mentioned anything bad about you. [22] However, we would like to hear what you think. We know that everywhere people are talking against this sect."

[23] On a designated day a larger number of influential Jews ⌊than expected⌋ went to the place where Paul was staying. From morning until evening, Paul was explaining God's kingdom to them. He was trying to convince them about Jesus from Moses' Teachings and the Prophets. [24] Some of them were convinced by what he said, but others continued to disbelieve.

[25] The Jews, unable to agree among themselves, left after Paul had quoted this particular passage to them: "How well the Holy Spirit spoke to your ancestors through the prophet Isaiah! [26] The Spirit said: 'Go to these people and say,

"You will hear clearly but never understand.
You will see clearly but never comprehend.
[27]   These people have become close-minded
and hard of hearing.
They have shut their eyes
so that their eyes never see.
Their ears never hear.
Their minds never understand.
And they never turn to me for healing." '

[28] "You need to know that God has sent his salvation to people who are not Jews. They will listen."

[30] Paul rented a place to live for two full years and welcomed everyone who came to him. [31] He spread the message about God's kingdom and taught very boldly about the Lord Jesus Christ. No one stopped him.

THE APOSTLE JOHN IS GIVEN DIVINE VISIONS

Revelation 1:9-18

⁹ I am John, your brother. I share your suffering, ruling, and endurance because of Jesus. I was ⌊exiled⌋ on the island of Patmos because of God's word and the testimony about Jesus. ¹⁰ I came under the Spirit's power on the Lord's day. I heard a loud voice behind me like a trumpet, ¹¹ saying, "Write on a scroll what you see, and send it to the seven churches: Ephesus, Smyrna, Pergamum, Thyatira, Sardis, Philadelphia, and Laodicea."

¹² I turned toward the voice which was talking to me, and when I turned, I saw seven gold lamp stands. ¹³ There was someone like the Son of Man among the lamp stands. He was wearing a robe that reached his feet. He wore a gold belt around his waist. ¹⁴ His head and his hair were white like wool—like snow. His eyes were like flames of fire. ¹⁵ His feet were like glowing bronze refined in a furnace. His voice was like the sound of raging waters. ¹⁶ In his right hand he held seven stars, and out of his mouth came a sharp, two-edged sword. His face was like the sun when it shines in all its brightness.

¹⁷ When I saw him, I fell down at his feet like a dead man. Then he laid his right hand on me and said, "Don't be afraid! I am the first and the last, ¹⁸ the living one. I was dead, but now I am alive forever. I have the keys of death and hell.

GOD'S NEW WORLD

Revelation 21:1-4

[1] I saw a new heaven and a new earth, because the first heaven and earth had disappeared, and the sea was gone. [2] Then I saw the holy city, New Jerusalem, coming down from God out of heaven, dressed like a bride ready for her husband. [3] I heard a loud voice from the throne say, "God lives with humans! God will make his home with them, and they will be his people. God himself will be with them and be their God. [4] He will wipe every tear from their eyes. There won't be any more death. There won't be any grief, crying, or pain, because the first things have disappeared."

Revelation 22:20

[20] The one who is testifying to these things says, "Yes, I'm coming soon!"

Amen! Come, Lord Jesus!